HELMUT SCHMIDT

HELMUT SCHMIDT
Helmsman of Germany

Jonathan Carr

St. Martin's Press   New York

Library of Congress Cataloging in Publication Data

Carr Jonathan.
    Helmut Schmidt : helmsman of Germany.

    Bibliography: p.
    Includes index.
    1. Schmidt, Helmut, 1918 Dec. 23–   . 2. Heads of
state——Germany (West)——Biography. 3. Germany (West)——
Politics and government. I. Title.
DD260.85.C37   1985   943.087′7′0924 [B]   84-24190
ISBN 0-312-36744-9

CONTENTS

INTRODUCTION

In the bad old days, leading Nazis had villas on Schwanenwerder, a peninsula poking into the Wannsee lake on the outskirts of Berlin from wooded shores. It was a good place to relax, conveniently close to the heart of the Reich.

Nowadays Schwanenwerder is on the fringe of the free world. A few minutes' boat trip away are the watch-towers and barbed-wire marking West Berlin's border with communist East Germany. Just the other side lies the town of Potsdam where Roosevelt, Churchill and Stalin held their summit conference after the German capitulation in 1945. It was the last of their three meetings to try to settle the shape of post-war Europe. The Cold War followed, the division of Germany and, sixteen years later, construction of the Berlin wall by the communists.

Since 1974, Schwanenwerder has been the home of the Berlin offshoot of the Aspen Institute, a privately financed American organization which runs conferences on world affairs. The site offers the quiet of a cloister, a sense of history and a sharp reminder of East–West division – small wonder that Aspen Berlin has held many productive meetings over the last decade. But one in particular stands out, held in the bitter days of February 1979, and attended by the West German Chancellor, Helmut Schmidt.

Expectations ran high among the politicians, diplomats, publicists and academics invited to the gathering. Schmidt's prestige was probably higher than that of any other world leader – as a defence and economics expert, as an 'Iron Chancellor' who just over a year earlier had won a key battle in the war against terrorism. Moreover, the Chancellor was not called 'Schmidt *Schnauze*' ('Schmidt the lip') for nothing. Some participants gleefully looked forward to one of the infamous 'off the record' briefings, in which Schmidt scorned politicians of whom he thought little. The most likely target seemed to be the luckless US President, Jimmy Carter.

Nothing of the sort happened. Discussion of the conference topic, 'The Federal Republic of Germany – its place in world affairs', was well under way when the Chancellor turned up. He gave a brief greeting, then settled back to hear what the score or so of other participants had to say. Once or twice he glanced through the big picture-windows in the Aspen conference room to the Wannsee and beyond. When he finally made a brief comment or two, Shepard Stone, Aspen's irrepressible director, had to urge him to 'Speak up, Chancellor'.

Many of those present were disappointed. They had come to listen to Schmidt and instead Schmidt, flatteringly but unnervingly, had listened to them. Perhaps, it was felt, the Chancellor was saving biting comments on political and strategic matters for an after-dinner speech he had promised to give that evening. But again there was a surprise.

Schmidt loosened up his audience with a joke or two, then said he planned to talk about 'The Europe of the Day after Tomorrow'. He did not mention Soviet missiles or East–West force cuts or the dismal economic state of the (Western) European Community. Instead he spoke of a greater Europe with a common cultural identity from the Atlantic to the Urals. Tolstoy and Chekhov, Chopin and Bartók belonged just as much to this community as Dante and Shakespeare, Beethoven and Kant. This underlying union of ideas, ideals, of the spirit, was stronger than the political division of the continent and would outlast it. The barriers would not come down quickly, but no one should doubt that they would do so one day. In that context the German people too, politically split in the heart of Europe, would come together again (Herr Schmidt did not use the word 'reunite' with its political ring).

Schmidt's talk aroused conflicting views which emerged in private next day. Some listeners were deeply impressed. One politician said it was 'all blah blah' meant to convey the impression that 'the Chancellor has an artistic dimension too'. A lot of leaders put on that sort of show, he added, when they began to wonder what the history books would say about them. Yet another view was passed on by a senior diplomat over lunch: he had long ago heard that Schmidt was complex, artistic, personally vulnerable and often subject to deep depression; the picture of the 'Iron Chancellor' was not even half-true.

'Do you think that's right?' he was asked.

'After last night it wouldn't surprise me. Nothing surprises me any more. But you need much longer to form a proper judgement.'

1

YOUTH AND WAR

'I love this city with its scarcely hidden Anglicisms; its pride in tradition; its mercantile pragmatism combined with an endearing provincialism. But I love her with sadness for she sleeps, my beauty, she dreams. She is vain about her virtues without really using them. She luxuriates in today and seems to take tomorrow for granted.'[1]

The city is Hamburg, Germany's biggest port – but who is the disappointed lover? A lot of readers asked the same thing when they came across an unsigned article, from which the above excerpt is drawn, in a Hamburg newspaper in 1962. Surely, they felt, it could not be a local writer. The flowery style had nothing in common with true Hamburg understatement.

They were wrong. Three years later the surprising truth slipped out. The author was Hamburg's Senator (local minister) for Interior Affairs, a man renowned for his quick thinking and sharp tongue, for his expertise on many topics from transport policy to defence. Few people thought he had a poetic streak in him. His name was Helmut Schmidt.

In later years Schmidt said he had deliberately written in purple prose to cover his tracks. He wanted to wake Hamburg up a bit to the chances of playing a bigger role in national policy-making. A forceful, anonymous article seemed one way of getting a debate going.

For all the calculation, Schmidt surely put a lot of heart into that piece about his home city. Hamburg helped to make and sustain him in a switchback career with at least as many troughs as pinnacles. He studied there, married there, got his first civilian job there and retired there when life in political opposition in Bonn, the federal capital on the Rhine, seemed to have brought him to a dead end.

He was proud of Hamburg's cosmopolitan atmosphere; its history as a member of the Hanseatic league, which for centuries dominated trade with Russia and Scandinavia; of its role as a 'city state' in its own right. As Chancellor he had to receive most foreign visitors in Bonn. But those leaders he particularly esteemed were invited up north to his small house in Hamburg's Langenhorn district, on the city's outskirts ten minutes' drive from the airport.

Langenhorn does not figure much in the guide-books. It has no elegant villas and boutiques like the Pöseldorf district close to Hamburg's Alster lakes, nor splendid views of the River Elbe like trendy Blankenese to the west. Its solid citizens live in comfort, not luxury. The main Hamburg tradition alive there is lack of ostentation. If the distinguished visitors to Langenhorn (among them Presidents Leonid Brezhnev of the Soviet Union and Valéry Giscard d'Estaing of France) were nonplussed by the Schmidts' suburban idyll, they had little trouble hiding it. They knew that the Chancellor on his home ground was likely to be more open and relaxed than in Bonn. A chat while strolling round the garden and peering into the goldfish pond at Langenhorn could help unravel problems which defied solution in more formal settings.

Half an hour's brisk walk from Langenhorn towards the city centre takes you to an altogether tougher area, 'Red' Barmbek. At the start of the century it was famed as a working-class stronghold, and for the cheekiness of its children which no amount of earboxing seemed to cure for long. Nowadays, Barmbek is better known as the district where Helmut Heinrich Waldemar Schmidt was born – on 23 December 1918.

A month earlier the First World War had ended and Kaiser Wilhelm had abdicated. But Germany remained united, its armies still in relatively good order, its people already whispering about political betrayal – a stab in the back! The Peace Treaty of Versailles, imposing conditions and reparations which many Germans felt intolerable, was still six months away. Germany's first, ill-fated experiment with democracy, the Weimar Republic, had not yet begun.

Helmut Schmidt was four years old when Adolf Hitler staged his abortive *putsch* in a Munich beer cellar. The same year, 1923, inflation was at its height; workers collected paper wages daily in wheelbarrows and the price of a restaurant meal rose as you ate. He was ten in the year of the great Wall Street crash of 1929, and just thirteen when German unemployment passed the five million mark. One month after Schmidt's fourteenth birthday, Hitler was appointed Chancellor of the

Reich in what Germans still tend, inaccurately, to call the '*Machter-greifung*' or 'seizure of power'. A year later the Nazis had consolidated their hold, political parties and trade unions had been banned, books burned in the streets and the first concentration camps had been built.

Schmidt was thus one of those who were too young to be fully politically aware in the years leading up to Nazi rule, but who were old enough to go to war in 1939. Willy Brandt, Schmidt's predecessor as Chancellor, was only five years older, but those years made all the difference. At the age of sixteen Brandt became a member of the Social Democrat Party (SPD), the labour movement founded in the second half of the nineteenth century. At nineteen, when Hitler came to power, Brandt joined the Underground movement, fled abroad and stayed there throughout the war years. Helmut Kohl, Schmidt's successor as government leader, was a youth of only fifteen when Hitler's 'Thousand-year Reich' collapsed in 1945. There is plenty of evidence, including a particularly bitter outburst in Parliament in 1958, to show that Schmidt suffered deeply from being part of what he called the 'generation between the generations'.

Schmidt's father, Gustav, was a teacher who prized toughness, self-discipline and hard work above all. Those 'Prussian' qualities had not made him rich. The Schmidts lived in a simple four-room dwelling. But Gustav was sure that without them you could obtain nothing worthwhile in life. It was a message he drummed into his two sons, Helmut and his younger brother Wolfgang, almost from the time they could crawl. These were two Barmbek boys who did not answer back their father, who were taught not to cry if they fell over and to be diligent without expecting praise.

Their mother, Ludovica, was just the opposite. Artistically gifted, she took the children to concerts and museums and helped organize madrigal singing with relatives at home once a week. But Gustav ruled the household and young Helmut went in fear of him for years. An early photo, brown and faded, shows a group of dishevelled Barmbek urchins with Helmut Schmidt in the centre clutching a wheel and stick and peering nervously at the camera as though expecting a rebuke. A later photo, taken at the age of seven, shows a more determined-looking boy, jaw set and hands clasped tightly before him as though readying for an argument.

From his father's side, Helmut thus gained some of those qualities which helped carry him through setbacks to the top in politics. From his mother he won an early interest in music and visual arts. He also had the good luck from the age of ten to attend a school where both sides of his character had a chance to develop.

The Lichtwark-Schule (named after a former director of the Hamburg Art Gallery) was a liberal institution, remembered with affection by ex-pupils decades later. It was co-educational, open to the children of rich and poor alike, and struck a balance between the academic and artistic. Above all, it encouraged a critical instinct and self-reliance. Small wonder that the Nazis finally shut it down, although the red-brick building itself still survives on the edge of Hamburg's city park.

Helmut Schmidt was a Lichtwark-Schüler from 1929 until 1937, two years before the outbreak of war. He was smaller than other boys of his age, hence his nickname – the diminutive 'Schmiddel'. But what he lacked in size (then and later) he made up for in energy and the ability to organize. His exam results were excellent, including written and oral English. But he had no French and years later was to regret the lack of it. He spoke to Giscard d'Estaing in English, a language both shared, though Schmidt was more practised; but for Schmidt's talks with Giscard's successor, François Mitterrand, an interpreter had to be present. That allowed a more formal precision, but worked against a real *tête-à-tête*.

The school encouraged each pupil to undertake one major creative project a year, and in his mid-teens Schmidt carried out three which show his all-round interests. One was an extended essay on competition between the ports of Antwerp, Rotterdam, Bremen and Hamburg; another, a survey of the Renaissance in the Weser region of North Germany. In the third, he turned into a modest composer, transcribing twenty chorales for four-part singing. It was during these school days that he developed both as a pianist and painter. Later, in wartime Berlin, he took up the organ as well.

Schmidt also became head of the rowing team – a model pupil, in fact, the perfect all-rounder. But a future leader of the country? No one seems to have thought so, least of all Schmidt. He gradually came to the conclusion during those school years that he would like to become an architect; better still, a town planner. He loved art and could draw quite well, but he felt he would never be able to make a living from it. So architecture seemed a good compromise. That ambition remained until the war's end when force of circumstances set him on quite

7

another course.

What would he have thought had someone stood before the assembled Lichtwark schoolchildren in the mid-1930s and forecast that, 'One of you, Helmut Schmidt, will one day be head of government'?

'I would have thought he was crazy,' Schmidt says.

Hannelore Glaser, 'Loki' for short, would probably have reacted the same way. She was an electrician's daughter, long in Schmidt's class without, it seems, taking much notice of the small, clever but rather 'uppity' boy sitting a few desks away. That changed when they were both around fifteen. They began to flirt, the relationship deepened, then lapsed when Helmut went for military service. They re-established contact in 1941, were married the following year and have been together ever since. From the start they shared an interest in music, art and reading – but neither initially seems to have had much time for politics.

Even given his youth, was not Helmut Schmidt's virtually non-political attitude in those days a bit odd? What did his family think of the collapse of the Republic into dictatorship? Didn't his father influence him politically one way or another? Schmidt gave the following answer in the 1960s and it could stand for that of many young Germans of that time. His father, he said, was no Social Democrat, and certainly not a Nazi. But nor was he a resistance fighter.

'I imagine that during his life he drifted between the [centrist] German People's Party and the German Democratic Party of the Weimar era. But he was cautious, and perhaps he had reason to be cautious. . . . I was influenced atmospherically by my father *against* the Third Reich, but not *in favour* of anything else.'

Again, he said, that when the Nazis came to power 'I had no positive concept of democracy. It was clear to me that the scornful rejection of Western democracy by the Third Reich couldn't be correct. But I had no concrete impression of what a democracy looked like, how a state based on the rule of law should be organized.'[2]

Those comments underline one reason for the fall of Weimar, quite apart from the lack of scruples of the Nazis, the short-sightedness of the First World War victors and the economic chaos. The democracy of the 1920s had no roots. Many Germans of the time did not, perhaps could not, identify with it. So what politically did they have to offer their children?

But there was another crucial point about the Schmidt family which was long known only to very few. When Helmut Schmidt said that perhaps his father 'had reason to be cautious' he went no further into the matter. In fact Gustav Schmidt had a very good reason. His father, Helmut's grandfather, had been a Jew.[3]

Helmut Schmidt first learnt this in about 1935 or 1936 – he cannot recall exactly which year. His mother took him aside and told him that the man he had so far known as Grandfather was not his real one. She told him of his part-Jewish ancestry and warned him not to breathe a word. Gustav said nothing at the time to his sons, let alone anyone else. Had the truth come out, he might have ended up in a concentration camp. His family would have suffered too.

The tale does not end there. It is worth recounting in full because of the light it sheds not just on the Schmidts but on Germany under Nazism, the way in which the state probed into even the most private sphere, but was still not quite all-powerful.

During the war, Helmut Schmidt returned from combat on the Russian front determined to marry Loki Glaser. To do so he needed, among other things, an official declaration that his parents and grandparents were of Aryan stock. It was all part of the Nazis' effort to ensure that the German race would be 'pure'. He went to his father and for the first time they discussed the 'false' and the 'real' grandfathers. Gustav confirmed the tale, but added he had been born illegitimate. Because of that, the Nazis had not been able to discover who his real father was. Gustav then produced an official document, stamped with a swastika, saying in effect 'father unknown'.

The document was an at least partial insurance against further snooping into the background of the Schmidt family. But it looked as though it might be too little to allow Helmut to go ahead with his marriage. According to military rules, Helmut had to present his prospective bride to his commanding officer, who had to confirm that the necessary papers for the marriage were in order. Not the least piquant part of the story is that at that time Schmidt's commander, Oberstleutnant Kurt Andersen, was in Bonn. So it was that Helmut Schmidt made his first visit to the future Federal German capital where he was to become Chancellor more than three decades later. At that time it was a pleasant, rather sleepy, university town happily unaware of the greatness to be thrust upon it.

With foreboding Helmut and Loki went to Andersen, who was

quartered on the Venusberg hill above Bonn. Would he approve the papers? If not what could they do? They need not have worried. Schmidt recalls with a wry smile that Andersen was a 'tough disciplinarian but no Nazi. I was lucky. None of my superior officers was a Nazi.' Andersen took one look at the papers, then signed a stamped document saying Schmidt's Aryan stock had been proven to him – and briskly wished the couple well.

Before he learned of his Jewish background, Helmut Schmidt had become a part of the Hitler Youth. His rowing club was assimilated in 1934, like thousands of other organizations countrywide, as the Nazis extended and tightened their hold. One week the boys were rowing for their own club, the next, as it were, for the Führer.

It was art which brought Schmidt into direct conflict with the Nazis. He may have had no 'concrete conception' of democracy, but he knew very well which painters he admired, above all the German Expressionists. Forty years later he was proudly to display their works on the walls of his Chancellery in Bonn – pictures by Emil Nolde and Franz Marc, by August Macke and Käthe Kollwitz. To the Nazis these painters were 'degenerate', their works fit for occasional display only as examples of artistic and moral decay. Helmut Schmidt thought that view was rubbish. What's more, he said so openly, to the concern of friends who urged him to keep his mouth shut (never a task Schmidt found easy!). He escaped reprisals until, in 1936, he daubed a phrase about 'freedom shining like a beacon across the world' on a wall of the room where the rowers gathered to sing shanties. He was promptly suspended from the Hitler Youth, causing him, he admits, both relief that he had moved a step away from direct Nazi influence and fear of possible repercussions.

If the Nazi officials considered taking further steps they did not carry them out. Another year passed, Schmidt left school, and began the regular two years of military conscription. His course seemed clear. When he returned to civilian life he would still not have turned twenty-one. He could then begin his training as an architect sometime in late 1939.

But the initial job in 1937 as a recruit to an anti-aircraft battery was the start of a period of continuous armed service which lasted eight years, six of them in war. It was also the beginning of a lifelong involvement in things military, as a parliamentarian in the 1950s and 1960s, as Defence Minister in the early 1970s and as Chancellor into the

1980s.

Schmidt's first two war years passed quietly enough, in service in Bremen an hour's train journey down the coast from Hamburg. Then in 1941, promoted to lieutenant and attached to the anti-aircraft unit of a tank division, he was posted to the Russian front. Nearly forty years later he was to stand in the Kremlin as Chancellor, criticize the Russians for invading Afghanistan and argue strategy for hours with the top Soviet nuclear missiles expert. But on that first visit, Helmut Schmidt was himself an invader, initially in the assault on Leningrad, later on Moscow. The smell of death, of burning flesh, was often in his nostrils, the cries of the wounded in his ears.

Transferred to Berlin he worked as an officer responsible for anti-aircraft training in Hermann Göring's Reichsluftfahrtministerium (the Air Ministry) until 1944. He was then moved on again, this time to the Western front.

Retreat followed, then capture in April 1945 by British forces on the Lüneburg Heath, the spot where only weeks later Field Marshal Montgomery was to receive the surrender of all German forces in North Europe. Four months after his twenty-sixth birthday, Oberleutnant Helmut Schmidt, battery commander and holder of the Iron Cross, was bundled into a prisoner-of-war camp.

It is easy to give a brief review of Schmidt's war career. It is much harder to know what was in his mind and heart during those years. Of his period in the Berlin air ministry he says, 'I had more insight into things than one had on the front, and heard more too . . . . It became clear to me that this was a criminal government.'[4] He was also detailed to sit in on one of the notorious 'People's Court' trials of those implicated in the attempt to assassinate Hitler in July 1944. Schmidt, shocked by the prosecutor's threats and screams of abuse at the defendants, asked his superior to be spared a second day's attendance.

Not only was Schmidt aware of what was happening, he felt he knew how it would end. He says that 'particularly during the last years of the war, my wife and I and a few friends really had no doubt that it would end in a terrible external, internal and moral collapse. I must admit that we imagined the collapse to be even more dreadful than it turned out to be.'

What conclusions were drawn by those Germans who realized the national cause was wrong and disaster inevitable? Some joined the Resistance, hence the abortive assassination attempt on Hitler. Most, like Schmidt, carried on despite an inner conflict, as he put it 'on the one hand knowing we had to defend the country, which we did willingly, and on the other hand knowing that every day, every week, in which we put off final defeat meant prolonging a damnable regime'.

Against that background – Schmidt's Jewish ancestry, as well as his experience as student and soldier under the 'Third Reich' – one address he gave as Chancellor takes on special relevance. It was delivered at the synagogue in Cologne in November 1978.[5]

Speaking of the Nazi crimes against the Jews, Schmidt began with a quotation from Isaiah: 'How the faithful city has played the whore, once the home of justice where righteousness dwelt – but now murderers!'

'The truth is', Schmidt said, 'that a great many Germans disapproved of the crimes and wrongs; by the same token there were a great many others who learned of nothing or almost nothing at the time.

'The truth is that all this nevertheless came to pass before the very eyes of a large number of German citizens and that another large number of them gained direct knowledge of the events.

'The truth is that most people, faint of heart, kept their silence.'

The Chancellor went on to quote the German-Jewish philosopher Martin Buber who said, 'This heart of mine, well aware of the frailty of man, refuses to condemn my neighbour because he failed to find the strength to become a martyr.'

Most of those present that day were impressed by the speech, surely one of the finest Schmidt has given. Some of them thought they detected an unusually personal note. They were right.

For Helmut Schmidt, capture by the British marked both an end and a beginning. His period as a fighting soldier was over with the defeat he had expected. But behind barbed-wire, from April 1945 until his release in August, his life as a conscious political democrat began.

In the earlier war years he and his wife used to have the Utopian dream of a 'simple life' with no slogans, no ideology, indeed no politicians. Ironically, it was only as a prisoner of war that Schmidt was able to discuss openly with fellow soldiers how and why Germany had toppled to disaster. Passionate arguments lasting far into the night emerged among men who had never been trained to debate much anyway, and who for years had been subject to military discipline. It was there, in the camp, that Schmidt's dream of the 'simple life' faded and his first concrete impressions emerged of what a future German democracy could look like. He went to university later, but he surely did not again go through so concentrated a period of learning and change as he did in that summer of 1945.

At that crucial moment he was influenced by one or two older officers in favour of social democracy. One of them in particular, Oberstleutnant Hans Bohnenkamp, Schmidt remembers as a 'religious socialist' of unusual conviction. Increasingly Schmidt came to believe that if a democratic Germany could emerge in the post-war period, then the key role should belong to the SPD with its tradition of social justice and opposition to fascism. At the same time, at least one part of his war experience seemed to Schmidt to match a principle on which the SPD had been founded. He had known the comradeship of those facing a common threat, the help one soldier would give another to pull through even at the risk of his own skin. Was the mutual support of comrades in arms really so far removed from the solidarity so highly prized among the 'comrades' of the SPD?

Schmidt thought it was not and often said so. But for all his apparent conviction, there were some in the SPD after the war who wondered whether his 'conversion' was genuine. It is easy to see why. Whatever tactical mistakes the party might have made in the Weimar era, whatever the internal divisions which undermined its national strength, its record in opposing Hitler was a proud one. As the Weimar democracy crumbled in early 1933, it was the SPD leader, Otto Wels, above all, who had hurled defiance at jeering Nazis in a Reichstag ringed by brown-shirted thugs. 'You may take our freedom and our lives,' Wels told those who were shortly to do just that, 'but our honour you cannot take. We dedicate ourselves in this historic hour to the basic principles of humanity, freedom and socialism.' Within months the party had been banned, and its leading members went into the Underground, prison or exile.

Traditional supporters of a party which suffered as the SPD did under the Nazis were bound to feel at best cool, at worst downright hostile, to Wehrmacht officers like Schmidt who joined at war's end. True, inwardly convinced Social Democrats fought for their country in the Second World War as they had in the First. But to a lot of them it must have seemed that the new officer recruits in 1945–6 slid all too easily into social democracy as they slid out of their leather greatcoats.

Schmidt overcame some of their reservations quickly but part remained. His peremptory manner did not help. For him the road to social democracy began in captivity. But years later an SPD leader could still arouse nods of accord from party colleagues with the bitter remark that 'Helmut Schmidt learned his socialism in the officers' mess'.

By the end of the war, social democracy had started to mean a lot to Helmut Schmidt, but Schmidt meant virtually nothing to the SPD. Kurt Schumacher was the key figure around whom the party crystallized. He was a person of evangelical fervour and unbreakable will, who lost an arm in the First World War and later had a leg amputated, but still survived years in Nazi concentration camps. Schumacher, who had once dared to define Nazism to Goebbels as that 'which appeals to the swinish element of human nature', battled for control of a democratic Germany in the first post-war years – battled, but lost.

Then there was Herbert Wehner, who had abandoned communism after years of critically dangerous work on its behalf from Moscow to Paris. 'I am one of those who was burned,' Wehner said of his communist period. From that experience emerged a consuming passion for democratic socialism. It was probably Wehner more than anyone who coaxed, cajoled and occasionally whipped the SPD down the long post-war road to governmental power. He was a grand strategist who, many claimed, was a Chancellor-maker and breaker too.

Schumacher was born in 1895, Wehner eleven years later. There were other leading SPD figures surviving from the Weimar days too. The name Helmut Schmidt would have meant nothing to them in that summer of 1945. Schmidt was simply one of the hundreds of thousands of ex-soldiers trudging home to bomb-shattered towns through waves of ragged hungry refugees.

With the benefit of hindsight so much that followed the war's end seems almost predetermined: the growing confrontation between the Western allies and Moscow; economic reconstruction; establishment of a democratic Western Germany; rearmament as the Cold War froze harder.

But how did the world seem to young Germans like Helmut Schmidt in that 'Stunde Null' ('Zero hour') as it was called? On what basis were they to build their lives? In the Western allied countries, service-people were going home as well, to all the problems of adjustment to post-war civilian life, it is true. But few doubted they would eventually settle into a niche in the system they had defended and which, whatever its faults in detail, was worth defending.

German soldiers were retreating defeated, the country occupied, the Führer of twelve years a charred corpse in the rubble-heap of Berlin. There was no system to re-enter, no shared achievement, only the bitter consciousness of largely wasted years. Who was responsible? Was it their own fault, that of their parents, of the divided Weimar democrats, of all together?

Small wonder that so many from Schmidt's 'generation between the generations' had become deeply suspicious of slogans, had an antipathy towards political visionaries, favoured pragmatism and, if anything, understatement. They found it hard to relax, to indulge in small talk and other so-called 'social graces'. For them school had given way to the military, the military to prison, prison to 'Stunde Null'.

In later years Helmut Schmidt was sometimes called the 'Feldwebel', the sergeant-major, by European partners irritated by his curt, authoritarian tone. Other critics, mistaking the pragmatic approach for lack of vision, called him the 'Macher', implying someone who gets things done without thinking about the future. Much of the explanation for Schmidt's abrasive character lies in his tough home upbringing, military experience, and in that accident of age which denied him a youthful break from the grim business of war and work. It is not surprising that as minister and Chancellor he often found young people hard to understand, especially, it seemed, the idealistic young in his own party!

Despite all that, the 'Stunde Null' and the period which followed were not just ones of privation and bitterness. Many Germans who lived through it look back with the kind of nostalgia with which Londoners recall the camaraderie of the Blitz.

Never again did even Germans work so hard or live their private lives so intensely, making music and listening to it, reading books and looking at pictures long banned, above all discussing and arguing interminably as Schmidt and his fellow prisoners had done. A dam had burst and a wave of political, philosophical and artistic debate, pent up for years, burst forth. Did it peter out too quickly, as the apartment blocks and factories rose from the rubble, as the Germans created that so-called 'economic miracle' which was the admiration, and envy, of the world? Many feel that it did, that the country and its people gave themselves too little, or perhaps were allowed too little, time to digest the Hitler experience before making a new start.

It is fascinating to speculate on how post-war Europe might have developed had those last months of the Second World War gone differently. Suppose, for example, that the Western allies had reached Berlin before the Russians. Or suppose that the Russians had been able to push more quickly to the west and north, engulfing Schleswig Holstein, Denmark and Helmut Schmidt's Hamburg. They came very close to doing so. The border between East and West Germany, and hence between the NATO and the Warsaw Pact alliances, runs only fifty kilometres to the east of Hamburg, less than an hour's drive from the city centre.

Likewise, suppose that Schmidt had had the chance to study his beloved architecture in post-war Hamburg. Would he have opted for that instead of economics, which he initially took up without much enthusiasm? Might that in turn have drawn him away from politics altogether? But Schmidt found there was no architecture course available in his home city. Instead he would have had to travel regularly the 150 kilometres south to Hanover, no easy task in those first chaotic post-war days. The prospect of spending so much time 'on the road' after years of nomadic life with the military did not appeal one bit. Besides, he would be able to matriculate more quickly in economics than in architecture and have more time to earn on the side. This was a key point since he and his wife had virtually nothing to call their own.

With their wedding 'documentation' problems resolved thanks to Oberstleutnant Andersen, Helmut Schmidt and Loki Glaser had married in Hamburg in June 1942. A wedding photo shows a relaxed, smiling bride, lightly linking arms with her husband, a garland of white flowers on her long, dark hair. Helmut Schmidt, back from the Russian front, stands stiffly to attention in full uniform, his hands clasped before him – looking away from the camera, it seems into the far distance.

Luckier than many wartime couples, the pair was able to spend a lot of time together thanks to Schmidt's subsequent posting in Berlin. For more than a year they lived near the little town of Bernau, twenty kilometres north-east of the capital. But they experienced a personal tragedy, too. Their first child, Helmut, died when only a few months old. He lies buried in a cemetery in what is now communist East Berlin

The Schmidts had a second child, a daughter Susanne, born in 1947. By that time some order had replaced the post-war chaos, but life was still very tough. The family lived in one rented room, with simple furniture part of which Schmidt himself had knocked together. Fuel was hard to come by. Initially coal supplies were augmented by what could be 'lifted' from railway trucks. But that soon became too dangerous. The trucks were better guarded and 'lifters' shot at.

The main source of income was Loki's earnings as a teacher, the job she had taken up at the start of the war and which she held through all the ups and downs of her husband's career until the late 1960s. Loki also picked up money doing sewing in the evenings. Helmut earned too – helping others with their tax returns and analysing statistics.

At first the sheer battle for existence took up most of Schmidt's time and energy, but the debates during his imprisonment stayed vividly in his mind. For him, as for so many others, the crippled Schumacher was the dominant political figure, and when Schumacher re-constituted the Social Democratic Party in 1946, Schmidt quickly joined. Later he was to express deep admiration for the SPD leader, even call him a genius, a term he rarely applied to other politicians. Above all, he recalls how on an early trip with a party friend to Hanover to see Schumacher, he had been fascinated by the older man's temperament and analytical skill, his ability to communicate and convince.[6]

Schmidt was already showing some of the same qualities himself in the German Socialist Students' Federation (SDS), a body which became very left wing long after Schmidt had moved on. A few dozen young socialists used to meet regularly in Hamburg, and participants still recall how Helmut Schmidt easily became the central figure. Partly it was the range of his knowledge, partly his 'gift of the gab', partly his air of complete conviction even about what others felt to be relatively minor points. Whatever the topic, Schmidt seemed to emerge both as the catalyst of the discussion and as the one who summed up. It was not long before he became formal leader of the Hamburg group, later rising to take the overall chairmanship of the Federation.

One of Schmidt's longest, firmest friendships began during this period with the young socialists. The name of Karl Wilhelm Berkhan will mean nothing to people outside Germany, but 'Willi' Berkhan has been a constant support to Schmidt for more than three decades, as an informal down-to-earth adviser and as a patient listener. Like Schmidt he was born in Hamburg, in 1915; they both did war service, they both shared an apartment in Bonn as parliamentarians, and they both own small stretches of the same lake in the far north of the country.

But it is easy to see that Schmidt was already considered a difficult customer by some of his socialist 'comrades', and not simply because of his officer's background. Even in that students' organization (admittedly, many of the 'students', like their leader, had seen war service), Schmidt made it clear that he thought nothing of debating clubs which came to no firm conclusions. In an open letter to members of the Hamburg group in 1948, for example, Schmidt strongly warns against drifting into nebulous, ideological discussion which overlooks, or ignores, social reality. In another article the same year, Schmidt says that a lot of Social Democrats seemed content to criticize the universities as 'reactionary' without even trying to say what should be done to put things right. Schmidt goes on to outline a six-point programme for reform, stressing that if society had to wait for professors to change the university system, it would wait indefinitely.

Schmidt was able to write at least partly from his own experience. From late 1945 until 1949 he was enrolled in the economics faculty of Hamburg University, and passed out with a thesis comparing the Japanese and German currency reforms. It might thus be thought that in those four years Schmidt swotted in his chosen field, imbibing much of the economic and financial expertise he was to show as Chancellor. The reality was different. Schmidt and many other 'students' were in their late twenties and had six years of war behind them. Quite a lot were married with children. All had to struggle even for the most basic necessities. To say the least, it was no ordinary campus and no common 'student–professor' relationship

Schmidt had his political activities as well. When he could, he devoured the works of authors he had never come across before, like Hemingway and Sartre. He also broadened his knowledge of philosophy and history, not least the history of the American revolution; economics books were on the programme too. But he applied himself really whole-heartedly to his official course of study only towards the end, when exams were looming.

During Schmidt's time at university, his path first crossed that of a man who was to play a big, and turbulent, role in his career. Professor Karl Schiller arrived in Hamburg from Kiel with a high reputation as an economist, though still only in his mid-thirties. He worked his way up the political ladder during the 1950s and 1960s, becoming Economics Minister in Bonn in 1966, then 'Superminister' of Economics and Finance in 1971. He resigned a year later after bitter arguments in cabinet. His successor was the man often called his 'former student' – Helmut Schmidt.

Schmidt rejects the idea that he 'sat at Schiller's feet' (or indeed at anyone else's) while at university. He was already half-way through his course when Schiller arrived on the scene and, in any case, he attended few lectures or seminars. He praises Schiller as 'one of the best economists Germany has produced', but he also sees him as vain and difficult.[7] Many people would share that view of Schiller, but note that Schmidt does not have an easy temperament either. It was probably inevitable that two such men whose careers came so close would get in one another's hair.

If Schiller did not loom very large at university for Schmidt, the Professor evidently saw that Schmidt had talent. Schiller was head of the Hamburg office (Ministry) for Economics and Transport as well as holding his university post. When Schmidt graduated, Schiller promptly offered to take him on at the ministry. So it was that, at the age of twenty-nine, Schmidt got his first steady civilian job.

Schmidt began work on the general economic policy side but switched over to transport, rising to head the section in 1952. It was a typical move for him, away from broad theory, fascinating though that could be, towards the solution of practical problems. Besides, in wrestling with the problem of bringing more order to Hamburg's transport system, Schmidt was not very far from his youthful ambition of town-planning. At any rate, it was the closest he ever came to it.

As he worked his way up in the Hamburg administration, so his reputation spread in the SPD. Already known as a quick thinker and good speaker, he began to get invitations to address party gatherings throughout northern Germany. Not everyone liked the trenchancy, tinged with arrogance, with which he spoke on economic and social issues, but no one was bored. Helmut Schmidt became something of a regional SPD star, 'good value' to draw the comrades into draughty halls on cold winter evenings. It was only a matter of time before he was urged to stand for Parliament.

It is hard to believe that in those half-dozen years of growing recognition in and around Hamburg, Schmidt had never seriously considered a career in national politics. So many other people during that period thought of Schmidt as unusually capable, that it would seem odd if Schmidt had not thought the same himself – and looked ahead a bit. But when he talked later about his breakthrough to Bonn, it was as though he had been a person more acted upon than acting. It was suggested, he says, that he stand for a seat and the idea appealed to him, 'without my having the slightest idea how that decision would alter my life'. Once in the Bundestag (the lower house of the Federal Parliament) he was compelled, by law, to give up his post as an employee of the Hamburg government. 'So it is that one can be made into a career politician – without really aiming for it.'

Schmidt stood for a Hamburg constituency in the general election of 6 September 1953. His chances looked good. The seat had gone to the SPD in the 1949 election and, in a message thrust into voters' letter-boxes, Schmidt sought to capitalize on his local fame as a transport specialist. He complained that there had been a failure at national level to come to grips with the problems of rail, road and waterways. If elected, he declared, he would devote himself to this sector in particular. But transport was not, in his view, the only field where the ruling Christian Democrat (CDU)-led coalition was failing. The social security system was in a mess and tax regulations an almost impenetrable jungle. General economic policy lacked a sense of direction. Schmidt concluded with an appeal to voters to trust their judgement and hearts, not political slogans. Perhaps this idealistic advice was not altogether wise. In any case, a majority decided in favour of Schmidt's opponent from the liberal Free Democrat Party (FDP).

It was a bitter, but not fatal blow. Under the complicated German system, voters have two ballots each. The first goes to a constituency candidate who is elected by a simple majority. Schmidt lost on that one. But the other vote goes to a party rather than a person. The second votes are counted and seats divided proportionately. Each party has a list of candidates for the seats available. The higher you are on the list, the better chance you have of getting into Parliament. Schmidt was high enough to scrape through. In this way he began his parliamentary career, shortly before his thirty-fifth birthday.

2

TO BONN AND BACK

To win a Bundestag seat in 1953 was one thing. It was quite another to feel that, as a Social Democratic parliamentarian, one was doing something useful, influencing policy, building a career.

The Christian Democratic Chancellor, Konrad Adenauer, dominated the scene with the impassive authority of an aged Indian chief. In the 1949 general election he had led his new and disparate party to a narrow victory over the SPD, a shock from which Schumacher perhaps never inwardly recovered. In the 1953 poll the Christian Democrats, together with their Bavarian allies, the Christian Social Union (CSU), lengthened their lead. They picked up an extra five million supporters and took more than 45 per cent of the vote while the SPD remained static with less than 30 per cent.

Part of the reason was economic. At Adenauer's right hand sat Ludwig Erhard, personifying the 'economic miracle' with his big cigars, roly-poly bulk and contented air. It was Erhard who had fought for removal of economic restrictions after the currency reform of 1948, pinning his faith on the creative power of market forces. The initial results confirmed to the Germans, and the world, that he was right. So long as the '*Dicke*' (the 'stout one') was there, many believed, nothing could really go wrong with the economy. That view was to change in the 1960s when recession set in and Erhard floundered. But in election year, 1953, steel production was well over fifteen million tonnes (triple the 1948 figure), unemployment again dropped sharply, more than half a million flats were built, the foreign trade account was in surplus for the second successive year, and the central bank's gold and foreign exchange reserves topped DM8 billion. Few people thought socialist planning and control could have done as well.

But there were foreign policy reasons for Adenauer's success too. The CDU Chancellor had made clear from the first that his top priority, even before German unity, was to tie the Federal Republic firmly to the Western community of nations. Hence Bonn's decision to take part in the European Coal and Steel Community, formed in 1952, and its readiness to contribute to Western European defence. The SPD, on the other hand, feared that every step, especially militarily, taken to bind the Federal Republic to the West would solidify the division of the country and make German reunification less likely. With the benefit of decades of hindsight that position may seem unrealistic. But those were the days well before the building of the Berlin wall, when the Russians were repeatedly dangling the prospect of a united (but neutral) Germany before the West. It was a time when many Germans, even in Adenauer's own ranks, deeply deplored the idea of taking up arms again, for any alliance, under any circumstances. After all, Hitler had been dead for less than a decade.

The Korean war, which started in 1950, helped to change that. It swung some West Germans over to Adenauer's argument that alliance strength was needed to resist communist pressure. But much more persuasive was the abortive uprising in East Germany in June 1953. Hardly three months before West Germans went to the polls, they saw East Germans taking to the streets and demanding free elections, only to be crushed by force of arms.

Schumacher saw neither the uprising nor his party's subsequent election defeat. He died in August 1952, a great outsider with no friends in the East and few among the Western allies. As Willy Brandt said, he was Russia's number one enemy because he refused to permit any collaboration between Social Democrats and communists. He wanted a Social Democratic and free Germany, not a Soviet puppet state. At the same time 'for the Americans he was too socialistic, for the English too aggressive, for the French too German. They all found that he was too independent.'[1]

He was succeeded by Erich Ollenhauer, who was decent but relatively ineffectual. The SPD's attitude to defence remained confused and its economic and social stance was weighted with the ideological ballast of the late nineteenth century.

Such was the SPD, and the quality of its leader, when Helmut Schmidt arrived in Bonn in the autumn of 1953. Schmidt was far from alone in believing the party had to bring itself up to date if it was ever to win governmental power. Others, better known in those days like Herbert Wehner or Carlo Schmid, were working for change – though it was to be years before the party drew the formal consequences in a new programme, and more than a decade before the SPD entered government.

But on the issue of the SPD's attitude to defence and rearmament, Schmidt made an impact from his earliest days in Bonn. Later he explained that when he arrived on the scene, the SPD's spokesman on defence issues, Fritz Erler, was becoming ever more involved in broader foreign policy questions. So there was a vacuum which Schmidt helped to fill – not with the idea that he might one day become Defence Minister but simply, as he says, as a chance to do something concrete in those opposition days.

No doubt there is something in that explanation. Many SPD deputies had already been in Parliament for four years, they had established reputations, and it was hard for a new recruit to make his mark among the 'old hands'. Schmidt quickly became involved with transport problems where he was an acknowledged expert. But that field on its own must have seemed limited to an energetic back-bencher, no longer youthful, facing a full four-year term. What could seem more natural than that Schmidt, with his military experience, should move into a defence 'vacuum' which few other party members seemed disposed to fill?

But that is surely not the whole story. There are many signs that Schmidt felt the SPD was making a major, perhaps historic, error by spurning military matters, and that from the first he set out to help change things. From the involvement over his party's relationship to the armed forces grew a broader interest in East–West strategy. Within only a few years he was making proposals for balanced arms control and disarmament, well before the era of superpower *détente* in the 1960s, let alone Bonn's '*Ostpolitik*' of the 1970s.

Schmidt developed and refined that concept of 'balance' as the key to security, but he never abandoned it, no matter what new weapons systems emerged or what power changes occurred in Moscow and Washington. His support for the controversial NATO 'twin-track' decision of 1979, to help correct the East–West imbalance in nuclear weapons is a case in point. Not many people (even in Germany) realized that his stand, far from being a new one, was the logical extension of a concept he had held for roughly two decades. Probably still fewer people realized how close a connection there was between balanced arms control, relaxation of tension in Europe, and the reunification of Germany; yet Schmidt had been underlining that point too for years.

This is moving ahead a little. When the young parliamentarian Helmut Schmidt took issue with his party on military affairs in the mid-1950s, he was doing so at least as much for domestic as for foreign political reasons. In a nutshell his message to the SPD was, 'You have to lick the army – or it will lick you.' This emerges loud and clear from an article he wrote in the magazine *Sozialist* in 1954.[2] In it, Schmidt said he knew many party members hated talking about defence policy at all, but sooner or later the Federal Republic would have armed forces, like it or not. (The Bundeswehr was, in fact, formed the following year after West Germany became a member of NATO.) Social Democrats could not afford to opt out of responsibility, Schmidt said. They had to overcome their basic dislike of the issue and answer questions like, how could parliamentary control over the military be assured, how should officers be chosen, what scope should there be for conscientious objection. The errors of the Weimar era must not be repeated, when politicians, including Social Democrats, failed to keep a grip on the armed forces.

A furious reply to *Sozialist* from an SPD member shows how little Schmidt's arguments were shared by the rank and file. The writer said formation of a West German armed force should not even be open to discussion. Whoever suggested otherwise undermined SPD foreign policy and, specifically, the hope of German reunification. It was unworthy for a German to fight for a divided country, the letter said. Defence efforts should be made only when there was something worth defending.

Schmidt stuck to his views and later was to make fears about Social Democrat abstinence in defence matters more specific. In 1960 he reminded trade unionists that, at the end of the Weimar Republic, the Reichswehr had been a major political factor although it numbered only 100,000 from a population of sixty-five million. West Germany, Schmidt noted, would shortly have armed forces totalling 300,000 from a population of fifty-three million. It was clear that a potential domestic power-factor was emerging and that it could not be controlled by people standing on the sidelines and slandering the forces year after year. Schmidt appealed to his listeners to overcome their suspicion of the military and establish a dialogue with soldiers whenever possible. 'They're not madmen,' he declared. 'They weren't born in a barracks.

They're normal people you can talk to – and influence.'[3]

In retrospect, after decades of West German integration in NATO and stable civil government in Bonn, fears of an 'unholy alliance' between the political Right and the military may seem exaggerated. But in those early years it was far from clear that Bonn would succeed where Weimar had so dismally failed. Schmidt said in 1958 that no one should be deceived by the democratic form of the Federal Republic into thinking that the democratic substance was secure. Indeed the bitterness of many Bundestag debates in those days spoke not so much of government, opposition and 'honourable members', as of hostile forces each believing the other would wreck the system.

That hostility was due partly to differences over practical policy issues, above all in the foreign and defence fields; but it was also due to deep mistrust between the generations represented in the Bundestag. Schmidt identified four broad categories in those early days. The oldest parliamentarians had gained their views of state and society during their youth under Kaiser Wilhelm. The youngest, like Schmidt himself, had been at school when the Nazis came to power but had been old enough to go to war. Then there were two groups of deputies who had already been politically aware during Weimar. The members of one had actively fought against the dangers facing the democratic system, but had failed to head off the Nazis. The members of the other had gone along with developments, not necessarily aiming for the collapse of the system, but not doing much to try to stop it either.

All these elements, the policy differences, the generation gap, the mutual hostility of Left and Right, emerged in particularly sharp relief in a four-day debate on atomic weapons in the Bundestag in March 1958. The high-point, or as the government parties felt, the nadir, was the speech by Helmut Schmidt, witty, emotional and chilling by turns. The speech was the first to make Schmidt really well known to a national audience. It also made him, very briefly, the darling of his party.[4]

By that time, Adenauer had won another general election, piling up a lead in 1957 of 50.2 per cent for the CDU–CSU to the SPD's 31.8 per cent. West Germany was a member of NATO, the Bundeswehr was gaining strength, and the SPD felt the government, despite denials, aimed to gain control over atomic weapons. In the 1960s, Schmidt said he would no longer care to try to prove that really had been Adenauer's intention; but at the time it looked to the SPD as though West Germany was due to embark on a dire course, and in that parliamentary debate it was Schmidt who captured his party's mood better than anyone else.

From the first there were boos and catcalls from the government party benches, as Schmidt accused the CDU–CSU of mass psychosis in its 'ecstatic determination' to gain atomic weapons. But real uproar broke out when Schmidt added that it was 'the political forbears of this Adenauer coalition' who, twenty-five years earlier, agreed to the laws making Hitler all-powerful. 'I and many others here were just schoolchildren – fourteen years old,' Schmidt shouted into the tumult. 'Your assent to [Hitler's] enabling legislation took us and millions of others to the slaughterfields of Europe and into the cellars of our cities, millions more into the concentration camps and death chambers.'

Furious government deputies screamed back that Schmidt's political forbears were to be found in communist East Germany. They called him 'a grave-digger of democracy' and 'the rudest lout in the house'. One shouted 'Schmidt *Schnauze*', roughly translated 'Schmidt the lip', a description which stuck. But Schmidt, now in full flight, was not to be put off. He jabbed a finger towards members of the government parties who, he said, might have set youth an example of opposition in the 1930s, but instead had lain low, leaving the SPD alone.

'We tell the German people with solemn conviction', Schmidt declared, 'that the decision to arm both parts of our Fatherland against one another with atomic bombs will go down in history as just as fateful as was the enabling legislation for Hitler.' As the President of the Bundestag (Speaker of the House) frantically rang his bell for order, Schmidt drove home the assault on the CDU–CSU: 'When you talk about the unity of NATO you mean atom bombs for the Bundeswehr. . . . Give up your German megalomania once and for all, your German national megalomania.'

When Schmidt stepped down from the rostrum, a standing ovation from his party almost drowned the shouts and whistles from the government side. Ollenhauer, followed by other SPD deputies, sprang forward to shake Schmidt's hand and clap him on the back. Few Social Democrats bothered to listen to Kurt Georg Kiesinger of the CDU (later to become Chancellor) when he rose to say that Schmidt's words had been a disgrace to Parliament: 'The speech we have just had to listen to was nothing more than a rubbish bin emptied over this house.'

Many of those who witnessed the scenes in Parliament that day felt they had been present at the birth of a new star – one who would clearly go far in the SPD, perhaps rise to the very top. But only seven months later Helmut Schmidt, in disgrace with his colleagues, was voted out of the SPD parliamentary party's executive. He had been a member of it for only a year.

The reason was simple. In October Schmidt, with his Hamburg friend Willi Berkhan who had gained a Bundestag seat in the 1957 election, took part as volunteers in manœuvres of the Bundeswehr reserve. Many of the SPD 'comrades' were thunderstruck. Could this be the same Schmidt who had pounded the government to such good effect in the atomic weapons debate? Nor was it only members of the party who were astonished. Schmidt later said his wife too thought he was crazy when he went off for four weeks' military service, although he was under no compulsion.

But Schmidt's action was fully in line with the stand he had taken from the start. Opposition to atomic weapons for the Bundeswehr and criticism of CDU–CSU defence policy did not mean the SPD should cut itself off from the soldiers – quite the contrary. Moreover, Schmidt's experience in those four weeks with the military strengthened his conviction that he had been right. Every day from 7 a.m. to 6 p.m. he did his regular service – and every night, until the early hours, he found himself surrounded by soldiers, curious at having a parliamentarian in their midst. The thirst for discussion about politics in the broadest sense, not just about arms and defence, was unmistakable. At the end of his month Schmidt, exhausted by his efforts day and night, slept the clock round before returning to his family.

A few months after his military service and his exclusion from the party leadership, Schmidt turned forty. Had he gone into private industry a decade earlier, when that unprecedented period of sustained economic growth was starting, he would surely already have been well up the managerial ladder. Instead he found himself in an uncomfortable corner of a party which seemed doomed to opposition, presumably not for ever, but how old would Schmidt be when the SPD finally made it into government?

The very next year, in November 1959, the SPD took a step which greatly improved its chances of escaping from the '30 per cent ghetto' of the electorate. It drew the conclusions from almost a decade of failure at the polls, and adopted a new programme. This moved the SPD firmly away from being a 'workers' party' with a strong basis of Marxist ideology, and towards becoming a middle-of-the-road 'people's party'.

It is hard to say who was most responsible for the SPD's new-look 'Godesberg Programme', named after the spa of Bad Godesberg, next door to Bonn, where the document was adopted. Wehner among others had a big hand in it, but the change was clearly to the liking of Helmut Schmidt. For one thing the Godesberg Programme supported national defence while opposing atomic weapons. For another, it dumped a lot of ideological ballast including the concept of 'historical necessity', and recognized that human beings, their ideas and ideals, could move events. For Schmidt and most of his generation this had long been self-evident. But the formal recognition of it by the SPD seemed to bode well for future electoral success, especially since the so-far invincible Adenauer was showing signs of losing his touch.

The SPD's reasoning was broadly right, but the CDU–CSU was too far out in front to be quickly overhauled. In the general election of September 1961, the CDU–CSU slipped quite a bit to 45.3 per cent of the vote and the SPD rose to 36.3 per cent; but for all the improvement in support, it was the SPD's fourth election loss in a row. Helmut Schmidt faced more years on the opposition benches in Bonn and decided he could not stand the prospect. When Hamburg offered him the job of Senator for Interior Affairs, he jumped at the chance. The post was newly created and gave its holder responsibility for many matters previously scattered between different departments. Schmidt had plenty of experience; now he wanted a challenge. He soon found he had a bigger challenge than he had bargained for.

In the night of 16–17 February 1962 – less than two months after Helmut Schmidt had taken over his new Hamburg job – a hurricane hit much of northern Europe, including Germany. Winds of more than 150 kilometres an hour swept down the tidal River Elbe, piling the waters to nearly six metres above their normal level and bursting over the dykes in Hamburg in the early hours of the morning. Scores of people were engulfed as they slept, many more as they sought to flee. The warning sirens sounded but few heard them in the tempest. Telephone and power-lines were ripped down, whole districts cut off from the outside world. Roughly one fifth of Hamburg lay under water.

The disaster struck as Schmidt was returning to Hamburg from a conference in Berlin. He raced to the police presidium and took control of the situation in a way that was to bring him greater fame than anything he had done in Bonn over the previous eight years. The image of Schmidt the 'crisis manager' was born.

No one seems seriously to have contested Schmidt's authority at the time, even though he clearly exceeded the limits of what a provincial minister was permitted. He quickly raised and co-ordinated a small army of more than 40,000 rescuers, including Bundeswehr and Western allied troops, police, Red Cross and other civilian workers. At the height of the action, about 100 helicopters were taking part at Schmidt's behest, although the winds were twice as strong as the maximum in which the pilots were allowed to fly. Who gave Schmidt the authority to bring these forces together? 'They weren't assigned to me,' he declares. 'I took them over. There was no other choice.'

When Schmidt had already been dictating rescue operations for hours, the Mayor of Hamburg, Paul Nevermann, arrived on the scene. He had been on a cure in an Austrian spa but hurried home when he heard the news. The following conversation that took place in the police presidium belongs to the history (or at least the folklore) of the Hamburg flood disaster:

> *Schmidt* 'Mr Mayor. You're in my way here.'
> *Nevermann* 'But I take it the Hamburg constitution is still worth something, or . . . ? '
> *Schmidt (impatiently)* 'Paul, once and for all shut up. Can't you see I've urgent orders to give.'

It is a nice tale, and sounds the kind of thing that Helmut Schmidt might be expected to say in the circumstances. But he insists he did not,[5] and the origin of the story is obscure. Schmidt agrees that Nevermann turned up (unavoidably) late and 'he may have made a suggestion I did not find very helpful. But I would not have humiliated him before a crowd of people. I thought a lot of him.'

Whatever his Senator for Interior Affairs may or may not have said to him, the Mayor does not seem to have taken serious offence. Four days later in the Hamburg Parliament, Nevermann praised Schmidt for his 'clever and energetic measures' to deal with a catastrophe such as the city had not seen since the wartime bombing.[6] Most people felt the same about Schmidt's action. More than 300 people had died in the floods, but well over 1,000 in immediate danger of drowning had been saved, and 18,000 who lost their homes were brought speedily to shelter. It was not surprising that a local opinion poll showed Schmidt to be even more popular than Hamburg's football star, Uwe Seeler.

Schmidt played down his role in the action at the time. Later, recalling the Hamburg floods, he was to express misgivings about how easy it was to keep pursuing a course technically illegal, once the first step was taken. Perhaps, too, he realized what the consequences would have been for him had the action he ordered in those dramatic hours not paid off in lives saved. Fifteen years later he was to face another crisis, when terrorists hijacked a Lufthansa jet with ninety-one people on board to Mogadishu and tried to blackmail the government. Again, many lives depended on his decision and again his career hung in the balance.

3

DEFENCE AND UNITY

That might have been the end of Helmut Schmidt's national career. The prodigal son of the Free and Hanseatic city of Hamburg had returned home after eight years in the wilderness, and promptly brought off something of a miracle. He must have stood a good chance of becoming mayor before long, and most true Hamburg citizens consider that that job is better than anything Bonn can offer.

Schmidt even had a weekend and holiday home on his own stretch of a lake in Schleswig-Holstein, Germany's northernmost state between Hamburg and the Danish border. If that sounds as though the Social Democratic Schmidt had slipped into luxury, anyone who has visited the lakeside dwelling will soon correct the impression. From the outside the bungalow has the air of a barracks, though it is a lot more cosy inside. The heating is primitive and the building hardly habitable in winter. But the Schmidts spend at least part of their holidays there every summer.

It was a chance meeting on a train stuck in the snow between Hamburg and Bonn in the winter of 1957–8 which led Schmidt to his holiday home. He struck up conversation with a businessman from the Schleswig-Holstein capital of Kiel, and the talk turned wistfully from the vile weather to vacation prospects. The Kiel man knew of a fine stretch of lakeside land for sale – an ideal spot for sailing, even for swimming by those with a tough constitution. The plot was 10,000 square metres, far too big and costly for Schmidt even if he shared the purchase with his new acquaintance. But Willy Berkhan promptly agreed to come in on the deal and the land was divided in three. Schmidt's bungalow went up first and Berkhan's a year later, with both men doing a lot of the building work on one another's property.

The separate dwellings at least dealt with one problem which Schmidt had found flat-sharing with Berkhan in Bonn. Schmidt was a 'night owl', often working well past midnight and preferring to sleep late. Berkhan was up at the crack of dawn and loved singing in his bath – 'usually out of tune' Schmidt recalls with mock dismay. At least on holiday, Schmidt was far enough away not to be woken up by the singing.

The existence of this handy bolt-hole, his extraordinary post-floods popularity in Hamburg and the call to the top job there – all that, as well as the chance to have more time for his family, might have kept Schmidt out of Bonn politics. Was it simply personal ambition that drove him back to the capital on the Rhine after four years of administration in Hamburg?

Schmidt's ambition, or the lack of it, is a hotly disputed topic, best examined at that point in his tale where he becomes Chancellor. But certainly by 1965, another general election year, he was a much more considerable figure than that 'transport expert in search of a role' who had entered the Bundestag twelve years earlier. He was highly competent – he knew it, and everyone else admitted it (some of them unwillingly). He had made a success of a senior government post, in a provincial administration it was true, but even that was more than almost all his SPD colleagues and rivals had done. Just as important in politics, he was an actor and public speaker of uncommon ability. He was already a good amateur in the late 1940s, he developed into a professional in the 1950s, and later he became one of the great political actors of our time.

That does not imply that he is, or was, an empty demagogue. Schmidt often says a political leader needs the ability to analyse problems thoroughly, to take independent decisions and, a tiresome but crucial stage in a democracy, to convince others. He has at least his fair share of the first two qualities. But in his capacity to communicate and convince he surpasses almost all his contemporaries.

Whether facing an audience of steel workers in Essen or bankers in New York, potentially hostile members of the British Labour Party or philosophers at a conference on Kant, somehow he manages to have them eating out of his hand within minutes. On election campaign swings, he can vary his tone, pace and vocabulary from one gathering to another within the hour, always throwing in some local detail to make each audience feel he had been waiting for weeks to address them. Amid all the later international praise for Schmidt as a 'grand military strategist' or a 'world economist', this extraordinary dramatic flair tended to be overlooked or at least underrated. Yet without it, it is doubtful whether he would ever have become Chancellor or, having done that, have stayed in office for so long.

In the 1950s several of the Schmidt hallmarks were already powerfully present, among them the rich vocabulary, the fire and the love of repartee. Schmidt hates having to read a prepared speech and, as many harassed journalists can testify, if he has a text he often embellishes it. He prefers to keep one eye on notes, one on the faces in the audience and his ears cocked for interjections. That way he can adjust to the mood, snap a few crisp retorts and keep the flow of his ideas without having to search for his place in a text.

Schmidt's remarks in that atomic weapons debate of 1958 give an idea of his talent for verbal combat. But in translation they can give no feel of his relish for language, of how he would caress one word, spit out another. Take one example, drawn from later years when the CDU opposition leader, Helmut Kohl, had accused Schmidt of being a prisoner of his own party. Schmidt's off-the-cuff retort runs, 'Who is he to talk about the alleged Babylonian imprisonment of others – this Herr Kohl who rattles his own chains about a bit, but who is too weak to throw them off.'

The sense is clear enough, but even non-German speakers may gain an extra flavour by reciting the original. Schmidt began sharply, his voice rising, '*Was tönt eigentlich der Herr Kohl mit seiner Sprache über die angebliche Babylonische Gefangenschaft anderer,*' then dropped into a note of contempt for '*der seine eigenen Ketten ein bisschen rasselt*', ending in a weary whisper '*aber abzuschütteln zu schwach ist*'. The very absence of a gesture from Schmidt as he rolled out the sentence added to the effect, as though Kohl's charge was hardly worth the effort of dismissal. In his early Bundestag days, Schmidt gesticulated a lot more than he did later. Photos of him in the 1950s show him leaning over the speaker's dais, one hand just a blur as he emphasizes a point. Later he conserved his energy better, and when he finally made a sweeping gesture it impressed all the more by being rare.

Above all, he mastered television. That was not very important in the 1950s, of course, but in the 1970s it contributed crucially to his popularity, which surged far ahead of his party's much of the time. In his television interviews Schmidt is always the thoughtful statesman – weighing every word, often pausing and gazing far beyond the camera as though taking a new, grand survey of world problems. The technique lends an air of gravity even to fairly minor matters. It gives the impression that things are under control or that, at least, if they are not, then it is not due to any weakness of Helmut Schmidt. If a questioner seeks to draw him onto dangerous ground, Schmidt is expert at slipping away. 'I would formulate that another way,' he says, and goes off at a tangent to safety, packing his answer with enough facts and figures to make many critical viewers forget that he has really been asked something else.

His good looks help too: the firm jaw, the intense grey eyes, the sudden, brilliant almost voracious smile. He is quite a small man – only 1.72 metres in height, but that does not emerge on television and never seems to have affected his popularity with the ladies. Well before Schmidt became Chancellor, a Hamburg newspaper pronounced him 'Germany's Number 1 Sexy Man'. He had charm, cleverness and was handsome too, according to 40 per cent of the paper's women readers. Two pop singers, themselves no mean television performers, were well behind him in the polls.[1]

Only one man, over three decades or so, has been able to compete with Schmidt as an orator; only one constantly produces the same thrill of anticipation when he rises to speak. That is the Bavarian, Franz Josef Strauss.

In some ways the men are opposites. Schmidt comes from the far north of Germany, Strauss from the deep south. Schmidt belongs to a party of the Left. Strauss personifies one of the Right, the Christian Social Union, whose outbursts of wilfulness have often strained ties with its generally more moderate CDU ally in Bonn. Strauss, with his bull neck and broad shoulders, is in his element when clinking beer mugs with party friends at a noisy Bavarian get-together. Schmidt usually seems withdrawn at the big SPD rallies, and if he has a favourite drink then it is probably Coca-Cola or tea. Strauss is a fund of funny stories. Schmidt does not have much of a talent for humour – at best, as he says, for 'silly, satirical jokes, and one shouldn't make those when one is in public office'.[2]

But there are parallels too. Strauss, three years older than Schmidt, also fought in the artillery on the Russian front. Like Schmidt he became Defence and later Finance Minister. Like Schmidt he used a firm provincial base to re-launch himself into national politics after a setback in Bonn.

Strauss had been held responsible for police raids in 1962 on the office of the Hamburg news magazine *Der Spiegel,* which published an article alleging that NATO had betrayed state secrets. In the ensuing uproar he was accused of deceiving Parliament and had to give up the defence post. He retreated to Munich, the Bavarian capital, took a university course in economics (like Schmidt) – and bounced back to the Bonn cabinet in 1966. He was never Chancellor, but he and Schmidt fought one another for the top job in the 1980 general election.

If Schmidt's polemical speeches are like machine-gun fire in their precision, Strauss's are more like shrapnel, hurling a lot of potentially deadly material over a wide area in the belief, usually justified, that some at least will find a target. Latin quotations (Strauss was a brilliant classical scholar), scraps of Bavarian folklore and pungent attacks on 'Reds' mingle with economic and strategic theory in a brilliant, if not always illuminating, cascade.

'A Bavarian power-station which often blows a fuse,' is how one commentator described Strauss. That is much in line with Schmidt's view. In the 1958 debate on atomic weapons, Schmidt said that Strauss, already Defence Minister for more than a year, had 'a splendid memory, quick understanding, a not inconsiderable education – and vitality, oh yes indeed! But the man is guided only by feelings, by impulse . . . . I believe Strauss is a dangerous minister precisely because of his surpassing ability.'

That comment shows that despite his reservations, Schmidt from quite early days had a marked respect for Strauss. In an interview in 1966, Schmidt was to go further: 'The only one who really knew a lot about military problems in those days was Strauss,' he said. 'All other politicians were relatively badly informed.' He repeated that he felt Strauss could be dangerous, but added, 'On the other hand I can see that he is making an effort to take a grip on himself. And I must admit that after all these years I've still got a certain feeling for the charm he displays once in a while.'[3]

Just as Schmidt felt that the armed forces domestically should not be influenced only by the political Centre-Right, so he believed that Strauss must not be left as an almost solitary parliamentary pundit on strategic matters. Had Strauss been a less brilliant minister, and hence less of a challenge, perhaps Schmidt would not have thrown himself so intensively into the study of military strategy, and its foreign policy implications. But only a year after the tumultuous atomics debate, what seemed to be a new Schmidt appeared before the Bundestag.

Exceptionally, he stuck closely to a long prepared text, so long in fact that many government deputies either told him to 'be quicker about it' or yawned and left the chamber. The speech acquired none of the notoriety of its predecessor, but in retrospect it looks more important. Schmidt '*Schnauze*' was not dead, only sleeping, but Schmidt the strategist had arrived on the scene.[4]

Citing numerous foreign experts, from Field Marshal Montgomery of England to 'the American Professor Kissinger', Schmidt appealed for the creation of a Central European zone of arms limitation and control. He stressed that the step did not imply either that the Federal Republic would leave NATO or that Eastern European states would desert the Warsaw Pact. A basic change in military blocs could only come much later in the context of a 'collective European security system' including 'a political solution of the German question'.

What he had had in mind, Schmidt said, was a zone from which almost all foreign (i.e. Russian and Western) troops would be withdrawn. Only a small, symbolic number would remain, plus the national forces of those countries which made up the zone. The result would be a Central European balance at a lower force level, and hence greater East–West security.

What countries would be included in the zone and how would a 'balance' be defined? The two questions were closely linked. Schmidt made it clear that he was not talking about exact parity in the number of troops, tanks and aircraft. All factors relevant to defence capacity had to be taken into account, including population numbers, economic strength and the lie of land where battles might be fought.

That in turn made it clear that no real balance could be achieved in a zone covering the two German states alone. The Federal Republic on its own was, strategically, a far more important customer than its Eastern neighbour. On the other hand, a zone covering the whole of Western Europe and extending to Russia's western border would weigh the advantage too heavily in favour of the East. Schmidt suggested, without firmly committing himself, that a balance might be found in a zone covering West Germany on one side, and East Germany, Poland, Czechoslovakia and Hungary on the other. He noted in passing that the Poles had already implied that they saw a possible balance involving almost the same countries but excluding Hungary. It was a point worth following up in negotiation, Schmidt said.

He then ran over the objections which could be raised to his idea. True, almost all the non-German forces of NATO (above all those of the United States) would have to withdraw behind the Federal Republic's western border. But Soviet forces would have to fall back still further to the east. It was also true that the Russians could in theory break the accord and march back into the zone. But in that case NATO would have more time to react than it did at present, with Russian troops right up against East Germany's border with the West. Besides, Schmidt added pragmatically, NATO troops could move back east more quickly on West German roads than Russian troops could move back west on Polish ones.

Schmidt denied that his plan involved wholesale disengagement of the US from European defence. Some American troops would remain in West Germany as part of the symbolic force, more would be deployed in other parts of Western Europe (though Schmidt agreed this could bring 'absorption' problems), and the US Sixth Fleet would remain in the Mediterranean. Schmidt admitted he was not 'over-optimistic' that the Russians would agree: 'We know that step-by-step withdrawal from the DDR [East Germany] and other states in the East would undoubtedly have political consequences over there – and, after all, should do so. That is the point of the thing.'

That is indeed the point, and a key problem which was later to haunt the East–West Mutual and Balanced Force Reduction talks (MBFR) droning on through the 1970s and 1980s in Vienna. Six years before Schmidt spoke, Soviet troops had helped put down an uprising in East Germany. Three years before, they had crushed one in Hungary. In 1968 they were to do the same in Czechoslovakia. Russian forces were in Eastern Europe at least as much to occupy as to defend. What could Moscow stand to gain by withdrawal from such unruly and unreliable neighbours? Perhaps it could hope thus to detach West Germany from the Western alliance – but at what price? With superpower troops withdrawn, the 'German question' would be wide open again.

The hour was late when Schmidt ended his speech and the number of government deputies left in the chamber was small. The Bundestag President, Eugen Gerstenmaier, who a year earlier had sought to stem Schmidt's tirade against the CDU–CSU, this time had some kindly words for him. 'I could imagine', he declared 'that on the basis of this carefully prepared address a new discussion could begin in this House.'

Schmidt did not trust to the Bundestag alone to give his ideas an

37

airing. He began to expand them into a book, writing bits when he got the time on trains, aeroplanes, and at his Bonn flat. The result was *Verteidigung oder Vergeltung* (*Defence or Retaliation*) – first published in 1961 and at once praised in the German-speaking world as a major, probably *the* major, German contribution to the study of East–West strategy. The next year the book appeared in translation in London and New York, and Schmidt's name became known to a much wider circle of politicians and defence experts in both countries. By that time the 1961 general election in Germany had been lost and Schmidt was back in Hamburg. The new star seemed to have been only a comet after all, vanishing almost as it appeared.

But many things were starting to change in West German domestic politics and in East–West relations. For one thing the Bonn government's touch became less certain at home and abroad. Adenauer at last stepped down as Chancellor in 1963, but the ruling coalition had begun to creak and groan well before that. He was succeeded by the less awesome Erhard, whom Adenauer did not favour and whom he lost few chances to belittle from the sidelines.

Willy Brandt, long a popular Governing Mayor of West Berlin, had meanwhile risen to the top of the SPD. He succeeded Ollenhauer as a new, more charismatic leader of the party in 1964. But even before the 1961 general election Brandt had been 'Chancellor candidate', that is the man the SPD wanted as head of government if the party came out on top at the polls.

In contrast to Adenauer, Brandt had shown marked resource and determination when the communists built the Berlin wall in August 1961. Brandt's performance had still not been enough to carry the SPD to victory in the elections the following month, but there was at least a fair chance that his leadership, combined with the government's own problems, might carry the 'post-Godesberg' SPD to success in 1965. When Brandt looked round for a Shadow Defence Minister before the election campaign began, Schmidt was the obvious choice. His international standing as a strategic expert was a bonus to the party, even if some comrades still nursed grievances over Schmidt's active stint in the Bundeswehr reserve.

At the same time, an era of superpower *détente* had opened, which at least partly explained the discomfiture of the Bonn government as it sought to adjust to the new situation. Schmidt himself saw it as the third key phase in East-West relations since 1945. In the first, the

potential threat of the Soviet Union's huge, non-demobilized conventional forces in the immediate post-war years was counterbalanced
by the unique position of the US as a nuclear weapons power. In the
second phase, Moscow too became a nuclear power, upset the balance,
overestimated its capacity and caused several international crises,
culminating in the Cuba confrontation with the US in 1962. Cuba
ushered in the third phase, in which both superpowers realized they
had parallel interests. President Kennedy's 'Strategy for Peace' was
one example of this recognition, the Moscow Nuclear Test Ban Treaty
of 1963 another. The policy of 'rolling back communism' followed by
the former US Secretary of State, John Foster Dulles, had changed to
one of 'containment'. The Soviet Union had not given up its hopes of
extending its hold across the world, but its tactics had changed. The
aim, as the Soviet leader Nikita Khruschev put it, was for 'victory in
peaceful competition with capitalism'.

This left the West German government in a jam over its own policy
towards the East, and above all to East Germany.

In 1955 Bonn had announced the so-called Hallstein doctrine
(named after Walter Hallstein, then State Secretary at the Foreign
Office) under which West Germany would have no diplomatic ties with
any state recognizing East Germany. Bonn was determined to
underline its right to speak for all Germans and to keep the door open
for reunification. The Hallstein doctrine was at least consistent and
fitted well enough into the confrontation era. But as superpower
relations thawed, so Western states generally began to become
impatient with Bonn's rigid position. Besides, there seemed to many
West Germans to be something deeply unsatisfactory about a stand
which cut them off from contact with their closest neighbours in the
East, Soviet satellites or not.

The CDU Foreign Minister, Gerhard Schroeder, put the problem in a
nutshell in 1965: 'Today the predominant and general interest in
preserving peace', he said 'has taken pre-eminence over the specific
interest in [German] reunification. True, agreement on the goal [of
unity] still exists; but it has become more difficult for German foreign
policy.'[5]

Schroeder took several pragmatic steps to try to ease relations with
the East. It would be fair to call him at least 'one of the Fathers' of the
Ostpolitik, the policy of improving ties with Eastern Europe and the
Soviet Union. But it was really the SPD which, by the mid 1960s, had

the men and the policies most fitting to the new situation. One was Herbert Wehner, fired by a sense of Germany's guilt for Nazi atrocities in Eastern Europe, particularly Poland. Another was Willy Brandt, shocked by the West's inaction when the Berlin wall was built and convinced that Bonn itself had to take a new course to keep open the issue of German unity.

Yet another was Schmidt, though in later years this tended to be forgotten. In the early 1970s it was almost inevitable that Brandt, as Chancellor and Nobel peace winner, was most widely seen as the architect of the *Ostpolitik*. He even became the embodiment of the policy in the eyes of the world, thanks not least to his dramatic gesture in falling on his knees before the memorial to the victims of the ghetto uprising in Warsaw. Walter Scheel, Brandt's Foreign Minister, naturally had a major hand in pushing through Bonn's treaties with the East, so that the expression 'Brandt–Scheel' *Ostpolitik* became common. Schmidt in those days was Defence Minister and not many identified him any more, if indeed they ever had, with Bonn's political thrust to the East. By the time Schmidt became Chancellor, most Eastern treaties had been signed and ratified.

Yet Schmidt's 1959 speech on troop reductions in Central Europe shows that even then he was trying to think beyond the confrontation era. Nor were his thoughts confined to the military field. The same year he produced a theoretical study of how an economic and monetary union might be achieved between the two German states. Many people know of Chancellor Schmidt as an architect of the (Western) European Monetary System (EMS) in the late 1970s. Few are aware of the effort twenty years earlier by back-bencher Schmidt to work out something similar for his divided country.[6]

Schmidt proposed that the process start with removal of restrictions on delivery of West German goods to the East and the establishment of an All-German Investment Fund. It was to end with a customs union, a joint tax system, free movement of capital and freedom of enterprises to invest and establish themselves in both parts of Germany. Schmidt recognized that Germany's neighbours would look askance at this new economic giant in their midst. He therefore said the Germans would have to provide some counterbalance, for example by special payments to finance investment in countries less well off than themselves. A crazy scheme? Perhaps, but not unthinkable in the context of that Central European military disengagement Schmidt was also urging.

It is very doubtful whether Schmidt believed either his military or monetary proposals would be put into practice in just a few years. In both cases, he warned of the big problems involved. But he stuck to the view that a new, more flexible approach to East–West issues was needed, and by the mid-1960s he and Brandt were clearly thinking along the same lines. Indeed, large parts of a speech on *Ostpolitik* and the German issue which Schmidt delivered to an SPD conference in 1966 might have come from Brandt himself.[7]

Schmidt stressed that it was not only the Russians who opposed German unity. Western democractic leaders formally supported Bonn's aim but they were responsible to electorates who often saw things differently. 'The fear of the risk of a change in the *status quo* in Europe is far greater than the wish to see Germany reunited. In other words, the policy of strength [i.e. forcing change through confrontation] has clearly collapsed once and for all.' On the other hand, Schmidt said, the Federal Republic had neither the right nor the desire to abandon the unity issue, leaving East Germans alone to pay the price for the last war with their enslavement. What should Bonn's new course be?

Again Schmidt underlined that the precondition for progress was maintenance of an East–West military balance, with bigger efforts made to reduce force levels. But Bonn should use every chance emerging from superpower *détente* to seek trust and understanding from its neighbours in the East. It should not make maximum demands, or sit tight on legalistic positions, or make agreement in one sector dependent on accord in another. The Hallstein doctrine must be applied more flexibly. Bonn could not formally recognize the (East) 'German Democratic Republic', but, apart from that one point, it should try in every practical way possible to improve ties between the two German states. The key to success, Schmidt stressed, was to reduce the fear of Germany. 'We Germans want peace, freedom and reunification. Everyone believes we want the last two. Not everyone believes we want the first. . . . Reason tells us that peaceful reunification will never emerge as though by a judge's sentence in a courtroom, but only through the assent of the world powers and of all our neighbours.'

Shortly before, Schmidt had also spoken on German unity to students in Hamburg. In doing so he quoted the words carved over the great gate in Lübeck, the Holstentor, '*Concordia domi foris pax*'. Roughly translated that runs 'External peace depends on domestic concord'.

Schmidt meant that the German people would never overcome the division of the nation if they were wracked by bitter political differences at home. A minimum of common ground was needed between government and opposition. He clearly had in mind the fierce parliamentary battles of the 1950s. Was he also aware of how much Schmidt '*Schnauze*' had contributed to them?

By the mid-1960s Schmidt was striving to achieve that 'self-control' whose absence he so deplored in Strauss. He did not always succeed, then or later. He talked much about 'balance', but his sporadic outbursts, even during his Chancellorship, showed how hard he found it to achieve that condition in his own temperament.

In 1965 Schmidt seemed ripe for national office – and the SPD for governmental power. It was clear that if the SPD won the September election, then Brandt would become Chancellor, but Schmidt was high on the list of those behind him. A British newspaper even hazarded the guess that in ten years' time Debré would be President of France, Lindsay President of the US and Schmidt Chancellor of West Germany.[8] The forecast was way off the mark on the first two (perhaps few people can still remember who Debré and Lindsay were). It was right about Schmidt.

But the SPD lost – yet again. It picked up 39.3 per cent of the vote, its best result so far, but the CDU–CSU won 47.6 per cent and the liberal FDP 9.5 per cent. Ludwig Erhard became Chancellor for the second time running, and Brandt, deeply depressed, swore he would never stand for the job again. He remained party leader but retreated to Berlin. It had been a dirty campaign and Brandt seemed physically and mentally worn out. In contrast to the 1961 campaign, there had been fewer obvious jibes about his illegitimate birth. But there had been attacks on his past as a refugee who had taken Norwegian citizenship. 'Where was Brandt in 1948? In safety,' read a (factually inaccurate) banner strung between two planes and drawn across the sky as the election drew near. It was typical of efforts by some of the political Right to smear Brandt as a coward and traitor, a more vicious counterpart to those on the Left who shunned Schmidt as an ex-Wehrmacht officer. Germany's tortured past erupted in some such way in every election, even into the 1980s!

Schmidt put on a bold face at the election defeat. He told an interviewer there had not been enough time for voters to overcome deep-seated prejudices against the SPD. Besides, Schmidt added brightly, opposition was not that bad. He should know since he had had eight years of it.

Despite all this, Schmidt toyed with the idea of staying in Hamburg as Interior Senator, and it took quite a lot of pressure from party colleagues to persuade him to come to Bonn. Among the most persuasive, as ever, was Herbert Wehner who was anxious to shore up the SPD in the wake of Brandt's retreat and disillusionment. For the same reason, Wehner tempted Karl Schiller, Schmidt's former economics and transport boss in Hamburg, to give up his post as Berlin Economics Senator to strengthen the SPD ranks in the Bundestag.

Was Wehner grooming Schmidt to take over the reins if Brandt really refused to stand again for the Chancellorship, or even stepped down as party leader? Certainly, when Brandt was first chosen as the SPD's 'Chancellor candidate' in 1960, Wehner was among the sceptics, and he never seems to have shaken off all his misgivings. On the other hand, Wehner was not a whole-hearted Schmidt fan either. He was one of those who looked askance at Schmidt's military background. The relations between these three key Social Democrats over decades were hardly ever free of friction, with respect and rivalry, warmth and wariness all playing a role. In the late 1970s a leading SPD parliamentarian joked that with its ruling troika, Chancellor Schmidt, Chairman Brandt and Bundestag floor-leader Wehner, the party had the most stable leadership in the world. 'Schmidt would never dream of resigning while Brandt and Wehner remain at their posts,' he declared. 'But Brandt will never step down before Schmidt and Wehner, and "Uncle Herbert" will not go before Schmidt and Brandt. Checkmate.'

Wehner's overriding ambition was to see the SPD gain government power and retain it. The aim was not power for its own sake but to press for social reform at home and a new approach to the East. This was far more important to him than any career ambitions or personal feelings about this or that individual. The only really important question was, would the party be well served or not. This 'old volcano spitting fire and fury' had a dedication to duty (as he saw it) no less passionate than that of ex-officer Schmidt.

In May 1966, Schmidt received another blow, even harder than the general election defeat eight months earlier. He stood as a candidate to lead the SPD in Hamburg and lost narrowly. It seemed scarcely credible! Had the party forgotten his services to the city, above all in the great flood? Moreover, the SPD voted in as its leader Paul Nevermann, that same Nevermann who, as Mayor, had been abroad when the flood began and had returned to find Schmidt in command.

There were probably personal reasons involved in the defeat. Perhaps, too, the Hamburg party wanted someone who would be on hand in the city the whole time. At any rate, it was a speech by Wehner (who also had a Hamburg constituency) which swayed the balance. Wehner paid tribute to Schmidt's vitality but judged that it was trying to do too much to take on Hamburg as well as Bonn politics. Later, Schmidt said stoically that 'you learn from your defeats – and gain new strength from them', but in the summer of 1966 he was in one of the deepest troughs of his career. He could not know (and even the prescient Wehner can hardly have guessed) that only a few months separated the SPD from the governmental power in Bonn it had sought for seventeen years.

4

PARLIAMENTARY LEADER

Since his general election victory in 1965, little had gone right for Chancellor Erhard. Potential rivals within the CDU–CSU were undermining his authority and the liberal FDP, junior partner in the coalition, was becoming ever more restless. But it was Erhard's failure to deal with growing economic and financial problems which most caused his undoing. Ironically, the 'father of the economic miracle' seemed incapable of devising a new strategy to head off approaching recession.

By the grim standards of the 1970s and 1980s the economic problems of 1966 look mild. But for West Germans, used to years of strong and continuous economic growth with price stability, the signs were alarming. Industrial production was falling, especially of coal and steel; the foreign trade surplus was the lowest since 1952 and the inflation rate the highest (3.5 per cent) for fifteen years. Flagging industrial orders spoke of worse to come. Indeed, in 1967 for the first time Gross National Product contracted in real terms (after allowing for inflation) and the number of jobless tripled to nearly 500,000, more than 2 per cent of the labour force.

Erhard thought nothing of state expenditure programmes to try to boost the economy. His instinct, and his experience during the post-war reconstruction, told him it was market forces, not the state, which could create a durable economic upswing. He might have favoured offering investment incentives to private industry but no spare government funds were available to finance that. A gap in the 1966 budget had been plugged only with difficulty. By the autumn, a bigger hole was looming in the 1967 budget, partly because tax revenue estimates were being revised downwards as economic activity slowed. The Basic Law (constitution) insisted on a balanced budget, and made it hard for the government to borrow funds to make up a shortfall.

It was this budget deficit problem, closely linked to the economic downturn, which finally toppled the government. Erhard proposed tax increases to close the emerging gap, but the FDP demanded spending cuts, in defence among other things. On 27 October the four FDP ministers resigned from Erhard's cabinet and the party went into opposition. That left the CDU–CSU with only 245 seats in the Bundestag against a potential 251 for the SPD and FDP if they voted together. At the end of November Erhard stepped down.

Sixteen years later the FDP was to withdraw from another government alliance; again the economy was in poor shape, again there was a battle over the budget and again the FDP demanded spending cuts. But in 1982 the coalition partner was the SPD, and the Chancellor who fell was Helmut Schmidt.

Whatever feelings Schmidt had about the FDP on the day he lost office, surprise cannot have been among them. Even in 1966 Schmidt deeply distrusted the 'liberals' who had withdrawn from Adenauer's coalition in 1956, then again in 1963 (over Strauss and the *Der Spiegel* affair) and finally had brought down Erhard. He was sure that the FDP would not be a reliable partner for the SPD any more than for the CDU, and he played a key role in convincing most SPD parliamentarians of that fact.

This was not easy. After the collapse of Erhard's coalition there were three possibilities. One was that the FDP might form a further alliance with the CDU–CSU under its newly elected 'Chancellor candidate', Kurt Georg Kiesinger. Coalition talks were held between the two sides, but came to nothing.

Second, the SPD might join with the FDP, although the two parties would have only a razor-thin majority in the Bundestag. It was a dangerous course but had strong supporters, among them Willy Brandt who had successfully led an SPD–FDP coalition in Berlin. By late 1966 Brandt had been easily re-elected SPD Chairman and had recovered from his depression after the 1965 election. It was not the last time that friends and foes alike were to be astonished by Brandt's powers to recuperate after being virtually written off politically.

Finally, the SPD could form a 'grand coalition' with the CDU–CSU. Wehner, above all, had long been working for this. He not only shared Schmidt's views about the FDP, he also believed that a big parliamentary majority was needed to carry through major domestic and foreign policy reforms. He felt that the SPD could only overcome the reservations many West Germans still had about it, if it shared power for a time with the CDU. In others words, the grand coalition was to be the SPD's golden bridge to governmental respectability.

The Wehner–Schmidt line finally prevailed, but there were deep misgivings right across the political spectrum. Some traditional supporters of the CDU–CSU could not stand the sight of a coalition with Social Democrats, and switched to the far-right National Democratic Party (NPD). Their shift, combined with the fears aroused by economic recession, helped account for the sudden but temporary boost in support for the NPD in several regional elections in the second half of the 1960s.

On the Left the reaction was still more sharp. SPD members marched through German cities brandishing banners demanding Wehner's resignation and opposing alliance with the 'bankrupt CDU'. Young people in particular felt alienated and helped swell the ranks of the student revolt of the late 1960s. But even older people who remembered the bitter duels between Adenauer and Schumacher rubbed their eyes over the extraordinary ministerial line-up of the CDU–CSU–SPD sworn in on 1 December 1966.

The Chancellor was Kiesinger, Prime Minister of Baden Württemberg and a former (albeit non-active) member of the Nazi Party. The Vice-Chancellor and Foreign Minister was Brandt, a former refugee from the Nazis. The Finance Minister was Strauss, described in the SPD as 'the toad we had to take to bed' if the coalition were to be put together at all. Strauss was not only a minister of experience but also Chairman of the CSU, and hence could hardly be left out. The Economics Minister was Schiller, keen to bring more order and planning into a field where so far doctrinaire belief in 'the self-healing powers of the market' had prevailed. The Justice Minister was Gustav Heinemann, who had resigned from Adenauer's cabinet and joined the SPD in protest at West German rearmament. The All-German Affairs Minister was Herbert Wehner, main architect of the alliance and tirelessly working to hold it together both in and outside the cabinet.

Schmidt had no cabinet job although he might have gone to the Foreign Ministry if he had pressed for it. During the coalition negotiations, Brandt had said he did not insist on becoming Foreign Minister. He felt his work as SPD Chairman and Vice-Chancellor would be heavy, and that he could well make do with a relatively minor cabinet post, for example Research. In retrospect the offer seems surprising. Brandt put much effort and apparent enthusiasm into his foreign policy job over the next three years despite setbacks. It is odd to think he was ready to step aside so easily. Brandt's colleagues, including Schmidt, argued him out of the idea, insisting that the party chairman must have the top ministerial post too.

Schmidt could clearly have handled Defence, but coalition balance in the distribution of portfolios meant that job went to Gerhard Schroeder of the CDU, the former Foreign Minister. Schmidt was then offered Transport, but he refused. His days as a transport specialist were over, besides he did not really want to act as a specialist at all. The job he was really keen on, and the one he got, was leader of the SPD parliamentary party. He had already become deputy leader after the 1975 election. When the grand coalition took office he became acting leader, standing in for his much-admired friend and mentor Fritz Erler, who had cancer. After Erler died in February 1967, Schmidt took full control – and kept it until the general election of September 1969.

Those years as SPD floor-leader turned out to be among the most rewarding of Schmidt's career. They prepared him at least as well, and probably better, for his future Chancellorship than any ministerial post could have done. He was very much his own master, cheerfully stressing that 'there is only one leader of a parliamentary party, but twenty ministers in a cabinet'. He had to grapple with every topic which came before Parliament, from economics to defence, from legal reform to unemployment benefit. And of course, the job gave him many opportunities to display and develop his oratory. All those elements – the independence, the policy range and the polemical skill – emerged in his first major speech in the Bundestag after the grand coalition took office.[1] It quickly became clear that floor-leader Schmidt would not only be a fierce critic of the FDP opposition, but an uncomfortable figure for the government too.

He began by heaping scorn on the FDP, provoked by an ironic interjection by the liberal leader Erich Mende, for whom Schmidt had very little regard.

'For seventeen long years we vainly laid siege to the government fortress,' Schmidt told the FDP. 'Now they have had to open the gates to us. During those seventeen years you were sometimes outside, sometimes inside, then out again, then in again – and now you are out once more.'

'We took part in the siege with you for some of the time,' called an

FDP deputy, stung by the implication that his party had not acted honourably.

'Yes, it was never very clear on which side you really stood,' retorted Schmidt, referring to past splits with the FDP itself. 'Some of your colleagues took part in the siege, and others were among the besieged.' As applause and laughter burst forth from the government party benches, Schmidt added, 'I don't want to go on with this. It was just that Herr Mende provoked me. . . .'

The smiles were quickly wiped off the faces of many in the CDU–CSU. Schmidt proceeded to give what amounted to an extension, and partial critique, of the government declaration which Chancellor Kiesinger had already made in Parliament. Schmidt made clear the SPD would have liked more clarity in Kiesinger's statement on *Ostpolitik* and regretted that too little had been said about defence policy and the Bundeswehr's future role. He urged speedy action to tackle the economic problems which 'as Chancellor Kiesinger correctly noted' were due to past (government) neglect. Legal, financial and other reforms must be implemented during the current legislative period. For anyone who had not fully taken in his message, Schmidt stressed that the grand coalition did not mean the end of parliamentary control over government. It did not even mean that the forty-nine deputies of the FDP would be left alone to exercise that control. 'We will hold the government to its responsibilities,' he declared, 'not just the whole government to general policy lines but each minister in his own field. We expect results from our own ministers in particular.'

On the economic recession, Schmidt urged, as any Social Democrat would, that working people must be given back confidence that their jobs were secure. But he also stressed that employers must regain confidence in economic policy so that investment could be boosted and new jobs created.

Schmidt was not the only SPD leader to adopt this even-handed approach to management and labour alike, but over the years he built unusually close relations with both sides. In his days as Chancellor, it was quite common to hear praise of Schmidt from many industrialists and businessmen who had no intention of voting for his party. The ironic comment from Schmidt critics in the SPD was that 'he is the best CDU Chancellor we have ever had'.

On the other hand, Schmidt had wide support in the trade union movement and counted several union leaders among his personal friends. At least part of that support was won during the grand coalition period, when Schmidt fought for a say by more workers in the running of business. An SPD team he headed aimed to extend '*Mitbestimmung*' ('co-determination') as practised in the iron, steel and coal industries. After a lot of work, he and the SPD brought their proposals to the Bundestag, where the CDU–CSU and FDP joined in rare alliance to throw them out.

Even in a country where the 'conservative' parties (under Adenauer) built up the social security system, and where many Social Democrats acknowledged the need for company profits, Schmidt's political position was unusually hard to define. Part of his activities seemed to belong to 'the Left', other parts to 'the Right'.

Schmidt said, well before the grand coalition came to power, that he believed he 'probably' belonged to 'the Left' because he favoured 'progress through social democracy'. But, truth to tell, he found expressions like 'Left' and 'Right' were not helpful. 'Let's not use hazy expressions in political debate,' he urged, 'but state in concrete terms what we want, how, when, under what conditions, for what purpose, at what cost and taking what secondary effects and disadvantages into account. Likewise, let's say clearly what we don't want.'[2]

This is the voice of a man who hates 'blah blah' and who will come down hard on those who produce it. So it proved in the SPD parliamentary group after Schmidt became its leader. Those deputies who drifted away from a point were quickly brought back to it; those who talked but seemed to have no point were told to shut up. 'A lot of people think democracy is a matter of endless debate,' Schmidt said. 'I believe that democracy consists of debate, and then decision on the basis of the debate.' He hurt feelings and hence stored up trouble for himself. But there are still those in the SPD who think the parliamentary party was never better led than during the Schmidt era. They say that when a thorough debate was really needed, Schmidt would neither seek to dominate it nor to cut it off prematurely.

One major issue during Schmidt's time was whether to approve legislation allowing the government special powers in a national emergency. In principle the action seemed necessary and sensible. In a hangover from the occupation period, the three Western allies – the US, Britain and France – still had the legal right to take control of the Federal Republic if there was a major natural catastrophe or if the 'democratic constitutional order' was threatened. Among other things, the allies could tap telephone lines and open private mail. The object was to hand on these powers, circumscribed with parliamentary safeguards, to the Bonn government.

This was done in 1968, but not before fierce protests throughout the country and anguished debate, not least in the SPD parliamentary group. Some felt that the legislation, whatever the built-in safeguards, smacked of the kind Hitler had used to win full control of the Reich. Others believed that the measures were at least ill-timed. In 1968 the student revolt was under way, partly directed at the US and the Vietnam war, partly at the education system, partly it seemed at the democratic order itself. The passage of emergency legislation would be seen as aimed at the student rebellion, however much the government argued it had been seeking the new laws well before the unrest began.

These fears and more emerged during the debate within the SPD parliamentary group which went on for weeks. Detailed changes to the legislation were proposed, compromises thrashed out. Schmidt coaxed and argued, fighting for some of the changes, warning against others, rekindling the debate when it seemed to him some things had been left unsaid. He could not pull everyone round and he knew it, but he was determined that no SPD deputy would go to vote with the feeling that the issue had not been given the time and effort due. In the event the legislation passed easily but with fifty-three SPD deputies voting against (among them Kurt Gscheidle and Hans Matthöfer, both future members of a cabinet under Schmidt).

Leading the SPD was hard enough in itself; co-ordinating with the CDU–CSU parliamentarians was an added hurdle. Many SPD deputies had doubts about the grand coalition from the first although they reluctantly accepted the arguments in favour of it from Wehner and Schmidt. But as the months passed their reservations grew. Kiesinger's popularity increased and his party did well in a series of regional elections. The SPD lost ground and many of its deputies began to wonder whether they were going to pay for the grand coalition with their seats in the next general election. Parliamentary co-operation with the CDU–CSU could easily have suffered and undermined the government itself.

Schmidt recognized the danger and it was one of the reasons why he kept the SPD group on a very tight rein. At the same time he established an excellent working relationship with the leader of the CDU–CSU group, Rainer Candidus Barzel. The co-operation between the 'coalition brothers', as they were called, helped the government alliance over many difficult moments, but it was not regarded as an unmixed blessing in either coalition party or even by the Chancellor. When someone noted to Kiesinger that the two floor-leaders were 'very capable', he sourly retorted 'capable of anything.'[3]

From the start, Schmidt had publicly wagged a finger at the Chancellor, stressed what needed doing and, in effect, told the government to get on with it. As the first months passed and progress was slow, Schmidt's impatience increased. He and Barzel were holding the parliamentary troops together, now it was up to 'King Silver-tongue' (as both floor-leaders called Kiesinger) to sound the advance. The grand coalition had less than three years to show what it could do and the last of these would probably be dominated by the election campaign.

Kiesinger was uneasy about Barzel too and many in the CDU–CSU felt the same. Barzel had already been rival to Kiesinger in the bid to succeed Erhard as Chancellor. Earlier he had tried unsuccessfully to become Chairman of the CDU. He was a brilliant organizer, a clever speaker with a nice feeling for irony, and was still only in his early forties. Despite those early setbacks, Barzel seemed destined for the top once Kiesinger had gone.

Things did not work out that way. Barzel sought to topple Willy Brandt as Chancellor in a parliamentary vote of no confidence in 1972. He narrowly failed in and in 1973 gave up the CDU national leadership he had held for less than two years. Perhaps he had always been too obviously ambitious for his own good, giving his CDU–CSU rivals the chance to band together against him before they tackled one another. Maybe that was also part of the reason why he and Schmidt often seemed more relaxed with one another than either was within his own party. Each acknowledged the other's political stature and professionalism. Both felt, with some justification, that they were keeping the coalition ticking over if anyone was. But they were not competitors within the same party.

Their mutual respect long outlived the alliance of their parties. When Schmidt's Left–Liberal government fell in 1982 it was Barzel, alone of the CDU–CSU, who went up to his former grand coalition colleague in Parliament to express sympathy. Much earlier, Schmidt had said of his work with Barzel: 'Neither one of us tried to lead the other up the garden path, or to gain advantage by tricks. Often there were arguments and often it was hard to find a compromise. But despite much of what is said, or put into circulation, about Barzel, I found him to be a man who was fair and stuck to his word.'[4]

The Schmidt–Barzel tandem was one unexpected success of the grand coalition. Another, at least at first, came from the unlikely twins at the Finance and Economics Ministries. Few had thought that Finance Minister Strauss, csu, rightist champion of free enterprise, would get on well with Economics Minister Schiller, spd, professor and planner. But the two gave the impression they had been happily in harness together for years, swapping jokes in public, digging one another in the ribs and swearing allegiance to a common course. The public called them *'Plisch und Plum'* (more or less 'Tweedledum and Tweedledee') and they seemed to revel in it.

Within the first half-year of the government the budget deficit was plugged and a special credit-financed government investment programme approved to help combat the recession. Schiller introduced the 'concerted action' meetings, in which trade unionists and employers as well as government and central bank representatives jointly discussed economic prospects and tried to thrash out differences. Above all an economic 'Stability and Growth Law' was passed, laying the basis for longer-term financial planning, better policy co-ordination, and giving the authorities more weapons to fight slumps and booms.

The coalition had come to power promising to get the economy going again and it did so. By 1969, Gross National Product was growing by nearly 8 per cent in real terms, the inflation rate was under 2 per cent and the number of jobless had dropped to less than 200,000 (below 1 per cent of the labour force). It seemed just like the golden days of the 1950s, more golden in fact since the balance of payments was in record surplus.

In a way the coalition succeeded too well for its own good. The glowing trade figures and low inflation rate brought growing pressure to revalue the Deutschmark, even in 1968. The government tried to fight it off, partly by imposing a tax on exports and a subsidy on imports (a step hardly credible from the standpoint of the 1980s). It was to no avail. By spring 1969, the pressure was mounting again and brought sharp coalition differences. Schiller strongly favoured a revaluation, to help end the inflationary pressure from funds flooding into the Deutschmark from abroad. Strauss and the cdu fiercely resisted for reasons of principle and tactics. They were reluctant to interfere, as they saw it, with the fixed exchange rate system which had served the world well since the end of the Second World War. Those were the days before 'currency floating' and the Deutschmark had only been revalued once, in 1961. Furthermore, the Union parties thought revaluation would be unpopular with German exporters and hence clearly unwise so close to the autumn general election. In the event, revaluation only came a month after polling day – approved by a new government which included Schiller but excluded Strauss.

The growing differences over the economy and currency were only two of the elements prising the coalition partners apart. Abroad, the Warsaw Pact invasion of Czechoslovakia in 1968 had undermined the coalition's approach to *Ostpolitik*. Brandt and the SPD wanted to continue with vigorous efforts to forge new links with the East, Kiesinger and the CDU saw Czechoslovakia as a warning to proceed only with caution. At home, the student unrest convinced Brandt more than anything else that the grand coalition had had its day. The upsurge among the young had emerged throughout most of the Western world (and even part of the Eastern), not in the Federal Republic alone. But Brandt felt that another term of CDU–CSU–SPD government with no strong parliamentary opposition could spark still more serious youth rebellion in Germany and a further rise of the far Right. He wanted to head it off. He also felt the SPD stood to gain by scooping up and trying to channel at least some of the idealistic young who had been out on the streets. Finally, the jovial but determined Rhinelander, Walter Scheel, had succeeded Erich Mende as leader of the FDP in 1968. It was a change that Brandt felt made the liberals into a more reliable potential partner.

This view was widely shared in the SPD. It received further support in March 1969, when the FDP joined with the SPD to vote in the Social Democrat Gustav Heinemann as Federal President, instead of the CDU–CSU candidate, Gerhard Schroeder. But Wehner and Schmidt were among those in the SPD who still had strong doubts.

Partly this was a matter of arithmetic. No one believed the SPD could win a majority of Bundestag seats in the election and hence be able to govern alone. It was not even certain the FDP could clear the '5 per cent hurdle'. Under German law a party failing to gain at least 5 per cent of the votes cannot be represented in Parliament, a step intended to prevent the unstable government of the Weimar period. Even if the FDP did gain entry to the Bundestag it was unlikely to be by much.

54

Thus an SPD–FDP government would have only a slim majority, perhaps restricting its room for manœuvre and in any case demanding reliability from almost every member of the coalition all the time. Schmidt and Wehner strongly doubted if that could be guaranteed.

These fears were not groundless, as events showed. In the September election, the FDP won only 5.8 per cent of the vote, the SPD 42.7 per cent and the CDU–CSU 46.1 per cent. With the almost reckless courage of their convictions, Brandt and Scheel agreed to form a government alliance with only 254 Bundestag seats to the CDU–CSU's 242. Brandt was elected Chancellor with 251 deputies supporting him, just two more than the absolute majority he needed. His slim lead evaporated through defections over the next two years, making premature general elections necessary in November 1972. Only then did Brandt and Scheel emerge with a firm parliamentary base. How easily it might have gone the other way, with Brandt failing to gain election as Chancellor in 1969 and the Social Democrat–Liberal alliance dying at birth!

Apart from the technical, but crucial, issue of parliamentary numbers, Schmidt gave the grand coalition better marks than did Brandt. It had made a slow start in some fields and had not carried out all it promised. One casualty had been electoral reform, which the CDU–CSU had keenly wanted and which Schmidt and part of the SPD cautiously supported at the start. The idea was to introduce a voting system along the English lines of 'winner takes all' instead of the mixed system of (qualified) proportional representation. Advocates of the change said it would eliminate unstable coalitions, meaning in practice that the irritating FDP ('in again, out again') would be blotted out. By 1968, the SPD had decided to shelve the issue. For one thing, studies showed that the CDU–CSU probably stood to gain more from a change than the Social Democrats. For another, the FDP seemed to have increasing potential as a coalition partner for the SPD. The idea of killing it off thus lost attraction.

That apart, Schmidt acknowledged that the CDU–CSU–SPD alliance had done a lot of useful work: economic, financial and legal reform, the emergency laws and so on. He could hardly feel otherwise since he and Barzel had invested so much time and energy in whipping the government programme over the hurdles. Brandt's experience as Foreign Minister had been less happy, despite all his efforts. He felt that Kiesinger, who had a big interest in foreign affairs, often intruded on his ministerial patch. Brandt thought once or twice of resigning, but stuck it out because he did not want to be the one to bring down the grand coalition.[5] That was to be the job of the voters!

There was another difference between Schmidt and Brandt which became more marked later. Schmidt was highly sceptical of the idea that the SPD could boost its popularity by opening itself to the rebellious young. True, the party had to evolve, to be self-critical; but Schmidt felt that if it made its policy contours wishy-washy to gain new voters it would lose traditional supporters, above all in the trade unions.

It is easy to over-simplify and see Schmidt as a '*Macher*' and Brandt as a 'dreamer', but there has always been something of Chairman Mao about Willy Brandt, the Mao who urged 'let a thousand flowers bloom, let a thousand fields of thought contend'. In his Nobel Peace Prize speech of 1971, Brandt stated: 'I say to my young friends and to others who want to hear it: there are several truths, not merely the one which excludes all others. That is why I believe in diversity and hence in doubt. It is productive. It questions existing things.' Helmut Schmidt might have some sympathy with that as a philosophical statement but would certainly feel it to be a dangerous stance in practice for a political leader. At any rate Schmidt considered, throughout the 1970s and right into the 1980s, that Brandt kept the SPD on far too loose a rein. Not least, Schmidt believed that, as Chancellor, he had too little firm and continuous backing from his party on NATO's nuclear arms strategy. The SPD was torn between responsibility to government on the one hand and sympathy for the anti-nuclear 'peace movement' outside Parliament on the other. Brandt, as so often, hung between. The seeds of this problem were already present before the SPD–FDP coalition first came to power.

During 1969, Schmidt publicly kept his options open on what coalition might be most desirable after the election. In any case, it would have been foolish to give the CDU–CSU the impression that the SPD had no practicable alternative partner. If the grand coalition were to be re-constituted, then there would first be hard bargaining over future policy and leading positions including Schmidt's. The longer the SPD seemed at least to be keeping the door ajar for an alliance with the FDP, the more leverage it would have on the CDU–CSU.

When Brandt, with rare decisiveness, went like a bullet for the coalition with the FDP after the election, neither Schmidt nor Wehner shared the elation of many of their party colleagues. But once they saw the course had been set they did what they could to help.

In the days before the parliamentary vote which was to make Brandt Chancellor, Schmidt took drastic steps to see there would be no SPD absentees. He bluntly warned deputies that their careers would be at stake if they were not present, for any reason, to cast their vote. The margin between victory and disaster was too slim to allow the slightest avoidable risk. Meanwhile 'Brother' Barzel was doing much the same to round up the CDU–CSU opposition forces. In the event, only one deputy from a total of 496 failed to turn up, a seriously ill member of the CDU. Never before had the parliamentary presence for the election of a Chancellor been so high.

The almost-full house not only reflected the disciplinary powers of the respective floor-leaders. Most Germans in and outside Parliament felt that, for better or worse, 21 October 1969 would be an historic day if Brandt was elected. There had been no Social Democratic Chancellor since Hermann Mueller in 1930, and the CDU–CSU had never been out of power since 1949. That in itself was enough to justify talk about a 'new era'. But Brandt himself was the object of extraordinarily intense hopes and fears. His supporters saw him above all as the embodiment of their desire for domestic reform, although there was no clear accord on just what 'reform' involved. Some saw it as a step-by-step process of social improvement through legislation within the existing system. Others, especially among the young, felt it would be not just a 'wind of change' but a tempest to alter the system itself. Brandt would be able to go far to satisfy the first group – too far, it might be argued, in view of growing budgetary difficulties. But he was bound to disappoint the second.

Brandt's opponents had their fears on the domestic policy front but their biggest worry was over foreign affairs. Might not Brandt, free from the restraining influence of the CDU–CSU, move too far and too fast with the *Ostpolitik*, increasing risks not just for West Germany but for the West as a whole? This concern was not confined to the Federal Republic. The United States, Britain and France all shared this worry, although they naturally talked about it to one another rather than to the Germans.

Despite all that was at stake for him personally and politically, Brandt showed little emotion in the Bundestag plenum when his narrow victory was announced. Only later, when colleagues clapped him on the back and wrung his hand, did his eyes moisten. But he certainly did not underrate what he had achieved. 'Now Hitler has finally lost the war,' he told an interviewer.

Those early days of triumph for Brandt were not happy ones for Schmidt. There was more to this than 'sour grapes'; perhaps Schmidt felt he could have made an effective Chancellor for all his later insistence he never wanted the job. Now a man only a few years older was at the top, and perhaps for a long time.

None the less, Schmidt recognized that Brandt was a leader of uncommon, albeit inconsistent, distinction. Right through into the 1980s, Schmidt would repeat how well he thought Brandt had handled the post of governing mayor during the Berlin wall crisis of 1961. Schmidt had listened with growing admiration to a live radio broadcast in which Brandt calmed and encouraged thousands of near-rioting Berliners assembled before the town hall. That experience made an indelible impression on Schmidt. It was a proof of what Brandt could 'pull out of the bag' for the great occasion. On the other hand, it could not blind Schmidt to his growing differences with the SPD leader, above all on party policy.[6]

The immediate problem for Schmidt was that Brandt offered him the job of Defence Minister, which he did not want but could not easily refuse. At first sight his reluctance looks odd. Was he not pre-destined for the defence portfolio? Even his political opponents admitted he was unusually well equipped for it. There was his background in the Wehrmacht and as a reserve officer of the Bundeswehr. There were his books. He had just completed a successful follow-up to his *Defence or Retaliation* of 1961 called *Strategie des Gleichgewichts* (later translated into English and called *Balance of Power: Germany's Peace Policy and the Superpowers*). There were his sharp, frequent interventions on military matters in the Bundestag, which had brought mingled respect and anger from successive Defence Ministers.

But Schmidt was not keen to specialize. In his parliamentary post he had been both a leader and a policy all-rounder. That was where he would have liked to stay. The Foreign Ministry job would have offered diversity, and Schmidt's latest book underlined how far he had gone from being a military specialist to a foreign political strategist. But under the coalition accord, the Foreign Ministry went to the FDP leader and Vice Chancellor Scheel.

Schmidt took about a fortnight to make up his mind, then agreed to

Brandt's offer and passed on the parliamentary leadership to Herbert Wehner. For Wehner it was the start of thirteen years in the job, during which he partly revised his views about the unreliability of the FDP. He found that he could work well with Wolfgang Mischnick, the FDP floor-leader, and together they proved at least as indispensable to the 'small coalition' as Schmidt and Barzel had been to the 'grand' one. Hence it was a bitter personal, as well as political, blow to Wehner when Mischnick, of all people, helped promote the FDP walk-out which broke the alliance with the SPD in 1982.

As he handed over his post as floor-leader to Wehner, Schmidt produced a large bunch of flowers and managed to summon a brief smile. He had the distinction of being the first Social Democratic Defence Minister in Germany since Gustav Noske in 1920s Weimar, but he went to office on leaden feet.

5

IN CABINET

Schmidt had no illusions about what awaited him. Even in 1966 he had called the defence job a 'murderous' one which brutally exposed the failings of those who took it on. Later he noted that it could become an 'ejector seat' for a luckless incumbent. Schmidt's successor in the post, Georg Leber, had to resign and Leber's successor, Hans Apel, came close to doing so.

Even in Schmidt's time the sprawling ministry on the Hardthöhe hill on the outskirts of Bonn had a staff of more than 5,000, an annual budget of around DM20 billion, and was responsible for 650,000 people. In other words it was as big as the country's largest industrial enterprise, but was wracked by political and social problems from which most industrialists were happily free. This was partly a hangover from the bitter dissension over German rearmament of the 1950s. The need for the Bundeswehr had been accepted only unwillingly. Soldiers were called 'citizens in uniform' but they often felt more like outcasts and changed into civilian clothes the moment they were off-duty. Military service was compulsory and many young Germans approached it with dread, or fury that they were losing time they could have spent learning a job.

Schmidt saw the need for change but, just as important, he had a clear idea of the kind of leadership and teamwork which would be required to bring about change. During his four years as Interior Senator in Hamburg he had learned the bitter lesson that if you did not take a firm grip on bureaucrats then they would take hold of you.

Civil servants were bent on continuity, he reflected grimly in an essay on politics.[1] In principle that was no bad thing for the state – but it could spell calamity for a fresh, green minister full of plans but unaware of the resources with which officials would fight to maintain the *status quo*. Pressed to adopt a new course, they would argue that 'we have never done things that way' and raise extraordinarily complex legal objections. A minister rarely had the detailed knowledge to assess whether the objections were well-founded. If he then beat a retreat before the 'experts', he was lost. A minister could have excellent powers of analysis and know the best political solution to a problem, but if he could not control the administration he was lost.

Once installed on the Hardthöhe, Schmidt sought to outflank the bureaucrats in two ways. He let it be known that he welcomed suggestions and criticism direct from the armed forces, and spent about nine weeks touring the country and hearing complaints at first hand. He learned a lot, and officers and men could let off steam about problems which had been simmering for years. In one or two cases they let off a bit too much steam and Schmidt had to see that the lid was put back on again.

Schmidt also formed a small, brain-storming team of people he could trust, drawn mainly from outside the ministry. For the first time, but by no means the last, the expression 'Schmidt's Hamburg Mafia' was heard in Bonn. One member was Willi Berkhan, who became State Secretary responsible for liaison with Parliament (and later Ombudsman for the armed forces). Another was Johannes Birckholz, from Schmidt's former Interior Ministry in Hamburg. Yet another, fairly briefly, was Theo Sommer, deputy (and later chief) editor of the Hamburg weekly *Die Zeit*. Under Sommer's guidance the Defence Report ('*Weissbuch*') for 1970 was drawn up, the most readable as well as comprehensive survey the ministry has produced before or since.

One leading non-Hamburg member of the team was Ernst Mommsen, a senior industrialist from the Thyssen concern, whom Schmidt drew in to reorganize procurement of military equipment and get better value for money. The appointment of a 'Ruhr steel boss' raised some eyebrows among the Social Democrats but that did not bother Schmidt. He aimed to have the most trustworthy and efficient staff available. Political ideology played almost no role. As Chancellor, Schmidt was to appoint a Christian Democrat as his top foreign policy adviser and, for a time, had a man who was certainly no Social Democrat as his chief spokesman. He even enlisted a senior member of Strauss's Christian Social Union to head an enquiry into errors made in the hunt for terrorists. Appointments like the latter could well be justified as evidence of a non-party approach to a matter of deep national concern. None the less, Schmidt's readiness to look beyond the

SPD for key personnel was one further factor which caused growing friction with his party over the years.

This inner circle (which included the Bundeswehr Inspector-General, Ulrich de Maizière) was Schmidt's key instrument for forging policy as well as implementing it. Hour after hour was spent thrashing out problems to try to reach a consensus. Schmidt had plenty of his own ideas and in the end he was the boss, but he demanded constant input and argument from other members of the team. Theo Sommer recalled his initial astonishment at the amount of time and effort Schmidt was ready to put into discussion before coming to a decision. Many members of the ministry, who had been expecting a kind of political gun-man shooting directives from the hip, felt the same surprise.

This is far from the image of 'know-all Schmidt' who irritates cabinet colleagues (and even US presidents!) by apparent intellectual arrogance. But the battle in the SPD over the emergency laws had already shown that Schmidt could encourage comprehensive debate even lasting weeks when he thought it was worth it.

He was no different later as government leader. One new recruit to the Chancellor's team was told after a few weeks by a senior colleague that Schmidt was satisfied with him except for one thing: 'You don't argue enough. The Chancellor knows what he thinks, he expects to hear more of what you think.' Later the recruit was called in by Schmidt in the early evening, and they argued over a problem from every angle and considered the tiniest detail until after midnight. A lot of Schmidt aides had a similar experience, simultaneously exhilarating and exhausting.

The apparent contradiction between the two Schmidts, the intellectually arrogant and the inquisitive, is easily explained. When he feels someone is waffling he is quick to show it. All the more so if it is a person in high office and hence with a special responsibility for talking sense. Patience has never been Helmut Schmidt's strongest suit; but if he feels he is being told something sensible and new, he is not just interested but voracious. He is not happy until he has sucked in every scrap of available information. This intellectual curiosity and passion for detail, combined with extraordinary diligence, helped him rise to the top. If he had been better able to curb his tongue in private (without undermining his public oratory) he might have had an easier ascent, and a less uncomfortable time at the summit.

Schmidt was Defence Minister for about 1,000 days – time enough to start many reforms but not time enough to see all of them through. He cut the conscription period from eighteen months to fifteen, and reorganized the forces' system of education and vocational training. When he took over, there was a serious shortage of non-commissioned officers, the so-called 'backbone of the service'. By giving NCOs a better chance to learn a civilian trade, he made the Bundeswehr more attractive and was rewarded by a growing number of volunteers. On the other hand, a major study on structural change in the armed forces to face the challenge of the 1970s, proposed by Schmidt soon after taking office, only emerged as he was leaving. To help rejuvenate the Bundeswehr, Schmidt put many senior officers into early retirement and took steps to gain a better brief on pending promotions. In a more curious move to keep the Bundeswehr image up to date, he agreed that servicemen could wear long hair and beards. This action earned him a prize at the Aachen carnival for his 'German Hair Force' and sharp remarks from traditional supporters of the military 'short back and sides'. Schmidt's retort was, 'For me what matters is what goes on inside a man's skull, not whether there is long or short hair on top.'

He touched more dangerous ground when he warned, in 1971, that private cars would be drawn into military manœuvres the following year, as a test for mobilization. It was only a couple of sentences in a long speech in Kiel in the far north, but it immediately brought about a countrywide storm.[2] It is a golden political rule in Germany that you can get people to accept most sacrifices if you ask them the right way; but if you lay a finger on their cars – their 'lacquered lovelies', as one newspaper called them at the time – you are playing with fire. The Defence Ministry in Bonn initially seemed nonplussed by Schmidt's remarks and the fierce reaction to them. Only after two days did the Minister appear on television to ask what all the fuss was about. Fewer than 400 private commercial lorries were to be used, not millions of cars as people seemed to fear. In the event, only 160 lorries took part in the exercise and Schmidt's popularity did not suffer. He was lucky. A few years later he was to make another speech in the north about which his staff in Bonn knew little and could not quickly clarify. That time Schmidt was less lucky. His words about nuclear missiles were to reverberate from Moscow to Washington and back, above all bringing about a serious misunderstanding with President Carter.

Of more concern to Schmidt than criticism about bearded soldiers and commandeered vehicles, was the level of his defence budget. The

Finance Minister Alex Moeller, fighting against rising inflation, sought for months to rein in the spending of his reform-happy cabinet colleagues. He finally stepped down in May 1971, after failing to obtain the cuts he thought essential. Schmidt was one of those widely accused of fighting for every *pfennig*, and thus contributing to Moeller's fall. Schmidt insists that he had no 'exclusive' cabinet dissent with Moeller, whom he regards as an old friend.[3] Indeed, Moeller was trying to get everyone to save; but inevitably defence, which took the second biggest slice of the budget, was high on the list.

The figures show that both before and after Moeller's time, Schmidt fought for funds with some, not outstanding, success. In the three years he was Defence Minister, his budget rose by 2.6 per cent in 1970, by 10.3 per cent in 1971, and by 13.5 per cent in 1972. But the proportion of the total federal budget going to defence over that period remained static at about 22 per cent. Schmidt was getting more, but so were the other ministers.

Part of the increase in defence spending came from Schmidt's drive for internal Bundeswehr reform. Some of the changes might have been postponed, though at the cost of greater manpower problems later. But part of the outlay was for NATO commitments, including extra funds to help maintain the US presence in Europe. Here Schmidt was determined there must be no false economies. Never had the West had a better chance than at the start of the 1970s for productive negotiations with the communist East. But if NATO unilaterally weakened its defence posture, Schmidt was sure that the chance would go down the drain.

The so-called 'Brandt–Scheel' *Ostpolitik* was moving ahead quickly (treaties with Russia and Poland were both signed in 1970), but it was not doing so in a void. The West Germans were able to launch their Eastern initiatives with some confidence because they had the formal support of their allies in the West, whatever private worries those allies had about where the process might lead. This dependence was clearest on the Berlin issue. Bonn wanted a solution which would secure the position of West Berlin and end the chicanery to which travellers were often subjected on the transit routes through East Germany. But a Berlin settlement could only be reached by the four wartime victors who had jurisdiction over the city. Bonn could, and did, make its views on Berlin clear to the Russians. But it was dependent on the goodwill and negotiating skill of the US, Britain and France for a formal Berlin accord with Moscow which took account of West German interests.

Prospects for East–West force cuts seemed to be improving too. In June 1968 at a meeting in Iceland, NATO had sent its 'signal of Reykjavik' to the Warsaw Pact proposing talks on Mutual and Balanced Force Reductions (MBFR). The Soviet-led invasion of Czechoslovakia two months later put paid to that idea for a time; but in May 1970, in Rome, NATO reissued its call and in June the Eastern side gave what Schmidt called 'a less unsubtle and more forthcoming response than might have been expected'. The MBFR waggon seemed about to get on the road more than a decade after Schmidt's first Bundestag speech proposing 'balanced' force reductions and trying to define what 'balance' would entail. Successful MBFR negotiations would increase security and decrease pressure on the defence budget. In 1970 Schmidt was hardly optimistic enough to think that the benefits would emerge during his own time in the defence job, but he was sure they would come eventually if the West kept its nerve.

A potential threat to this process loomed in the US which was still in the throes of the Vietnam war. President Nixon was under growing domestic pressure to cut the US military presence in Europe, partly from those who wanted to divert more funds to Vietnam, partly from those increasingly opposed to an armed American presence anywhere abroad.

Schmidt was blunt about what he thought the consequences of this trend might be. In an article published in the respected US journal *Foreign Affairs* (and hence directed in particular at senators and others of influence in Washington), he warned that premature withdrawal of US troops would turn NATO's defence strategy into a shambles. It could also disastrously undermine public confidence throughout Europe.

Schmidt noted that a recent (1970) opinion poll had shown that two-thirds of all West Germans, and nearly 80 per cent of those in the Bundeswehr, believed a communist attack could not be repelled if the Americans went home. 'An American pull-out might indeed cause a psychological landslide and impel a despondent Western Europe towards its first major reorientation since the end of the Second World War,' Schmidt wrote. Schmidt agreed it was not 'Holy Writ' that US troop strength in Europe must never be changed; negotiations with the East on cuts might be looming on the horizon. But he warned that 'they may never become palpable political reality if the West throws away its

65

cards before going to the conference table or before getting agreements on mutual force reductions'.

Schmidt was aware that warnings were not enough. The European members of NATO (recently formed into the so-called EUROGROUP) had to give a signal that they were ready to shoulder more of the defence burden. He strongly canvassed his European colleagues and, in December 1970, the European Defence Improvement Programme (EDIP) emerged. Under it, the Europeans agreed to put up an extra $1 billion over five years to improve their own forces and NATO infrastructure – barracks, aircraft shelters and so on. West Germany pledged DM1.7 billion or nearly half the total. That did not remove Washington's worries, but it helped to ease them. Nixon promptly announced that, in view of the European defence efforts, the US would withdraw no troops unilaterally. Schmidt was not the only leader to recognize the dangers and press for an increased European contribution (of which the EDIP was only one part). But the urgency with which he argued his case, combined with the pledge that Bonn would pay so big a share, proved decisive.

There was a still more complex linkage in that series of East–West negotiations going on in the early 1970s. Bonn could not agree a treaty regulating its relations with East Germany until the four powers had reached a satisfactory Berlin settlement. The Russians were not keen to give ground on Berlin, which would give them problems with their East German ally. But they wanted a European Security Conference, indeed had been pressing for one for years. The US was determined not to give the go-ahead to a Security Conference, which it felt might benefit Russian propaganda, unless a Berlin accord were achieved first.

Finally, all were achieved – a Berlin settlement in September 1971, an East–West German Treaty in December 1972, and a 'Conference on Security and Co-operation in Europe' in Helsinki in August 1975. Just as important, the US and the Soviet Union reached a first accord in 1972 to limit their intercontinental strategic weaponry and discussed prospects for a second one. An end to the arms race in very long-range nuclear weapons was, of course, desirable in itself. But it also posed serious problems for Western Europe which were not widely appreciated until 1977 when Schmidt, then Chancellor, publicly underlined them and pressed for a solution.

That tale, and the friction it involved between the Chancellor and President Carter, belongs to a later chapter. In the early 1970s Defence

Minister Schmidt was the toast of the US administration. The American Ambassador to Bonn, Kenneth Rush, publicly stressed Schmidt's 'inestimable contribution to strengthening American–European relations'. Without him, Rush declared, the extra European efforts for NATO defence would have been far smaller.[4]

As Rush voiced this praise in January 1972, Schmidt lay in hospital with a mysterious illness. At first there was talk of a virus which he might have picked up during an Asian tour in late 1971. But close colleagues had been aware of a change for the worse in Schmidt before that. He suddenly began to look more tired and was much more irritable. Once he nearly collapsed after leaving a meeting but friends caught him in time. None of this was surprising in itself. He worked at least sixteen hours a day, poring over papers into the early morning with an almost fanatical concentration. Even in the Bundeswehr hospital in Koblenz, he had files wheeled to his bedside on a trolley. But that was not all. His complexion became grey and his eyes protruded in a way which surely was not caused by fatigue alone. Brandt was only one of those who wondered how long Schmidt would have the physical strength to hold down the Defence Ministry job.

In February, Schmidt returned to work pooh-poohing talk of a serious illness – but in April he was back in hospital again. This time the truth came out. There had been a serious virus infection but it had initially concealed the main problem: an over-active thyroid gland.

There was public speculation that the thyroid complaint, a condition which can have a psychological background, might have been caused by Schmidt's unhappiness about his job. Whatever the truth, neither praise from abroad nor popularity at home reconciled Schmidt to the defence post. Far from becoming listless, he seemed to try to make up for a lack of inner enthusiasm with redoubled effort. Were all those late nights at the ministry objectively necessary? From the descriptions of some who watched him, Schmidt at that time seems to have been like Tolstoy's Marshal Davoust, who made conditions hard for himself in order to provide an excuse for his innate gloom: 'How can I think of the bright side of existence when, as you see, I sit perched on a barrel in a dirty shed, hard at work?', the expression on Davoust's face seemed to say.'

From his hospital bed in early 1972, Schmidt must have felt that his political career might be close to its end. Yet, within a few months, there was a startling change in his fortunes, like the one in 1966 when he had suddenly been whisked out of opposition and into the floor-leader's job. Schmidt's thyroid problem gradually responded to treatment, though he has had to take medicine daily ever since, and in a cabinet reshuffle he was appointed 'Superminister' of Economics and Finance. It was a post which a lot of people at the time interpreted as that of a 'Chancellor-in-waiting'.

There had been no Superministry when the SPD–FDP coalition came to power. Karl Schiller kept the Economics job he had held with distinction since 1966 under the grand coalition, and Alex Moeller, also a Social Democrat, succeeded Franz Josef Strauss as Finance Minister. Optimism was in the air. Gross National Product grew by nearly 8 per cent in real terms in 1969, unemployment was low, industrial production and orders were booming. Even the revaluation of the Deutschmark by 8.5 per cent in October failed to dampen the spirits of the coalition partners. With economic growth apparently assured, it seemed reasonable to push ahead at full steam with that programme of social reform which was the domestic complement to the *Ostpolitik*.

But Moeller (formerly an insurance company director) was a cautious man. From the start he promised a 'solid' finance policy, meaning he was determined to battle inflation and would not let the state live too much off credit. Over the first year the government took several steps to stop the economy 'overheating' and the inflation rate was held to 3.3 per cent in 1970 (albeit up from 1.9 per cent a year earlier). But Moeller became more and more worried. Estimates showed that tax revenue would be lower than expected and meanwhile his cabinet colleagues were producing ever more costly plans for reform. Moeller constantly appealed to the Chancellor for support but got little help. An exasperated Schmidt no doubt went too far when he said later that Brandt found it hard to tell the difference between millions and billions, but it is clear that finance was never Brandt's strongest interest. Besides, when Moeller had his troubles, Brandt was deeply involved in *Ostpolitik*.

Moeller might have stood his ground all the same, but while being given a left hook at home, he received an uppercut from abroad. The international monetary system went into another of its periodic crises, threatening West Germany (among others) with big new inflows of speculative funds which could boost inflation.

As more and more people deserted the failing dollar for 'hard' currencies, upward pressure on the Deutschmark became irresistible.

As a result, the Germans decided, in May 1971, to 'float' the Deutschmark temporarily, that is to let it find its own (higher) level in the market. 'Floating' gave German monetary authorities a respite, but Moeller insisted the step had to be backed simultaneously by firm government savings measures. If the state did not show restraint on spending, then employers would show none on prices and the trade unions none on wage demands. That was his argument. He failed to carry the majority of his cabinet colleagues with it, and stepped down.

It was also a monetary crisis which gave the knockout blow a year later to Moeller's successor, Karl Schiller. But Schiller had already been on the ropes with his guard down when the blow landed. He had taken on Moeller's Finance post in addition to his own Economics one. That gave him the glorious title of 'Superminister' but also put him in a very difficult position. He had both to provide for steady economic growth and try to cut the government's financial deficit. These were not in themselves incompatible tasks, but they were hard indeed for one man to combine.

Brandt later said he had been wrong to give Schiller both jobs together, but it is easy to see why he took the decision. As Governing Mayor of Berlin in the early 1960s, Brandt had grown to like and admire Schiller, his Economics Senator. Later Schiller shone as Economics Minister in the grand coalition and his eloquence played a key role in the SPD's election campaign of 1969. Some people even talked about 'Schiller's election'. It began to look as though there was nothing the brilliant, dapper economics professor could not do. Small wonder that, when Moeller resigned, Brandt felt he could lay the irritating and obscure field of economics and finance wholly in Schiller's hands. Virtually no one in the cabinet questioned Schiller's technical competence but some were wary, even envious, of his power and most objected to his 'know-all' style. At the same time Schiller lost a lot of support in the SPD when he opposed proposals for tax reforms which he considered too left wing.

Things got much worse in the first half of 1972. Brandt had only narrowly survived a vote of no confidence in the Bundestag, the *Ostpolitik* was threatened by a parliamentary 'pat', and early new elections had become inevitable. At that moment, Schiller, warning of a new and bigger government deficit, slapped a long list of spending cuts on the cabinet table. Schiller's budget analysis was almost certainly right. But his timing and blunt presentation infuriated his colleagues.

It brought particularly sharp clashes with Helmut Schmidt who was being asked, again, to chop the defence budget.

A Schiller–Schmidt confrontation was almost inevitable – even leaving aside the defence spending issue. Both men were clever 'all-rounders', Schiller by virtue of his double-office, Schmidt by experience and temperament. No one else in the cabinet could match them. Both had sharp tongues. Schmidt was also battling against his thyroid problem which worsened his temper. It may be that resentment from the old Hamburg Economics Ministry days, when Schiller had the senior and Schmidt a junior role, played a part too.

Cabinet meetings at that crucial time for the SPD–FDP coalition were gloomy and often bitter. One participant later said that the Schmidt–Schiller conflict sometimes became so unpleasant that Brandt simply rose and left the room, leaving his ministers to fight it out alone. Another describes the pair as acting 'like a couple of prima donnas', but adds that Schmidt was often cutting to the point of rudeness even after Schiller had stepped down. When in a bad mood, Schmidt could snap and glower in a way which not all his colleagues would charitably ascribe to poor health.

However, when Schiller fell he not only had Schmidt against him but the whole cabinet. Schiller's budget warnings had become public, giving the opposition ammunition in the run-up to the general election, finally set for November. Schiller was well aware of this, but in his resignation letter he said he had not been ready to keep quiet about pressing financial problems simply for electoral reasons. Like Moeller, he felt he had too little active support from Brandt.

The final blow came in June. Again there was a monetary crisis and again inflationary funds were pouring into the Federal Republic. The Bundesbank this time proposed introducing capital controls and its president, Karl Klasen, took part in a Bonn cabinet meeting to argue the point. Schiller argued strongly against, saying such controls never worked properly and their imposition would send a dangerous signal to other countries. He warned that he would resign if Klasen's proposal was accepted. A vote was taken and no one supported Schiller. It is hard not to feel that Schiller's colleagues had been waiting for a chance to be rid of him, even if a resignation would do the coalition's image no good so close to elections.

Schiller only submitted his formal resignation in early July and by that time Schmidt was on an official visit to Turkey. He received an urgent, but not specific, phone call from Brandt, and flew back to Bonn where talk about a cabinet reshuffle was in full swing between the SPD and FDP partners.

What happened next is a matter of contention. Some German journalists at the time reported that Schmidt proposed three possible solutions, and at least one of the writers stands firmly by this version a decade later. According to these reports, Schmidt's first option was that he should become Economics Minister, and Hans Dietrich Genscher, the Interior Minister and deputy leader of the FDP, should take over Finance – thus splitting the Superministry. Failing that, he, Schmidt, should take over Economics *and* Finance. If that proposal too did not meet general acceptance, then he would take over Economics as well as Defence, while Genscher would receive Finance as well as the Interior. It seems unlikely, on the face of it, that any member of the SPD would have proposed the third option. It would have made Genscher unusually powerful and increased the cabinet weight of the FDP, which already had, among other things, the Foreign Ministry under Scheel. However, it is certain that this proposal was one of those being floated in coalition talks, albeit *before* Schmidt arrived back from Turkey.

Schmidt says that he did not present options to anyone.[5] He recalls that he arrived back in Bonn, went to see Brandt, was offered the Superministry and had only a few hours to decide whether to take it. He finally agreed, but produced a bombshell at the same time. In private conversation with Brandt, Schmidt said he would stick to the new job for the four months or so until the general election – then he would leave both cabinet and Parliament. He accused Brandt of turning the SPD into a 'Nenni party' – a reference to the Italian socialists who had no clear stance, failed to win broad support from labour and made little impact at the polls. He, Schmidt, did not want to continue to serve under Brandt in those circumstances. Schmidt says that after the election he planned to go into a management job in business or industry. 'I could certainly have done that. I had a lot of experience and a high reputation throughout the country.'

But things did not happen that way. The SPD–FDP coalition won the November elections handsomely. For the first time the Social Democrats became the biggest single group in the Bundestag, winning 45.8 per cent of the vote to the CDU–CSU's 44.9 per cent. The liberals pulled up from 5.8 per cent to 8.4 per cent.

The Superministry was then split for good. Hans Friderichs of the

FDP took over Economics and Schmidt went to Finance, taking several bits of former Economics Ministry responsibility with him, including international monetary affairs. Why did Schmidt stay on after telling Brandt he would go?

'That was a tragedy,' Schmidt says. After the election he recalls that Brandt, despite his personal success, had one of his periodic fits of depression, as well as a bad throat infection. He was rarely available for the coalition talks on forming a new government, sometimes did not even answer the phone. For a while he was in hospital. Schmidt says Brandt's illness left the task of negotiating with the FDP mainly in the hands of two people, Herbert Wehner and himself. He felt he could not walk out as he had planned, further reducing the SPD's leadership team at a crucial moment. Brandt gradually recovered and remained Chancellor for another eighteen months. But the distribution of cabinet portfolios was largely thrashed out in his absence, including the division of the Superministry.

Did Schmidt suddenly see a chance of replacing Brandt as Chancellor, the post many people claim he must keenly have wanted? Or did his resentment against Brandt increase because he felt duty-bound to stay in politics at the very moment when he had made up his mind to look for a new challenge? Whatever the answer, Schmidt's decision to stay on in an expanded Finance Ministry job was to have major repercussions for West Germany and Europe. When he took over he did not know a lot in detail about world monetary affairs.

'I wouldn't have trusted myself to pull a European Monetary System out of the font, as I did later as Chancellor,' he said years afterwards. 'But you learn in every office, through the challenges and partners you have. . . . I am very eager to learn.'[6]

Schmidt was not alone in his apprenticeship. Everyone dealing with monetary affairs in those days was uneasily entering uncharted territory. The general public saw international currency crises come and go with the baffling irregularity of volcanic eruptions. Western leaders could not agree on a diagnosis let alone a cure. The post-war system of fixed (but occasionally adjustable) exchange rates, established at Bretton Woods in the US, seemed to be in its death throes. It had accompanied, perhaps guaranteed, a period of unprecedented economic growth and rising living standards since 1945. What could replace it and with what consequences?

Schmidt was thus feeling his way like others in 1972–3. But he had already seen in cabinet the dramatic impact of international monetary turmoil, which had been one cause of the downfall of his two Finance predecessors. He also saw sharp price increases in virtually every country. He strongly suspected that a major cause of both, the monetary unrest and the inflation, was the lack of budget and balance of payments discipline by the United States. This suspicion gradually hardened into a conviction. It was the cause of much of his sharp criticism of US policy right into the 1980s. It also helps explain his efforts to form a zone of greater monetary stability in Europe.

The fixed exchange rate system had been founded on the US dollar, which was freely convertible to gold at a rate of $35 an ounce. Strictly speaking, that implied that the Americans would not run bigger balance of payments deficits than they could cover with their hoard of gold in Fort Knox. So long as this was the case the dollar was, literally, as good as gold. Even if the US went deep into the red for a time that would not matter much, so long as dollar holders had confidence in American policy to correct things. The real basis of the system was thus not only gold, but trust in the power of America's economy and the competence of its leaders.

Over the years the deficit widened and dollar holders became less confident that the US could put its house in order. The Vietnam war and the growing American budget deficit increased these doubts. It seemed that the US was financing the war by printing dollars not backed either by the production of goods and services or, any longer, by enough gold. To many non-Americans, President Nixon seemed to admit as much in August 1971, when he took steps to try to correct the US payments deficit and 'suspended' the dollar's convertibility into gold. In fact, convertibility was never restored.

Both before and after the Nixon measures, people off-loaded dollars and moved into currencies in which they had more confidence. Thanks to West Germany's relative success in controlling inflation and maintaining an external surplus, the Deutschmark was a favourite target. Sometimes the run became a stampede, putting fierce upward pressure on the German currency.

Under the fixed exchange rate system the Deutsche Bundesbank, like other central banks, had three main choices – all unpleasant: it could recommend the government to revalue the Deutschmark, which would make German exports dearer abroad; it could propose introducing currency controls (as Klasen successfully did at the end of the

73

Schiller era); or it could simply go on supporting the existing Deutschmark–dollar rate by buying up huge quantities of the US currency which speculators were off-loading. In the final years of the fixed exchange rate system this is what the Bundesbank found itself doing all too often. Its reserves (mainly dollars) rose from DM26 billion in 1969, to DM49 billion in 1970 to a (temporary) peak of DM91 billion in 1973. This massive inflow of funds threatened to boost inflation by swelling the domestic money supply and undermining the Bundesbank's control of liquidity and credit. That imported element of inflation would, in turn, encourage higher wage demands, eventually, and still higher prices.

There was a wider policy point too. On the one hand, Defence Minister Schmidt had been seeking more funds, not least for extra NATO commitments and to encourage a continued US military presence in Europe. On the other, Finance Minister Moeller had been trying to curb government spending, including Schmidt's, against the background of a dollar crisis. The problems of both ministers were thus complicated by the same factor, the external and budget deficits of the US.

This link between economy, finance and defence was not evident to many people in the early 1970s, but it became plainer later. As Schmidt put it a decade afterwards: 'The US's closest allies in particular are exposed to the effects of American economic policy. But it is on their economic efficiency and social stability that the strength and cohesion of the Western alliance depends. . . . Economic policy is thus, simultaneously, security policy.'[7]

Naturally Americans saw the collapse of the fixed exchange rate system differently. Increasingly they came to feel that the system meant too one-sided a burden on the US, and that criticism from allies and partners was not sincere. If countries in surplus were unhappy about the US external deficit, it was argued, they should revalue their currencies and so help restore a balance. If they did not do so, this implied that they really preferred to stay in surplus and the US to be in the red.

As for Vietnam and the budget deficit, successive US administrations argued that they were paying a high price to try to resist communist expansion. They felt that this cause, and its financial cost, deserved understanding from European allies, themselves on the fringe of the communist empire. Besides, most ordinary Americans felt that the budget deficit was America's business. Understandably, it was hard for them to see a link between Washington's housekeeping difficulties and Europe's economic problems. They found it no easier a decade later when the US budget deficit was far bigger, interest rates were soaring and the Europeans, Schmidt in particular, were laying much of the blame for recession at America's door.

A lot of Schmidt's analysis of US policy was shared by Valéry Giscard d'Estaing of France. He and Schmidt were Finance Ministers at the same time, and their professional esteem for one another grew into personal friendship. They were both in office during the final agonized contortions of the fixed exchange rate system. They took part, with varying degrees of misgiving, in the transition to general currency 'floating' in March 1973. Months later they faced the shock of the first oil crisis. Then, in May 1974, Schmidt became Chancellor and Giscard President within days of one another.

So began a partnership (critics called it an 'axis') which had a major impact on the European Community and on relations with the US through into the next decade. That does not mean the pair automatically saw eye to eye. Schmidt often had to persuade Giscard to modify some of his tougher positions, notably towards the US and Britain. It also seems likely that when Schmidt said he learned from 'partners' in office, Giscard was one of those he had most in mind.

Giscard, following a firm French tradition, was opposed to greater currency flexibility, believing this would increase economic problems, not relieve monetary ones. Accordingly, as Finance Minister, he made vigorous efforts to save the fixed rate system, and finally went along with 'floating' only with very grave doubts. Schmidt had reservations too, but pragmatically he saw no real alternative. In a new dollar crisis at the start of 1973, the Bundesbank had been forced to mop up nearly DM20 billion's worth of the US currency in just a few days. That could not go on.

Floating against the dollar emerged as the only practicable alternative, although in Europe several countries, including France and Germany, simultaneously tried to keep their currencies bound fairly closely to one another. Then came the oil crisis, bringing upheavals in balances of payments and capital movements, which would have destroyed the fixed rate system if it had not already been discarded. Even in 1975, Schmidt stressed that 'seen in the short term, this system of flexible exchange rates has functioned superbly'. But he added a note of warning that 'it is possible that even now it is causing harm which we cannot as yet detect clearly'.

Later Schmidt came to view currency floating as one stage in a fateful chain of events leading from the dollar crises of the 1960s to the deep worldwide recession of the early 1980s. He did not believe that the US alone was responsible. But he felt that US errors began a process which many other countries worsened by their own mistakes. Governments took advantage of floating to abandon financial and monetary discipline, which had already been faltering in the last turbulent years of fixed exchange rates. They then reacted to the rise in oil prices in 1973–4 by 'printing money' to try to spend their way out of trouble. The result was double-digit inflation, followed by lengthening dole queues.

West Germany made fewer mistakes than most of its partners. The catastrophic hyper-inflation of the Weimar era had made Germans more wary than other people of rising prices. They had an independent central bank dedicated to monetary stability and a relatively responsible trade union movement. They were also lucky to have in Schmidt a government leader who had Finance Ministry experience behind him and who was prepared to resist exaggerated demands for state spending from within his own party.

Right from the start of the SPD–FDP coalition, Schmidt had felt that the pace of domestic social reform was too swift and that costs should be more closely controlled. He made that publicly clear in July 1971, two months after Moeller had stepped down, pushing some unpalatable economic facts under the nose of his party at the same time.[8]

Schmidt recalled that in its first year the coalition had, among many other things, increased pensions, housing and family allowances, boosted state contributions to employee savings schemes and allocated more money for education and research. He agreed that much of this was desirable in itself, although the SPD should be on its guard against those people who wanted to turn the state 'into a self-service store'. But the speed of reform had pushed the state to the limit of what was financially tolerable. For the time being, the government should concentrate on measures which involved no extra cost, like improving the law governing workers' rights at shop-floor level.

In the longer run, Schmidt said, the coalition could bring in more reforms costing money, but only at a pace which did not exceed the growth of state income. That income depended greatly on the rate of overall economic growth, which in turn was determined by productivity and investment. In other words, neither government nor country could have its cake and eat it. If everyone wanted more, then the cake had to be made bigger first.

All of that could easily have come from Moeller and Schiller and is very much in line with what Schmidt would publicly seek to drum home, time after time, when he was Chancellor. But in the following year, 1972, Schmidt changed the tone a bit. He fiercely rejected CDU–CSU opposition claims that government spending was excessive and inflationary. On the contrary, he said that the opposition would impose a deflationary policy if it came to power, accepting much higher unemployment just to push the inflation rate down a bit. The phrase which Schmidt used, and which stuck to him long afterwards, was that the German people 'can put up better with five per cent inflation than with five per cent unemployment'. It certainly seems to stand in odd contrast to his insistence as Chancellor that inflation is a main cause of unemployment.

Much of the explanation for the change of tone is that 1972 was dominated in its second half by the general election campaign. The coalition partners were buoyed by growing public support for the *Ostpolitik* and Brandt's popularity. Even people who were not enthusiastic about the coalition felt that the CDU–CSU bid to unseat Brandt in a parliamentary vote of no confidence had been unfair.

On the other hand, Schiller's resignation and his dire warnings about the budget deficit gave the CDU–CSU valuable ammunition. Here, more than anywhere, was the government's open flank. Accordingly, Schmidt as new Superminister came under intense fire (above all from his old adversary, ex-Finance Minister Strauss) on the grounds that he was wantonly squandering the country's price stability. Schmidt gave as good as he got, and amid the noise and smoke of the campaign exchanges the real situation became hard to discern.

The truth was that Schmidt, whatever he might seem to be saying in public, followed a Moeller–Schiller savings policy. The moment he came to office he pushed through most of the budget cuts Schiller had vainly been fighting for, with an ease which seems to have given his predecessor some understandable irritation. Once the election was over, and partly because of big new dollar inflows, Schmidt produced two 'stability programmes', raising fuel and other taxes and cutting state borrowing. Brandt's government declaration in January 1973 was in much lower key than its predecessor in October 1969. 'There is little good talking of reform and using it as a camouflage for wage claims,' Brandt said, a sentence which might easily have come from Schmidt.

Then, in the autumn, the oil crisis struck. It not only put paid to what was left of plans for reforms costing money, it intensified an existing mood of disillusionment and speeded Brandt's fall as Chancellor. As part of fuel savings measures, the government banned Sunday driving and imposed lower speed limits. West Germans were suddenly faced with the uncanny spectacle of empty *autobahns*. Their fast cars seemed superfluous, their sense of economic vulnerability was greater than it had been for decades. People yearned for a leader who would provide pragmatic crisis-management, and Brandt, for many reasons, could not do so.

Brandt's method of government had always been more one of 'stop-go' than of the steady application of power. Periods of almost convulsive activity, in which the Chancellor was constantly in the public eye, were followed by long stretches in which he seemed to vanish. The style suited the coalition's first years with their sudden, dramatic breakthrough in foreign policy. But it was unsettling at a time of sustained economic threat.

Several of Brandt's public statements at the time made things worse. He tried to insist that public service workers be given wage increases of less than 10 per cent because the energy and economic crises demanded 'sacrifices' from everyone. But the workers went on strike and got their double-digit rise. Brandt also said that if the European Community could not agree promptly on a common energy policy, then it was worth nothing. But the Community reached no such accord, then or later.

It was not fair to blame the Chancellor alone for these setbacks. But by speaking out prematurely, he intensified a general mood of helplessness. Brandt seemed to be aware of this and thought of resigning when the public workers ignored his appeal. At at least one public meeting at the time he looked a lonely and beaten man – stumbling over his words, his face deeply lined, his hair blown into disorder by the wind.

He also had to face growing criticism from party colleagues. Herbert Wehner, feeling that the *Ostpolitik* was not moving fast enough beyond the treaty-signing stage, launched a scarcely concealed attack on Brandt during a visit to Moscow. The Chancellor, who was on a trip to the US, cut short his stay and flew back to Bonn to try to pick up the pieces. Meanwhile, the long-standing differences with Schmidt were again coming to a head.

Schmidt did not directly criticize the Chancellor in public, but even politically insensitive readers must have been struck by the ambiguity of an article he wrote in December 1973 for a West German magazine to mark Brandt's sixtieth birthday.[9] 'His colleagues in cabinet and his comrades in the party know that his initial silence only means he is willing to listen,' Schmidt wrote. 'His delay means that a matter is not yet ready for decision.' Schmidt also noted that despite Brandt's tolerance of those with different views, it was not always easy to work with him. Neither in government, party nor Parliament was co-operation 'free from tension and friction. We are none of us of a kind to make things easy for one another. The SPD is no Chancellor-party, thank God!' Schmidt never wrote truer words!

Schmidt's dissatisfaction reached a climax in March 1974, after SPD losses in local elections in Hamburg. In a television interview, he accused the party of being too lax with the hundreds of thousands of new members who had streamed in over the past few years. Then, in a private meeting of SPD leaders a few days later which was attended by Brandt and Wehner among others, Schmidt was more explicit. The 1972 election victory, in his view, had been a stroke of luck. The emotional atmosphere surrounding the *Ostpolitik*, and the failed vote of no confidence against Brandt, had concealed an underlying trend which was clearly against the SPD.

Schmidt said people all over the country were sick to death of seeing Social Democrats fight among themselves. The party had allowed all sorts of fringe elements to set the political tone, and in doing so it had *de facto* abandoned the political centre. For fifteen years the SPD had struggled to win understanding and support for its updated policies from broader sections of the population. Now it was giving up without a fight much of the ground it had won. Schmidt ended with a solemn warning against acting 'as though we're really the greatest and it's just the voters who haven't noticed. . . . That can only confirm a few more people in their view that they were right to vote CDU this time.'[10]

Much of the Schmidt-Brandt friction was thus sensed by the public and was quite evident within the SPD. But in March, Schmidt also drew personal consequences which did not become generally known at the time. He recalls telling Brandt he would stay on as Finance Minister until the end of the legislative term in 1976, then leave the cabinet. He was no longer thinking of taking a non-political managerial post as he had been in 1972, but of spending a last four years in Parliament.[11] Perhaps he hoped to get back his old 'dream job' from Wehner who, by the end of 1976, at the age of seventy, would have been SPD floor-leader for seven years and was perhaps ready to step down.

Schmidt was not just unhappy about the state of the SPD. He had made a speech warning in dramatic terms of the economic consequences of the oil crisis which struck in late 1973. Schmidt recalls that Brandt then ordered him not to make such alarming statements publicly. Schmidt reluctantly agreed, but felt frustrated that he could not speak out with the urgency he thought justified.

Less than two months later, on 6 May, Brandt announced he was resigning as head of government. An East German spy, Günter Guillaume, had been uncovered in the Chancellery and Brandt accepted 'responsibility for negligence' in connection with the affair. Guillaume had worked in the Chancellery since 1970, had often gone with Brandt on trips, even accompanied him on a holiday to Norway where he had access to top-secret NATO communications. Brandt's resignation stunned people in many countries and the spy affair seemed to most of them to be the cause. There was also a danger the embarrassing details of Brandt's private life might emerge and compromise his position as Chancellor. This point was less widely realized outside West Germany, although Brandt publicly hinted at it as he stepped down.

But to many people who watched the Chancellor's dwindling fortunes in his last year from close at hand, the resignation came as no surprise. Brandt had become increasingly isolated and demoralized before the Guillaume affair. The remarkable thing is how well he recovered once he had left government, retaining the SPD leadership well into the 1980s and winning, if anything, still wider international prestige as head of the 'North–South' group on Third World problems.

Brandt's misfortune and depressions also put a rather different light on another tale – that Wehner forced the Chancellor to step down and installed 'his Crown Prince' Schmidt in his place. Asked years later what he thought of this version, Schmidt answered simply, 'Nothing', the only point in a long interview where he replied with a single word.

Neither Wehner nor anyone else could have 'forced' Brandt to go if he had been in fighting mood and determined to stay. But once Wehner knew about Guillaume and became aware of the shadow of further scandal, he was determined that a decision must be taken quickly, one way or another. His first concern, as ever, was the SPD – already in poor shape and bound to become worse if Brandt muddled on, neither making a clean break nor fighting hard to overcome the new challenge to his authority.

In a meeting with Brandt in the country near Bonn on 4 May, Wehner stressed what he felt was at stake and urged Brandt to make up his mind within twenty-four hours. Wehner said he would support whatever Brandt decided, but Brandt (no doubt correctly) interpreted that as anything but a firm plea that he should stay in office. The next day he told a few senior party colleagues he had decided to resign and nominated Helmut Schmidt to succeed him. It is easy to guess with what feelings of bitterness and weariness Brandt must have made the announcement. Schmidt was one of those present who felt the reasons Brandt gave for stepping down were insufficient, and vainly tried to get him to change his mind. Indeed, Schmidt heaped abuse on Brandt for which he later said he was ashamed. 'But I was furious. I felt he had driven the cart into the mud and was leaving others to pull it out again.'[12]

Everyone knew that Schmidt was the clear successor, the person with the energy and experience to save the situation if anyone could. He was the right man in the right place at the right time as he had been thirteen years earlier when the floods burst over Hamburg. But that is different from saying that he was 'Wehner's Crown Prince'. Wehner condemned the fierce and increasingly public way in which Schmidt had criticized party failings, had even agreed on that point (though on almost no other) over a bottle of wine with Brandt shortly before the Guillaume affair erupted. But whatever Wehner thought of Schmidt's style, he could not but agree with much of the content. Brandt was slipping, the party needed Schmidt – so did Wehner.

On the morning of 16 May, the Bundestag elected Schmidt Chancellor by 267 votes to 225. Schmidt had once said he would certainly be too old to take over when Brandt finally stepped down. Now, at the age of fifty-five years and four months, he was the Federal Republic's youngest ever government leader. As the votes were being counted he sat apparently engrossed in documents, and only very close observers saw that his hands were shaking slightly. The Schmidt who had learned discipline and control at home, at school and in the military, fully displayed both as he reached the summit in politics. When he had taken the oath of office, he walked the few steps to the

Chancellor's place so recently vacated by Brandt, and plumped himself down almost absent-mindedly, as though he had had the seat for years.

INTERLUDE
Only a '*Macher*'?

'I didn't strive for this office,' Schmidt said in a public interview while Chancellor. 'Chance dictated things. I didn't reject it. I didn't reject other challenges either.

'I never planned to become Economics and Finance Minister; for two weeks in 1969 I resisted becoming Defence Minister. I was fully satisfied with my role in the Bundestag. I could just as well have gone on with that. I feel happy in Parliament – like a pig in clover.'[1]

Schmidt regularly made similar remarks indicating that his career virtually 'happened' to him. He says he stood for Parliament after friends suggested it; he took up defence issues because almost no one else in the SPD was willing to do so; he never really wanted the ministerial posts he was given and finally slipped, as it were, into the Chancellorship. He has even said privately he was afraid of taking on the top job because he well knew what had happened to the four previous incumbents – Adenauer who stayed too long, Erhard who was toppled partly by intrigue, Kiesinger whose coalition split, then Brandt. . .

That is surely only part of the picture. From his schooldays Schmidt showed an energy and drive typical of many people rather small in stature. He wanted to prove himself and, when he got the chance, he often came out on top. But for much of the time he must have felt he was in a blind alley, that life was cheating him.

First he had to abandon his hopes of becoming an architect because of the war; then there were the years in the opposition wilderness which drove him from Bonn back to Hamburg; later he reached the cabinet – but under Brandt, his senior by only a few years. Schmidt's own comments show his irritation with the way Brandt handled both government and party. He must have felt he could do things better, however much he recognized the hazards of the top jobs. It is not surprising that Schmidt suffered bouts of acute frustration which, perhaps, help account for his angry outbursts, his health problems, his thoughts about getting out of politics altogether before it was too late to make a successful career elsewhere.

Schmidt is not a man who simply did not 'reject challenges'. Ambition was there in plenty, backed by ability. But the widely held view of Schmidt as a ruthless '*Macher*', keen only on winning and retaining power, does not fit the bill either.

Schmidt tried to argue Brandt out of resigning on that dismal day in May 1974, with a passion others present felt sure was genuine. He certainly doubted Brandt's ability, but he believed no Chancellor should step down for the reasons Brandt gave. While head of government Schmidt himself came close to resigning more than once – and publicly threatened to go if the SPD deserted him on defence and security policy. He fought hard to stave off the collapse of the coalition which finally brought him down. But in the months afterwards he not only accepted his role as ex-Chancellor but embraced it with something like relief. His duty done, he could concentrate on other things for which he had had little time before. It was a surprise for all those who had argued that Schmidt found it difficult to live without power.

Many members of the SPD (especially the younger ones) accused Schmidt of being the 'manager type', meaning in their view someone concerned more with action than ideas, a blinkered pragmatist in fact. Schmidt's public manner often seemed to lend support to that judgement. As Chancellor he called himself the country's 'senior executive' and compared elections to shareholders' meetings.

Yet there is plenty of evidence too that Schmidt was at least as much 'an intellectual' as his critics and thought hard about the responsibilities and limits of political power. He frequently talked about the roles of church and state, making a careful distinction between 'basic rights' which the state had to do all in its power to defend, and 'basic values' which it should not even try to dictate. This point emerged in one speech or interview after another over the years. But because it had no 'hard news' value, and in any case did not easily fit the '*Macher*' image, it was widely overlooked.

On one occasion during his Chancellorship, Schmidt delivered a talk at a conference on the eighteenth-century German philosopher Immanuel Kant.[2] Those who noticed the event at all thought it was an odd way for Schmidt to be spending his time, with practical problems pressing in on him from all sides. But Schmidt saw no contradiction. He was not, and did not claim to be, a creative philosopher himself, but he had long found in Kant's works a valuable guide to the principles of political action. That applied especially to Kant's treatise 'On Perpetual Peace' which Schmidt admired for its logic and sense of realism, qualities he found all too lacking on both sides in East–West exchanges on security issues.

For Kant, Schmidt noted in his talk, 'peace policy does not consist merely of protestations of the will for peace, and least of all of hope for an age of international brotherhood. He pleads for the controlled handling of conflicts between states and for continuous efforts to settle them in the interests of all.' Schmidt recalled that Kant stressed the need for a balance of power to help maintain international security. But the Chancellor went on to say that 'balance is a necessary condition for peace but not a sufficient one. It must be complemented by a peaceful disposition, the will to show restraint towards others, the will to speak to one another and to listen when the other speaks. And it must be complemented by the will to understand the interests of the other side and to respect those interests.'

Schmidt sought to conduct his own foreign and security policy on those principles. But there was another, more abstruse, point of Kant's philosophy which influenced him too – the idea that a sense of morality must be accompanied by the ability and willingness to exercise reason: 'The politician', Schmidt said 'is not justified simply by the fact that he pursues morally right aims. That is at best only part of the justification. His political action must be preceded by a critical analysis of the situation and the various implications. If it is not then his actions have no moral justification whatever. Any mistakes he makes in his assessment of the situation or in his rational choice of the means he adopts to achieve a morally justified aim can have very tragic consequences. They can be just as terrible as the consequences of false moral principles. Both can disqualify the politician.'

That is not a lesson Schmidt learned only from Kant. As a young man he had stumbled across an edition of *Reflections on Myself* by Marcus Aurelius, the Roman emperor and stoic. Schmidt was deeply impressed, kept the book by him and constantly re-read it over the years. He was struck in particular by the comments on duty and fame – and the concept that a leader was responsible not just for his good intentions but above all for the consequences of his actions or omissions.[3] The book too helped form Schmidt's attitude to the business of politics. With that background and those convictions, it is no surprise that he did not get on at all well with the evangelical Jimmy Carter, a president of high moral aim and modest practical experience.

Quite apart from all that, there is another reason why the 'senior executive' self-description is inappropriate. It suggests that Schmidt could almost automatically have his policy wishes put into practice quickly. But while a modern German Chancellor has more power than his predecessors of the Weimar era, he still works under great constraints.

The Bundesrat, the second chamber of the Bonn Parliament, is not just a talking-shop. It is made up of representatives of the *Laender* (the federal states), its approval must be sought on all Bills and, on some (crucially those involving tax), it has the right of veto. During Schmidt's Chancellorship the Union parties, which formed the opposition in the Bundestag, had a majority in the Bundesrat because they did better than the SPD–FDP in regional elections. That made it especially hard and time-consuming for the government to get its legislation through Parliament. Even when a law has been through both houses, it is not wholly safe from correction or even refusal. If the Federal Constitutional Court, the highest in the land, declares legislation to be against the provisions of the Basic Law, the government has to go back and try again. This happened to Schmidt's coalition more than once.

Every Federal Chancellor, even Adenauer, had to face the problems of coalition government. But Schmidt's plight was worse because he rarely had his party whole-heartedly behind him. Latterly Brandt had had similar difficulties; but at first the *Ostpolitik* and the wave of social reform, combined with the disciplinary effect of a slim Bundestag majority, gave Brandt an easier ride with the SPD. Schmidt had no such honeymoon period.

Naturally the constraints on Schmidt were far more evident inside West Germany than outside it. Most non-Germans simply saw a man of great skill and will-power, an 'Iron Chancellor', taking the helm of the 'strongest country in Europe'. It had long been common to talk about the Federal Republic as an 'economic giant and a political dwarf'. With the Schmidt era, many people said the dwarf had grown up to match the country's economic might.

There was something in that judgement, but it was exaggerated all the same. Economically West Germany made a strong post-war recovery and always produces a healthy surplus on its visible trade. But it depends heavily on imports for its energy and raw materials and always runs a deficit on its 'invisibles' (like payments for tourism and the sums foreign workers in Germany transfer to their homelands). Although it has the most powerful conventional forces in Western Europe, it has no nuclear weapons of its own, unlike Britain and France. It is one half of a divided nation and has a long common border with the communist empire. Its room for political manœuvre was bigger when Schmidt came to power than it had been a decade earlier, but it was still constrained by the Nazi past.

Schmidt saw all that, though even he initially overestimated Bonn's scope to bring about the reforms it wanted in the European Community. Perhaps that recognition of the constraints at home and abroad was part of the reason for his private misgivings as he took over the Chancellorship. But from the outward show of confidence with which he set about his new job, it was not apparent that he had any doubts at all.

6

CHANCELLOR –
THE EARLY YEARS

The heat was terrific. In the grounds of the luxury hotel guests lay baking by the swimming-pool or sipped iced drinks in the shade of palm trees. The drivers of black limousines drawn up near the gates had retreated to a nearby café. The only person around showing energy strode to and fro behind an open window on an upper floor. He seemed to be talking ceaselessly, though the words did not float down to the drowsy onlookers, and once or twice he raised a finger of admonishment. At first he had a jacket on but later he was in his shirtsleeves, his only apparent concession to the climate. The uninitiated were told that the man was Chancellor Schmidt of the Federal Republic of Germany, and that somewhere in the darkened room behind him Italy's Prime Minister Mariano Rumor was believed to be present. It did not look as though Signor Rumor was having the chance to say much.

It was Schmidt's first trip to Italy as Chancellor – in August 1974. The Italians wanted to plug a gaping hole in their balance of payments. They expected aid from the European Community as a whole, but they also wanted a bilateral loan from the Germans. The Germans seemed very well off and the Italians were big buyers of their goods, 'Especially fast cars and Sekt [German champagne],' one Bonn government official said wryly. It was thus in German interest to help Italy keep its nose above water.

That, at any rate, was the essence of the Italian argument, but for a time it seemed to make no impression in Bonn. The government repeatedly said there would be no bilateral loan. The Italians were not discouraged. They proposed a top-level meeting at Bellagio, a resort of uncommon beauty on a promontory between Lakes Como and Lecco in Northern Italy. Surely such surroundings would soften the hardest hearts and open the tightest fists! *'Sono Arrivati I Marchi'*, ('The Deutschmarks have arrived'), trumpeted one Italian newspaper joyfully as the Chancellor arrived in Bellagio.

In the event the Italians got the money. They had to listen to a lecture from Schmidt about the virtues of economic and financial discipline, but no doubt they felt it was well worth it. They received a $2 billion loan from the Bundesbank for up to two years, guaranteed by part of the Italian central bank's gold reserves. The Germans insisted that this was a technical central bank operation, not a bilateral loan, but the public in neither country took notice of this distinction. Schmidt did not seem convinced by it either. He gritted his teeth and approved because he felt Italy might otherwise have dropped out of the Community. But he swore that West Germany would not be a party to a bilateral deal of that kind again. He feared that borrowers would resent Germany's ability to pay, even as they took the money, and that this could encourage an upsurge of scarcely latent anti-German feeling. Any future aid in Europe had to be given in a multilateral context even if, as seemed certain, the Germans would always be paying the biggest share!

Only a few weeks after the deal with Italy, Schmidt had to take another European lesson. In a move which shocked West Germany's partners, the Bonn cabinet rejected a European Community farm price increase of 5 per cent just agreed by the Agriculture Ministers of all nine member states in Brussels. The Germans stressed there were already big surpluses, especially of milk products. A 5 per cent price rise would encourage greater output and make things worse.

For many people this might seem to be no great cause for excitement let alone shock. But agriculture is the only sector where the member states have achieved a joint policy of substance (for better or worse) since the European Community was founded in 1958. The Common Agriculture Policy (CAP) thus takes up by far the biggest share of the Community budget, and the annual price setting is a ritual costing time and effort, even passion. No government had ever refused a price increase hammered out in Brussels until Bonn did so in September 1974. 'Finance Dictator Schmidt', was how a German magazine described the Chancellor.

With his '*Diktat*' Schmidt seemed above all to be putting good relations with Paris in question. The Community had been founded on an understanding that France would gain benefits for its many farmers in return for opening its borders wide to industrial imports, above all from Germany. Was Bonn trying to go back on that deal?

There is good reason to think that President Giscard d'Estaing was not unsympathetic to Schmidt's '*Nein*'. He too saw the need for change in the CAP. But many in his government thought otherwise and, naturally, the powerful French farmers' lobby raised a storm. More importantly, Schmidt struck serious trouble in his own coalition.

It was the FDP Agriculture Minister, the egg-shaped, bespectacled Bavarian, Josef Ertl, who had agreed to the 5 per cent rise in Brussels. True, the accord had been dependent on formal confirmation in Bonn, but Ertl confidently expected approval. Instead he found the SPD ministers and, above all, the Chancellor against him. His party leader, Foreign Minister Genscher, was away in the US and did not know what was brewing. When he found out, Genscher concluded the Germans were losing too much European goodwill for too little reason. He demanded that Bonn be more flexible.

Just over a week after imposing its 'veto', Bonn accepted the rise and the crisis was over. Schmidt could argue that Bonn had won a few points. For example, the other member states agreed that the latest increase should be 'taken into account' when prices were revised again the following year. Most experts were cynical about this pledge, rightly as it proved. More noteworthy, everyone accepted that there be a thorough 'stocktaking' of the CAP to deal with the problem of surplus production. One way or another the Community has been stocktaking ever since, but the CAP has never really been reformed and in the 1980s was still eating up around two-thirds of the Community budget.

The whole affair was a vivid illustration of the constraints to which Schmidt and indeed Giscard were subject at home. Later, during the creation of the European Monetary System, the two leaders skirted those constraints simply by letting almost no one know what they were up to!

Despite the setbacks, it was Schmidt and Giscard who together gave the Community what impetus it had in the mid- and late 1970s. This was partly because their countries complemented one another well. West Germany hung back from seeking a leadership role because of its past, while France would have loved to be leader but lacked economic weight. Together they stood to achieve a lot, even when they had simultaneously had leaders with very different temperaments, like Brandt and Giscard's predecessor as president, Georges Pompidou.

But Schmidt and Giscard established close personal ties as well. They phoned one another regularly (with no interpreters, since both spoke English). They sat side by side at international gatherings. They made unannounced, lightning visits to one another. The press, panting to keep up, called it 'The Helmut and Valéry Show'.

No doubt there was an element of 'show' about it; points of agreement were played up strongly by both and elements of discord uncommonly well hidden so that the '*Bonne Entente*', as Giscard called it, seemed all but complete. But there was more to the relationship than that. Schmidt described his co-operation with Giscard as 'unique' in the international field. It had developed, he once said, into a 'profound personal friendship which I believe will last all our lives'.[1]

On the face of it this is odd. Both men were quick-thinking pragmatists more or less of the political Centre, but their background and styles were quite different. The tall acquiline Giscard was a model of French élitist training who took to the pomp and circumstance of the presidency with easy self-assurance. Schmidt belonged to no élite, lived frugally and thought nothing of public display. Giscard's Elysée Palace symbolized the tradition of an often glorious past. Schmidt's new black steel and glass Chancellery (a building he took over in 1976 but never liked) had as much tradition about it as a computer bank. Perhaps it was exactly the difference which attracted Schmidt. Giscard personi-fied a national confidence and continuity to which a defeated and divided Germany could not aspire.

It was Giscard who got most of the credit for the invention of the 'European Council', meetings of Community state and government leaders three times a year to try to shape policy. It was natural that he should, since agreement to establish the Council was reached at a conference in Paris in December 1974, to which he had invited his European colleagues.

For much the same reason Giscard was often seen as the 'father' of the Western economic summit meetings. He pressed strongly during 1975 for a gathering of key Western industrial countries, which finally took place in November at Rambouillet, near Paris. The summits then became annual affairs.

But Schmidt had a key, perhaps decisive, influence on both initiatives. He fully shared Giscard's view that top Western leaders must find ways of meeting informally to discuss their most pressing problems. Existing forums were too unwieldy; Schmidt and Giscard favoured compact working sessions (there were only six small delegations at Rambouillet) interspersed with 'fireside chats' where leaders freed from red tape and bureaucrats could discover what was really on one another's minds. Sometimes the idea worked quite well, though both Schmidt and Giscard found to their chagrin that the summits generated a bureaucracy and publicity all their own.

The two leaders were thus at one on the kind of meetings they wanted, but initially they were not wholly in accord on the substance. Giscard wanted the Rambouillet summit to concentrate almost exclusively on monetary problems. He believed currency floating was responsible for many of the world's economic ills, and wanted to win support for an early return to fixed (or at least far more stable) exchange rates. Schmidt had his doubts about floating but felt it was too early to go back to fixed rates because countries' economic performances differed too much. More important, he knew the United States had no interest whatever in a return to fixed rates. Schmidt feared that a Franco–American monetary confrontation would emerge, with Germany under pressure to take sides. It might simply destroy chances of co-operation in broader economic fields, including energy policy, so vital after the oil crisis.

During the summer, Schmidt sought to influence both sides: the French to broaden the scope of the planned gathering and give more weight to economic issues, the Americans to be more open to discussion of exchange rates. In the event, Rambouillet emerged as an economic as well as monetary conference with Schmidt making the first address and steering a middle road between the extreme positions of Paris and Washington.

Schmidt and Giscard were not wholly at one over Britain either. A Labour Prime Minister, Harold Wilson, had come to power in London in February 1974, pledging to re-negotiate membership of the European Community, which Britain had joined under a Conservative government little more than a year earlier. Among other things, Wilson wanted a better financial deal for Britain and improved Community access for dairy products from the Commonwealth.

Schmidt was irritated by the re-negotiation demand, but he was ready to go a long way to try to keep Britain in the Community. Like many Hamburg citizens, Schmidt was an anglophile who admired Britain's democratic tradition and experience as a former world power. As a parliamentarian in the late 1950s he had even voted against the Treaty of Rome establishing the European Community because Britain was not a founder-member. He did not think much of Wilson, but he got on well with the Labour Chancellor of the Exchequer, Denis Healey, whom he had met when both were Defence Ministers. He also admired the Foreign Secretary (and later Prime Minister) Jim Callaghan for his toughness and reliability. The admiration turned to friendship over the years, despite policy differences.

In December 1974, Schmidt turned up in London to address a Labour Party conference which hotly debated the Community membership issue. The speech had been billed in advance by some newspapers as a political version of *High Noon*, when quick-firing Schmidt would 'shoot from the hip' at the anti-European Labour delegates. There had been talk of a likely walk-out when the Chancellor began his attack.

Schmidt knew very well what he was up against. A frontal assault would be counter-productive. He worked until the early hours on his text, weaving in a joke here, a bit of flattery there.

The speech, delivered in near-perfect English, turned out to be a triumph. His listeners relaxed from the start when Schmidt told them he felt like someone trying to convince the Salvation Army of the virtues of drink. He stressed it was up to the delegates themselves to decide about Europe, but Labour's comrades on the continent wanted Britain to stay in. They felt this was just as much in their own interests as in Britain's. In the name of 'solidarity' (that emotive word for the Left) Labour should bear this in mind. Schmidt backed up the point with a brief review of growing world economic problems. Without closer international co-operation the political stability of the Western democracies would be in danger.

Even the 'anti-Marketeers' (those against Community membership) were on their feet applauding at the end. The British press, which had often praised 'the good German' Willy Brandt, seemed even more admiring of Brandt's successor. 'Superschmidt' is how one newspaper summed him up. The word stuck.

Giscard did not have former President Charles de Gaulle's deep-seated suspicion of Anglo-Saxons, but he did not share Schmidt's marked sympathy for the British either. True, the West Germans (as the biggest single contributors to the Community budget) seemed bound to have the largest bill from any new settlement with Britain. But Giscard was opposed on principle to revising entry terms and making special financial arrangements for a single country. It is doubtful whether Giscard, left to himself, would have stuck to that principle indefinitely. But without Schmidt's behind-the-scenes inter-cession for continued British membership, Giscard would surely have been less flexible. The 're-negotiation' would have begun later and the bargaining would have been still tougher. Wilson might have found himself with little extra benefit to offer the British people made expectant by the 're-negotiation' process, and no alternative but to recommend withdrawal.

A deal was finally struck at a summit of Community leaders in Dublin in March 1975. Ironically, it was also the first session of what was seen as Giscard's brainchild, the European Council. Wilson got at least a respectable part of what he was after and, in a referendum in June, Britain voted to 'stay in Europe'. The Dublin meeting became known as the 'summit of pocket calculators' because the leaders spent their time haggling over things like New Zealand butter imports and Value Added Tax (VAT).

But the problems over Britain and the Community receded only very briefly and the next time round it was Schmidt who took the toughest line. Giscard simply lent occasional support to the Chancellor with the air of one thinking, 'I told you so.' At issue was Community representation at the so-called 'North–South Dialogue', a conference to be held in Paris between consumers and producers of energy and raw materials. At the time, after the first oil crisis, the conference looked like being very important (it turned out not to be) and the Community wanted to speak with one voice. Wilson said no. Britain wanted a separate seat at the gathering because it had North Sea oil, and therefore a special interest which no other Community member had.

The showdown, not so much like *High Noon* as *Gunfight at the OK Corral*, came at the European Council meeting in Rome in December 1975. It was held at the Palazzo Barberini, one of whose walls carried a fresco showing 'The Triumph of Providence'. All delegations thought this a good omen. On the second evening the conference dragged on well beyond its scheduled end. The flaming torches lighting the gardens expired but still the leaders did not emerge. At one point a member of the Irish delegation popped out from behind a bush to tell the press that Schmidt was 'crucifying Wilson on North–South'.

There were indeed some very sharp words – so sharp that for a while, at Schmidt's suggestion, Foreign Ministers and officials were sent out, leaving their leaders to battle on alone. Schmidt was furious. Was it for this that he had drawn on his credit with Giscard and fought to keep

Britain in the Community? He rejected Wilson's talk of a 'special interest' and said Britain's economy was so weak it could ill afford to do without Community goodwill.

After more than eight hours, it was agreed that there would be only one delegation to the North–South gathering. Britain would be able to add remarks at the conference but they had to conform to the position worked out by the Community. This was not much for Wilson, though he made the best of it and implied to reporters that it was virtually what he had been after.

Schmidt was still fuming when he addressed another late night press gathering. This was definitely *not* what he and Giscard had intended when they invented the European Council, he snapped. He already had on his scarf and marine-style peaked cap as though he could not wait to be off from a meeting which had taken so long to reach a position he felt should have been self-evident.

Schmidt's 'background' briefings to the press were often unusually enlightening. Most leaders would simply support their own positions before journalists with a cloud of generalities. Schmidt went more thoroughly into topics, was more concrete and often much more outspoken. Little more than a month before the Rome meeting he had invited to the Chancellery a group of journalists accredited to the Community in Brussels.[2] It turned out to be a lively affair, refreshing or shocking according to one's taste.

'I read in your articles that I am a bad European because I hesitate to spend money for nothing,' Schmidt said bluntly. 'Look at European Regional Policy. What has it really achieved so far?' The Chancellor said no one needed European integration more than the Germans, 'God knows'. But the Community's Regional Fund was just a mechanism for re-distributing finance 'clothed in a pair of bathing trunks with "regional policy" painted on them. You tell me what good will come of this for regional structure in Sicily or Scotland. Nothing. No one is obliged really to spend the money he receives on regional policy.'

Schmidt insisted that the Community was concentrating on the wrong issues. 'We have established market regulations for cork and cut flowers. Can you tell me how that promoted European integration?' As for the Common Agriculture Policy, year after year there were emotional battles over prices; subsidies were given to convert surplus milk into butter which was then sold to the Russians at a knockdown price. Public support for European integration was being misused for a 'fool purpose'.

Asked how things might be changed, Schmidt replied: 'Let the realists who know what they are talking about look after Europe, and spare us the opinions of people who could not even run a tram company for more than two years without making a loss.' This critical remark was taken to refer mainly to the European Commission (the Community's executive in Brussels).

Schmidt likened the Community to a convoy. With mutual consideration and aid the ships could keep together. But this depended in the first place on the skill of the captains and the support of the crews. Economically, the crucial question was – did national governments and other social groups have the strength to adopt balanced non-inflationary policies and the will-power to see them through? If not, there were no mechanisms in Brussels which, of themselves, could prevent the Community's economic collapse.

A transcript of Schmidt's briefing leaked out. Naturally it caused some hurt feelings, especially at the European Commission. But one non-German diplomat who obtained a copy wrote on it, 'Required reading! So unlike the press briefings of our own dear. . . .' He particularly marked the economic parts.

Many people felt that West Germany was producing a 'second economic miracle' with Schmidt as the magician. It seemed to them the Germans were forging along as though the oil crisis had never happened. This impression was exaggerated, as the sharply rising number of jobless in Germany (as elsewhere) showed perfectly well. But Germany was certainly managing the crisis better than most other countries. It more or less 'kept its head when all around were losing theirs'.

In 1974, the Germans imported less oil than they had done a year earlier, but because of the big price rise their bill for it more than doubled to around DM30 billion. Only the United States and Japan had to pay more for oil imports. Yet, despite this burden, West Germany still ran up a visible trade surplus of DM51 billion, its highest until then. Even allowing for 'invisible' deficits, the current account of the balance of payments was nearly DM27 billion in the black.

West Germany's success in controlling inflation was the envy of other countries too. In 1973, the Federal Republic's main partner countries in the Community saw living costs go up on average by more than 8 per cent. A year later Germany's inflation rate was still about the same but that of its European partners had nearly doubled. The US rate was up to 11 per cent, that of Japan had soared to 25 per cent.

It was natural for many foreigners, and quite a lot of Germans, to identify Chancellor Schmidt with this extraordinary success. After all, the full extent of Germany's economic lead became evident only after Schmidt took over as head of government in mid-1974. It was right to give Schmidt credit, but the origin of the so-called 'miracle' preceded his appointment as Chancellor.

In 1973, well before the oil crisis began, German authorities had put a brake on the economy to try to control inflation. Finance Minister Schmidt's two 'stability programmes' in February and May were key examples. Meanwhile, many of Germany's competitors were applying the accelerator, 'going for growth' and sucking in imports. So foreign orders soared for German goods at a time when the German domestic market was rather slack. German manufacturers pounced on the welcome chance to sell goods abroad for which there was relatively little home demand. Exports rose by nearly 20 per cent, bringing a trade surplus of DM33 billion.

In 1974 the trend was still more marked. Many countries responded to the oil crisis by trying to boost their economies still further. They hoped to ward off recession but instead fuelled inflation. Germany's exports increased by nearly 30 per cent and its imports (even including dearer oil) by 'only' 24 per cent. Despite the foreign trade success, the Bonn government stayed cautious. In his first policy declaration as Chancellor in May, Schmidt announced a course of 'Continuity and Concentration'. 'The chief concern of financial policy', he said, 'will be to accomplish urgent public tasks and to give consistent support to the policy of stability. To put it clearly: in the performance of this task the Chancellor will be on the side of the Minister of Finance.'[3]

That meant only gradually releasing the economic brakes, not going on a wild public spending spree. The government had already eased some of the restrictions imposed in 1973 and it took steps to help boost investment and growth in 1974. But compared with the stance of most other countries at the time, German economic and fiscal policy was a model of restraint. In late 1975 (with inflation at 6 per cent and falling further), the government announced new budget spending cuts and said taxes and unemployment insurance contributions would be raised.

Outside Germany that looked like self-discipline verging on flagellation, but there were many 'expert' German voices complaining that the government was actually being too lax.

The government was supported in its efforts for non-inflationary growth by the Bundesbank. It would be almost as fair to reverse the emphasis and say that the Bundesbank was backed up by the government. The German central bank is highly independent, more so than similar institutions in almost all other countries, and its first duty is to defend the Deutschmark (above all by crushing inflation). Any German government which tried to spend its way out of its difficulties by urging the Bundesbank to print more money than it thought proper would soon be given a thick ear.

At the end of 1974 the Bundesbank began what was at the time a unique experiment. It became the first central bank to announce a target for the growth of money supply for the coming year. In other words it told the nation how much extra cash it felt could be pumped into the economy to allow growth without feeding inflation.

Some say that Schmidt proposed the idea to the Bundesbank, others that the Bundesbank put it up to Schmidt. At any rate the Chancellor was in favour, and mainly for psychological reasons. He felt that by setting a restrained money supply target – around 8 per cent for 1975 – trade unions and employers would have an extra guideline in their annual winter wages bargaining. Arguably the Germans were thus the first 'monetarists', long before Mrs Thatcher's Britain or President Reagan's US produced more extreme versions. But neither Schmidt nor the Bundesbank viewed the target rigidly, still less as the prime answer to the country's economic woes. It was an aid – no more but no less. People became aware of it, but they did not hover anxiously over monthly, let alone weekly, money supply figures as Wall Street was to do in the 1980s.

The Bundesbank's action was probably one factor that encouraged lower wage settlements in early 1975 than there had been in early 1974. Another was a general belief that the public sector workers had overstepped the mark with their strike a year earlier which had helped topple Brandt. Yet another was growing unemployment, which made it harder for trade unions to push for a lot more money. Despite its highly visible export success, Germany could not isolate itself altogether from the world recession. The jobless total doubled to an average of nearly 600,000 in 1974 (2.6 per cent of the labour force) and in 1975 it crossed the psychologically important one million mark.

The moderate wage accords, combined with productivity improvement, gave the Germans a further advantage over their competitors. Labour costs in German industry rose in 1975 by only about one third as much as in other Western industrial countries. Because of the German success in controlling inflation and in exporting, the Deutschmark floated upwards. That made for higher German prices abroad, but not so high as to remove all the benefits German exporters won from low domestic costs. Besides, a stronger Deutschmark depressed the import bill and encouraged lower inflation. That, in a nutshell, was the 'second miracle'.

When Schmidt was asked how the West Germans were able to do better economically than most other countries he always gave the same answer. It was not that they worked harder (contrary to popular belief) nor that they were more clever, nor even (though he stressed this point less) that they had more effective government.

The key, for Schmidt, lay with the trade unions. Those labour leaders who built up the movement after the war had avoided the pitfalls of the Weimar era, when the unions were fragmented. The modern German unions were few in number (around twenty) – strong, united and mostly well led by political moderates. Bargaining on wages and conditions followed a set annual pattern and was often conducted at a high level of economic argument by both sides. The strike was a weapon of absolutely last resort, but one that employers had good cause to fear because the unions had plenty of money for a long fight. Sometimes a union went too far, as the public service workers did in early 1974, but this was rare. By the standards of most countries, German wages and productivity were unusually high, and strikes few.

Schmidt had forged close ties with leading trade unionists when, as SPD floor-leader, he had fought for a scheme to give workers more of a say in management. He saw organized labour as the backbone of the SPD, and the cabinet he put together in 1974 was especially strong on members who had a union career background. Some had already served under Brandt, like the Labour Minister Walter Arendt (from the miners' union) and the Defence Minister Georg Leber (from the builders). Others were new, including Hans Matthöfer (metalworkers) who became Technology Minister, and Kurt Gscheidle (postal workers), who took the double Transport and Post portfolio.

Erhard Eppler, one of the SPD's leading left-wing intellectuals who had been Brandt's Development Aid Minister, resigned after less than two months under Schmidt. He felt that West Germany had a moral duty to put up more funds for the Third World. Schmidt insisted that Eppler had to save like everyone else. He had already warned in his government declaration that the Chancellor would be 'on the side of the Finance Minister'; those who took no heed would have to go. There was very little doubt that the new Finance Minister would do what Schmidt wanted. He was Hans Apel, like Schmidt born in the Barmbek district of Hamburg, and thirteen years the Chancellor's junior.

Schmidt was clearly the boss. He had the cabinet team he wanted, at least as far as the SPD ministers were concerned. The atmosphere of drift and impending crisis, which periodically marked Brandt's Chancellorship, was absent. But one key support of the SPD–FDP alliance had gone too. Brandt had warm personal ties with the Liberal leader Walter Scheel, and this helped the coalition over many a hazard. But Scheel had announced in late 1973 that he would stand for the office of Federal President (thus giving up party politics) and by chance his election coincided with Brandt's resignation.

The cabinet thus had two new people at the top – Schmidt and Hans Dietrich Genscher, who succeeded Scheel as Vice-Chancellor, Foreign Minister and later as FDP Chairman. Genscher was a cautious Saxon with a brilliant lawyer's mind and large ears which seemed uncannily sensitive to the first sounds of approaching political danger. Relations between Genscher and Schmidt were normally businesslike, but plunged in the coalition's last years. They were certainly never warm; moreover, some in the SPD blamed Genscher for Brandt's resignation. As Interior Minister, Genscher had had responsibility for the counter-intelligence service which vetted Günter Guillaume before he got his job at the Chancellery. If anyone should have stepped down, so the SPD argued, it was Genscher. But the Interior Minister made no move to go and, if the SPD had tried to insist, the coalition might well have collapsed.

Brandt stayed on as SPD Chairman. To many in Bonn that seemed to be a bad omen for Schmidt, who had been SPD deputy leader since 1968. One official who served under both Chancellors recalls that in 1974, 'A lot of us thought Schmidt would go for the party leadership too. It was obvious that he would want to run a tight ship in government while Willy would take his old flexible line with the party. They had different visions, different natures. It couldn't work out indefinitely.'

Schmidt had another view at the time. He thought the Chancellor's job was quite enough without taking on the burden of the SPD leadership too. The division of labour with Brandt thus seemed the best available alternative. Years later he concluded he had been wrong,[4] but he never made a bid for the SPD chairmanship and it is far from certain that he would have succeeded had he tried. His support in the country was broader than his backing in the party, while Brandt's position was the opposite. 'I am not wholly satisfied with my party, nor it with me,' Schmidt stated in 1975. 'But I can find no better party and it has no substitute for me [as Chancellor]. So we must get along with one another.'

It was the kind of bitter assault that Schmidt launched at the conference of the Hamburg SPD in September 1974, which made 'getting along' with him so hard for many party members.[5] The Chancellor was deeply worried. The party had suffered heavy losses in the regional election in Hamburg in March, two months before Brandt resigned. It had a further setback in Lower Saxony in June. With a general election due in 1976, the SPD had to stop the rot soon, or it would go down in a crushing defeat. In the wake of the oil crisis, unemployment was rising everywhere. Yet in Schmidt's view many in the SPD prattled on with theoretical discussion which meant nothing to those worried for their jobs.

'What do you suppose the workers are interested in at the Witten steel refinery?' he asked the Hamburg delegates angrily. 'Or the people on short time at Volkswagen. Debates about theory are necessary – yes, one needs basic principles. But there is a difference between arguing over things in one's study among comrades and turning an intellectual wrestling match into the basis for a party of public consensus. Go to the meetings of the labour members of our party and you will see what workers are really concerned about. Don't try to get by with theoretical declarations of loyalty to their interests.'

The Chancellor added he did not 'care a hang' for waffle about what was on the political 'Left', what on the 'Right'. Oil cost 400 per cent more than it had a year earlier, all the goods landing in Hamburg port from overseas cost on average 30 per cent more. These crucial economic factors overshadowed everything. 'The world economy has been thrown into a state of crisis which you refuse to grasp,' Schmidt snapped, as though attacking political opponents on the campaign trail. 'You bother yourselves with the crisis of your own brains, instead of facing up to economic realities.'

The last phrase in particular incensed a lot of delegates and brought a sharp retort from a left-wing party member in an article soon afterwards.[6] 'Certainly we have no patent solution [to the economic problems],' he wrote. 'Now we know from Comrade Schmidt that he neither has one nor seeks one. He is no different in this respect from his predecessor. But Comrade Brandt at least had the advantage that he did not denounce thinking aloud in his party as the outpouring of crisis-ridden brains.'

Schmidt certainly found more elegant ways in 1974 ('Post Oil Shock Year One' as he called it) of warning about the dangers facing the world economy. In one article intended mainly for American readers he wrote that, 'What we are witnessing today in international economic relations – in the monetary field and now in the field of oil and raw materials prices – is virtually the same as what is going on between trade unions and employers' associations on the national level. It is a struggle for the distribution and use of the national product, a struggle for the world product.'[7]

West German experience, of course, suggested that the 'struggle' could be regulated. There were fairly clear ground rules and procedures to help reach a consensus between unions and employers. Schiller had invented the 'concerted action' meetings in the 1960s, to bring all sides round a table with the government to discuss the economic outlook. Schmidt as Chancellor brought in his own, informal variation of the 'concerted action' process which he felt had become 'too bureaucratic', always one of his most bitter criticisms.

Schmidt periodically called union and employers' leaders together for a 'chat' which often went on into the late evening. The sessions would start with a survey by the Chancellor of the world economic situation, how it affected West Germany and what he felt were the prospects for growth, inflation and jobs. This would last half an hour or so and the floor was then open for discussion. Schmidt always insisted he was not interfering in the free wage bargaining but he certainly influenced both sides, by his command of the subject and by his impartiality. The bosses knew Schmidt agreed with their stance that profits were essential for investment and jobs (as long as they did not exaggerate the argument). The labour leaders had plenty of proof that Schmidt supported a strong union movement and many of them got on well with him personally. That did not mean they could take advantage of his goodwill. When one union leader made a sharp interjection while Schmidt was talking, the Chancellor turned on him and said icily, 'Heinz. I didn't give you the right to speak. But if I had done, I would have taken it away from you for that.' There were no more interruptions.

Schmidt knew that this combination of formal procedure and informal dialogue to help divide up the national cake fairly existed in relatively few other countries. The prospects were therefore slim for establishing something similar at international level to regulate 'the struggle for the world product'. But the attempt had to be made. He had apocalyptic visions of international economic anarchy, a chain reaction of trade protectionism, spiralling inflation and mass unemployment on a scale so far unknown. He feared that that in turn could increase civil unrest and undermine the democratic basis of Western society.

That assessment came to seem exaggerated in the second half of the 1970s, especially in West Germany itself where economic growth resumed, inflation fell and unemployment at least rose no further. It looked much less far-fetched at the start of the 1980s after the second oil crisis with more than thirty million unemployed in the Western world, many developing countries hopelessly in debt and the international banking system in danger of dislocation.

It was with those dangers in mind that Schmidt supported the creation of the 'European Council' and Giscard d'Estaing's initiative for what became the Western economic summit conferences. He pressed for dialogue with the oil exporters, whom he admitted from the first had a good case for demanding higher prices (though none at all for ruining their customers!). He advocated a plan to stabilize the export earnings of the raw-materials-producing countries (emphasizing it must not become an expensive white elephant like the European Common Agriculture Policy). And he worked for a stronger International Monetary Fund (IMF), as the body most able both to lend to needy states while simultaneously imposing essential economic policy changes on the borrowers.

Time after time Schmidt talked about 'the interdependence of the world economy'. He was thinking not just of the international division of labour to produce goods and services, but also of the revolution in high-speed communications. A fearful whisper on one currency market could quickly bring panic selling on another half-way around the world, circumventing governments and overrunning central bankers.

'Many of you are on the phone every day to New York,' he told businessmen in 1975. 'Events there, attitudes, impressions are immediately communicated to Tokyo, Frankfurt, Düsseldorf and elsewhere. If it is true that economic policy consists 50 per cent of psychology, then what the present fight against recession is about is largely psychology in New York City.'[8]

The remark makes clear why Schmidt urged President Ford to bail out New York when the city was virtually bankrupt. If, as the saying went, the world caught flu when Wall Street sneezed, what would happen to the world economy if New York went bust? Many Americans thought Schmidt was exaggerating and poking his nose into their domestic affairs. Perhaps he was. Fortunately New York got extra funds and Schmidt's thesis was not tested.

These international economic issues loomed large virtually throughout Schmidt's Chancellorship, as the *Ostpolitik* had done during most of Brandt's. The shift of emphasis reflected both the impact of the oil crisis, and the fact that when Schmidt took office almost all Bonn's major bilateral treaties with the East had been signed. The novelty and drama of the *Ostpolitik* had largely gone. Schmidt had the less eye-catching task of building on the basis of the treaties, and of doing what he could to influence multilateral contacts between East and West.

In October 1974, five months after becoming Chancellor, Schmidt flew to Moscow for the first of what were to be regular meetings over the years with the Soviet leader Leonid Brezhnev. Progress was made on a plan under which West Germany would deliver atomic power-stations to the Soviet Union and receive electricity in return. The scheme foundered in its original form, partly because Bonn insisted that West Berlin be linked into the proposed East–West power line, which the East Germans found unacceptable. But a similar plan involving natural gas was carried out years later, despite opposition from the Reagan administration which felt that the Europeans were becoming too dependent on Moscow for their energy. By the time Reagan came into power the Americans had already gone sour on *détente*, which they felt had been chiefly of advantage to the Russians. But many Europeans, above all the Germans, did not see things that way. The Germans argued that they had to import almost all their energy anyway, that they were careful not to rely too much on a single source, and that Moscow had scrupulously honoured its gas contracts in the past.

The Germans not only benefited economically from closer ties with the East. Nearly two million West Berliners felt more secure than they had for decades, thanks to the four-power agreement and the East – West German Treaty. Further, hundreds of thousands of ethnic Germans living in the Soviet Union and Eastern Europe were granted permission to leave and re-settle in the Federal Republic. All that was bound to loom far larger in Bonn than in Washington.

One such humanitarian accord, under which about 120,000 Poles of German origin were allowed to travel to the West, was reached in August 1975. Bonn promised Warsaw credit and other finance in return. The agreement was thrashed out by Schmidt and the Polish leader Edward Gierek on the margins of the East–West Conference on Security and Co-operation in Europe, held in Helsinki.

The Americans under President Ford still favoured *détente* and took part in the thirty-five nation gathering. But they were sceptical about the practical value of the conference, for which the Russians had long pressed, with its high-sounding declaration on (among other things) respect for human rights. Schmidt had doubts too. But he felt the chance for dialogue had to be seized and hoped the Security conference might give a boost to East–West talks on force reductions.

Schmidt also used the margins of the conference for another get-together, far less productive than the one with Gierek, but historic in its way. He held brief talks with the East German leader Erich Honecker in the first top-level inter-German meeting since Brandt resigned over the Guillaume spy affair. Schmidt and Honecker did not hold really thorough talks for another six years. *Détente* was always slow, but between the two Germanies it moved at a snail's pace.

Schmidt had to face his first general election as Chancellor less than thirty months after taking over from Brandt. Viewed from outside Germany, it seemed hardly thinkable that Schmidt could be tipped out. In the East he had consolidated, with caution, what Brandt and Scheel had built. In the West he had shown outstanding economic competence. In the election year, 1976, the West German inflation rate was down to little more than 4 per cent, economic growth was at its strongest for six years and unemployment was falling slightly, though still high.

Many people abroad wondered what else the Germans could reasonably ask for. Surely not for Helmut Kohl, the opposition CDU leader who had taken over from Rainer Barzel three years earlier. Foreigners with an abnormally strong interest in German politics knew that Kohl had been a good Prime Minister of the wine-producing state of Rhineland Palatinate. He was big, amiable and transparently honest, often with a look of owlish concern which no doubt helped persuade voters he understood their problems. But could he oust Schmidt? Could he even defend himself for long against the machinations of the CSU leader Strauss, nominally his ally but in fact a fierce rival? It seemed highly unlikely.

The truth was different. Kohl was underestimated for years (at least until he became Chancellor in 1982), not only by the relatively few foreigners aware of his existence but by many pundits at home too. He had a thick skin, remarkable staying power and a political cunning belied by his 'friendly bank manager' appearance. Many 'opinion-makers' in the political hot-house of Bonn did not think much of him, but many voters did.

Schmidt's rating was high in the country, but the SPD's lagged well behind. Shortly after Schmidt's rebuke to the Hamburg comrades in September 1974, the party lost more ground in elections in Bavaria and Hesse. In March 1975, the CDU for the first time supplanted the SPD as the party with the biggest vote in West Berlin. More SPD losses followed in other provincial polls. Against that background, the result of the general election on 3 October 1976 should really have come as no surprise. The CDU–CSU won 48.6 per cent of the vote – its best result since Adenauer's time – the SPD 42.6 per cent and the FDP 7.9 per cent. The Union parties thus regained their position as the biggest single parliamentary group, which the SPD under Brandt had taken from them in 1972.

Kohl at once declared that the result gave him the moral right to become Chancellor. The government partners ridiculed the statement, but they had had a narrow escape all the same. In his last election campaign speech, Schmidt said he was hoping for a Bundestag majority of twenty to twenty-five seats. Instead the government had one of only ten seats, even fewer than when Brandt and Scheel had formed their alliance in 1969.

'After an election victory which was really nothing of the kind,' wrote one press commentator, 'and with a party which is not happy supporting his Chancellorship, Helmut Schmidt looks lonelier than ever.' Schmidt certainly looked worried on election night, although he sought to conceal his feelings with a glassy smile. A majority of only ten spelt trouble ahead, even though it might help to keep the left wing of the SPD in line too.

Serious trouble came even before Schmidt was re-elected Chancellor in the Bundestag. The so-called 'pensions fiasco' was a domestic affair at first hardly noticed outside Germany, but it deeply depressed Schmidt and brought him to the brink of resignation.

During the election campaign the government had announced that pensions would be raised by 10 per cent in July 1977. As usual, this would keep them virtually in line with wage increases and hence ahead of inflation. 'Indexed' pensions were not one of the expensive reforms of the SPD–FDP era but dated back to Adenauer's time. No party thought of overhauling the system, so long as economic growth generated the money to pay the bill. After the election the government received new data indicating economic growth would be lower than expected. That meant there would be more jobless and less cash paid into the national pensions insurance fund. If the pensions rise went ahead in July as proposed, the fund would face a deficit of around DM10 billion in 1977 alone.

The government initially decided to put off the increase for six months, but it was so shocked by the criticism which burst forth from all sides that it hastily abandoned the idea. Naturally, the CDU–CSU was in the forefront, claiming Schmidt was a 'pensions swindler' who had won the election under false pretences. But the trade unions, long Schmidt's firmest supporters, were hardly less derisive. The SPD parliamentary group refused to swallow the postponement, saying that if Social Democrats did not show solidarity for the weak then no one would.

Schmidt the '*Macher*', the 'economic and monetary wizard', thought of throwing in his job. 'I can assure you', he said later 'that in all my long years of political responsibility, in different posts, I never suffered more than during that period at the end of 1976, when we had to conclude that our prognoses for pensions finance were no longer correct.'[9] During the summer, Schmidt had sat with Apel, the Finance Minister, and Arendt, the Labour Minister, going over the pensions and economic growth figures. They thought they could make the announcement of an increase with confidence. They were wrong, and someone had to carry the can.

In the end the victim was Arendt, a tireless worker and one of the mainstays of the coalition since 1969. He was replaced in the cabinet Schmidt announced on 15 December. The same day, Schmidt was confirmed in office by 250 of the 496 Bundestag deputies, only one vote more than the simple majority he needed. No Chancellor since Adenauer in 1949 had been elected by so slim a margin.

In his government declaration, Schmidt confessed that the pensions problem had brought 'serious unrest' and strained confidence in the coalition. To hoots and jeers from the CDU–CSU Schmidt added, 'But no government is infallible. Only totalitarian regimes claim to be that.' It was one of Schmidt's poorest performances. He stumbled over words and seemed to lack confidence, as well he might. It seemed a bad omen for 1977 – a year when Schmidt again evaded resignation by a hair's breadth, but which also saw his popularity surge higher than ever before.

INTERLUDE
Schmidt's Chancellery Team

At the Defence Ministry Schmidt had put together a strong personal team of advisers to help him circumvent bureaucracy and inject new ideas. As head of government he took a similar approach with wider consequences. He drew around him a group of aides who gained a lot of influence on national policy-making, but who were not generally much in the public eye.

Naturally, earlier Chancellors had their special advisers too. But Schmidt armed himself unusually well with a team tailor-made to help him launch initiatives of his own and to block unwanted moves from elsewhere in his government and party. That does not mean Schmidt could do what he liked. The checks and balances on him at home and abroad have already been mentioned. But for diplomats and journalists trying to find out what was really happening in Bonn, or more interestingly what was likely to happen next, the Chancellery became more important than it had been since Adenauer's time.

For example, the plan for a European Monetary System was concocted in the Chancellery (and in Paris) initially without the knowledge of the Economics and Finance Ministries. Schmidt's personal representative (usually a Chancellery man) prepared the ground for the Western economic summit conferences. Several key foreign and defence policy moves were born in the Chancellery, developed with the specialist ministries and finally sanctioned by the cabinet. On the other hand, it was not uncommon for a policy scheme to be hatched in one of the ministries, float up through the bureaucracy – then vanish almost without trace when it reached the Chancellery. Schmidt's experts had analysed the scheme and given it the thumbs down. 'Impracticable' and 'too expensive' were frequent reasons for rejection.

You did not have to be a Social Democrat to be a leading member of the Schmidt team. You did have to be unusually competent and ready to work as long as the boss, that is for fifteen hours or so on many days. If you set high store by family life, it was best not to apply to the Chancellery at all.

At the core of the team was the so-called '*Kleeblatt*' (cloverleaf) group, made up of four people including the Chancellor. Schmidt used the regular sessions of the *Kleeblatt* for planning and brain-storming on everything from, say, the agenda for the next cabinet session to the content of a future key speech or the government's standing in the polls. The talks were intensive and, by repute, brutally frank as they only could be in a very small and trusted circle.

The outstanding member of the *Kleeblatt* was Hans-Jürgen Wischnewski, long-standing Minister of State at the Chancellery and Schmidt's biggest trouble-shooter. A portly, bespectacled Social Democrat, born in 1922, Wischnewski has a sure instinct for sniffing his way to the heart of a problem and grasping the chance for solution or compromise. 'Ben Wisch' (so called because of his close ties with the Arab world) became widely known when he played a decisive role for Schmidt in the terrorist crisis of 1977; but for years he worked diligently out of the limelight, not least at the thankless task of smoothing relations between the Chancellor and his party.

Klaus Bölling, born in 1928, looks more youthful than anyone who has served in the *Kleeblatt* for more than six years has a right to expect. A former German television correspondent in Washington, Bölling was State Secretary for Information and government spokesman for much of the Schmidt era. He displayed a striking gift for public circum-locution, and it may be that he relayed more essential information about the press to the Chancellor than he did about the Chancellor to the press. At any rate Schmidt listened carefully to Bölling's sug-gestions, and not just on media matters. When the important and delicate post of Bonn's representative in East Berlin fell vacant in 1980, Schmidt named Bölling for the job.

The *Kleeblatt* team was rounded off by Manfred Schüler, born in 1932, a brilliant administrator whom Schmidt discovered in the Finance Ministry and took with him to run the Chancellery apparatus in 1974. 'Everyone says he's very effective but nobody has ever seen him,' remarked Schmidt once, only slightly exaggerating. A little man with a big domed forehead, Schüler used few words and never seemed flustered, even when Schmidt's programme was at its most hectic.

Schüler was succeeded as Head of Chancellery in 1980 by an ebullient young Social Democrat, Manfred Lahnstein, born in 1937. A Rhinelander with an unusual array of talents (wine-making and trombone-playing are among them), Lahnstein is one of the few people to have held top positions in the Chancelleries of both Brandt and Schmidt. After a career in trade union work and at the European Commission in Brussels, he was appointed head of the Chancellery's economics section by Brandt in 1973. When Brandt fell, Lahnstein went too, working at the Finance Ministry for seven years and winning Schmidt's notice and confidence.

Back at the Chancellery, Lahnstein's union contacts and financial expertise were doubly useful as economic recession deepened and budget problems increased. Moreover his optimism proved almost unshakable, even in those last years when there seemed little to be optimistic about. In the final months of the Schmidt era he became Finance Minister and, when that post too vanished under him, he began a new career – this time in industry.

Schmidt managed to pluck a few of the brighter stars from Genscher's Foreign Office to head his own foreign policy section, including Jürgen Ruhfus (later Ambassador to London) and Otto von der Gablentz (Ambassador to the Hague). But probably the perfect 'Schmidt man' in the Chancellery team was Horst Schulmann, in charge of the economics department. A big, craggy individual with a strong background in economic theory and an analytical mind, Schulmann was assistant in the early 1970s to another 'workaholic', Robert Macnamara, President of the World Bank in Washington. Perhaps it was that experience which equipped Schulmann with the ability to stay up for nights on end without sleep. Usually mild-spoken, he can defend his arguments with disconcerting ferocity when pressed. It is not surprising that Schmidt chose him as the ideal aide to work on the creation of the complex and controversial EMS.

The Chancellery experts produced such a stream of detailed reports on so many topics that it seemed hardly credible that Schmidt could get through them all. But he did so despite the other claims on his time, helped by a fast-reading technique which allowed him to scan a page diagonally in a few seconds and miss nothing. Late at night Schmidt would still be sitting at his desk, chain-smoking menthol cigarettes, and ploughing through file after file of papers. He appended comments in green ink and woe betide the aide who let slip a loose formulation.

One official recalls being about to leave his office at 11 p.m. after a hard day when the telephone rang. It was Schmidt demanding clarification of a couple of sentences in a report. The Chancellor showed no surprise that the official was still at his desk; he apparently assumed he would be.

Another aide remembers being asked late at night for a report to be in Schmidt's hands early the next morning. He stayed up and finished the work just in time. Schmidt took the document, nodded and went off without a word. 'He took it for granted,' the aide recalls ruefully. 'He drove us and I often swore at him behind his back. But he drove himself more. He didn't just take over our formulations and ideas. He mastered the detail and produced a strategy of his own. He was the most creative political boss I ever had by far. I wouldn't have missed that Chancellery time for anything.'

Small wonder that Schmidt was the best prepared Chancellor ever to chair cabinet sessions. Not only did he have years of experience behind him at the Defence and Finance Ministries, and in Parliament. He did his 'homework' to keep himself up to date. He often knew more about topics than did the specialist ministers responsible for them. He evidently felt that only by having detailed knowledge in most policy fields could he keep the government reins firm and press effectively for progress.

The contrast with the loose way Brandt often ran cabinet meetings could hardly have been more marked. But Schmidt's method did not only bring benefits. 'Anyone who knows as much as the Chancellor and who shows it as obviously as he does is bound to arouse envy,' said one senior official, a great admirer of Schmidt. Another participant in cabinet sessions puts it less flatteringly. 'I would be invited to put my view and then after thirty seconds Schmidt would break in with questions which sometimes took us off at a tangent. A Chancellor shouldn't try to know everything or he will miss the wood for the trees.'

In other words, Schmidt made some of his colleagues feel like fools, and stored up trouble for himself by doing so. This also applied to the press. One example from many: Schmidt agreed to talk informally to journalists on his train after a heavy round of speeches during an election campaign swing. He soon made clear he thought almost all the questions daft and had most of the score or so of reporters writhing with hostility towards him. The hour was late and Schmidt had a bad cold which made him even more snappy than usual. He might legitimately have excused himself altogether. No doubt it was that sense of duty, the belief that an appointment made must be kept, which caused him to turn up. A less conscientious person would have gone home to bed and the press would not have held it against him for long.

7

CHANCELLOR
To the Plateau, 1976–80

On 5 September 1977, the German industrialists' leader, Hanns Martin Schleyer, was kidnapped in broad daylight on a drive home from his office in Cologne. Five members of the terrorist Red Army Faction gunned down Schleyer's driver and three bodyguards, bundled their hostage into a waiting vehicle and vanished. The next day in a letter to the government they demanded that eleven jailed members of the gang be released, given DM100,000 apiece and flown to a country of their choice. Otherwise Schleyer would be shot. Schmidt called ministers and the opposition leader to an emergency meeting. He was determined that the state must not give in to the demands. The best hope, but a slim one, was to play for time until the terrorists could be found and Schleyer freed. So began a battle of nerves which gripped the nation for six weeks, and ended in a bloody mixture of triumph and failure.

The Schleyer abduction was the latest in a string of atrocities by German terrorists ('urban guerrillas' as they saw themselves) going back about a decade. The movement had its origin in the student unrest of the late 1960s. Young extremists began by committing arson, then bank robberies and bombings, and later murder of carefully selected public figures. American servicemen and military installations were favourite targets – symbols, so the terrorists believed, of a fascist, imperialist order which had to be destroyed. What would they have put in its place? That was never clear. They could best be compared to Dostoyevsky's 'Devils', ready even to throw acid in a child's face if it would serve their anarchic, otherwise indefinable, cause.

By 1972 many of the leaders of the first wave of terrorists, including Andreas Baader and Ulrike Meinhof, had been caught and jailed pending trial. It was the Baader–Meinhof gang which coined the title Red Army Faction for itself, and Baader was one of the eleven whom Schleyer's kidnappers were trying to free. Meinhof hanged herself in her cell in 1976.

Those who had been captured were in different cells and prisons, but they still kept contact with one another and with terrorists outside. This was partly due to their ingenuity in devising secret communications systems, partly to the complicity of some of their lawyers who carried messages, and partly to the laxity of prison officials. But a growing number of Germans believed that the laws themselves needed tightening. People pointed out that some DM12 million had been spent building the top security Stammheim jail on the outskirts of Stuttgart. The authorities had boasted that 'not even a bird' could get in or out without a pass. Yet contacts between the terrorists went on in Stammheim and elsewhere, and the number of terrorist attacks grew.

In November 1974, West Berlin's Chief Justice was shot dead, evidently as a reprisal for the death of a terrorist who had been on hunger strike in prison. In February 1975, Peter Lorenz, leader of the CDU opposition in Berlin, was kidnapped and the freedom of six jailed terrorists demanded as part of the price for his life. For nearly a week the government delayed, then they gave way. Five terrorists were released (one refused to go) and flown to Aden. Lorenz was freed unharmed.

The Lorenz affair was a watershed for Schmidt. Angry and frustrated, he saw terrorists blackmail the state, use television to have their messages broadcast to the nation and get away with it. He feared, rightly as it proved, that those freed in Aden would return to Europe and commit more crimes.

When terrorists occupied the West German embassy in Stockholm two months later, took hostages and demanded the release of twenty-six Baader–Meinhof prisoners, Schmidt said no. Two German diplomats were shot dead during the raid and others were injured. Two terrorists died after explosives they were laying blew up, smashing part of the embassy walls and roof.

The government had stayed firm, but terrorist murders went on. In April 1977, the Federal Attorney-General, Siegfried Buback, was killed in a hail of machine-gun bullets when his car stopped at traffic-lights. Three months later, Jürgen Ponto, the Chief Executive of the Dresdner, one of the country's biggest banks, was shot dead at his home near Frankfurt. Then came Schleyer's kidnapping.

It is obvious why the terrorists singled out Buback; but they showed cunning in selecting Ponto and Schleyer as their victims too. Schleyer was simultaneously President both of the Federation of German Industry and of the national German employers' organization. He was a tough and skilled negotiator with the trade unions. He personified the spirit of West German business enterprise.

So, in a different way, did Ponto. He was a banker of wide interests, unusually well read and a keen supporter of the arts. Hans Friderichs, the Economics Minister and shortly to become Ponto's successor at the Dresdner, summed it up well at the memorial service in Frankfurt's Paulskirche. Ponto, he said, was 'a representative of an order which in its ideal form, by no means always achieved, combines economic success with social justice, hard work with active humanity, business instinct with cultural and social responsibility'. The terrorists hated that order, Friderichs said. That was why they shot Ponto.

There was another point, unspoken but in many minds. The terrorists talked from time to time about 'freeing the masses' but few of them had any idea of the lives, hopes and needs of ordinary working people. Most of the killers came from well-to-do backgrounds. 'I got sick of eating caviar at home,' one said when asked why she went into the underground. Ponto's killers only gained entry to his home because one of them was his god-daughter, from a wealthy Hamburg family. She arrived at the door with red roses and an unsuspecting servant let her in, along with two friends. The terrorists could not fairly be classed as products of the system they sought to destroy, but they were at least by-products.

Among those attending the Ponto memorial service was Schleyer. 'I shall be next,' he told a senior politician as they streamed out of the church. He was given a round-the-clock police guard, but it was not enough. Businessmen and public figures redoubled efforts to protect themselves. They changed their routes to and from their work. Their appointments were revealed only to the few who absolutely had to know. Bulletproof glass barriers went up at offices all over the country.

Bonn, the federal village, became an armed camp. Armoured cars rumbled through the streets. Barbed wire was laid around ministries where for years it had been possible to wander in with scarcely a check. Guards with sub-machine-guns were stationed at many buildings, politicians' homes were floodlit. Police stopped private vehicles frequently and searched them. Drivers without all their papers to hand faced immediate suspicion and tough questioning.

For weeks the Schleyer kidnapping was the top item on the television news in the evening and the headline story in the morning papers. The abductors did not achieve their immediate aim of freeing prisoners and humiliating the state, but they created an atmosphere of fear in which the government came under intense pressure to 'defend law and order' with drastic measures.

The longer the crisis went on, the greater became the strain on everyone, above all on the Schleyer family and Schmidt. New deadlines were constantly set as the government tried every conceivable ruse to win time, but the kidnappers could not be traced. In his first days as a captive, Schleyer indicated he was ready to accept what the government decided, whether it meant life or death for him. But, as the weeks passed, his anguish in letters and tape-recordings became clearer. Schleyer's son sought to force the government to accept the kidnappers' demands and save his father's life by appealing to the Constitutional Court; but the Court turned him down.

It seemed hardly possible that things could get worse, but they did. On 13 October a Lufthansa jet with eighty-six passengers and five crew was hijacked by four Arab terrorists while on a flight from Mallorca to Frankfurt. In an ultimatum to Schmidt, the hijackers – two women and two men – demanded that the conditions of Schleyer's kidnappers be fulfilled, otherwise they would kill everyone aboard. It had long been known there were strong links between German and foreign terrorists. The hijacking was the latest, most dramatic proof.

A new battle of nerves began as the hijackers too repeatedly set new deadlines, forcing the jet on a crazy 9,000-kilometre flight via Rome, Cyprus and the Middle East to Africa. Each time the plane landed, Bonn sought with the appropriate government to devise plans to free the hostages. Schmidt's key trouble-shooter 'Ben Wisch', Minister of State Wischnewski, flew to Dubai and tried to reason with the hijackers by radio from the airport control-tower. Schmidt phoned leaders in the United Arab Emirates and Saudi Arabia. President Giscard d'Estaing of France and Prime Minister Callaghan of Britain urged the Chancellor not to give in and promised what help they could. Even the Russians and East Germans agreed to use what influence they had in the region to end the hijacking.

None of this worked. On Saturday, 15 October, the captain of the hijacked plane, Jürgen Schumann, sent the following message to Schmidt from Dubai: 'The lives of ninety-one men, women and children on board this plane depend on your decision. You are our last and only hope.' On Sunday, after the plane arrived in Aden, the terrorists forced Schumann to kneel and shot him dead in front of the passengers. His body was left lying in the cabin, then flung out a day later after the jet flew in to Mogadishu, capital of Somalia.

The Lufthansa passengers and crew had now been under intense physical and psychological strain for about one hundred hours. The hijackers had murdered Schumann and might soon kill others. Schmidt took a big calculated risk. He phoned Somalia's President Siad Barre and urged that a night attack be made to free the hostages. The main rescue attempt was to be made by the crack German anti-terrorist squad GSG-9 (*Grenz-schutz Gruppe-9*), with backing from the Somalis. Barre might well have preferred delaying tactics, for fear of a bloodbath if the attack went wrong. Or he could have objected that use of a foreign armed force infringed Somali sovereignty. But to the immense relief of Schmidt, and the cabinet which approved the scheme, Barre finally gave the go-ahead.

Shortly after Schmidt's phone call, Wischnewski arrived in Mogadishu and bargained with the hijackers, gaining an extension of their latest deadline to 01.30 hours on the following day, Tuesday 18 October. The terrorists were evidently made to think they had won and that their comrades in Germany were being freed.

After nightfall, thirty men of the GSG-9 force flew in. With them were two British specialists equipped with stun-grenades, which can briefly paralyse the enemy with flash and noise. Hours of waiting began. Those in Bonn aware of the operation privately recalled the massacre at the Olympic Games in Munich in 1972, when Arab terrorists seized Israeli athletes. In a night-time rescue attempt by police sharpshooters, all the hostages had been killed. The GSG-9 had been set up as a result, but the odds against success in Mogadishu still looked long. Schmidt had already made up his mind about the consequences if the rescue attempt failed. 'I would have gone before the Bundestag on the following day and announced my resignation,' he says. 'No one would have persuaded me otherwise. I was firmly determined.'[1]

At five minutes past midnight the attack on the plane began under the codeword '*Feuerzauber*' ('Magic Fire'). As the stun-grenades exploded outside, German commandos burst into the jet at front and rear. Two terrorists were shot dead at once, another moments later. The fourth was seriously wounded. One Arab hurled a hand-grenade, but it rolled under an empty seat and exploded harmlessly. As he went down in a spray of bullets, he threw another grenade which went off, slightly injuring some of the hostages.

In seven minutes the action was over and Wischnewski was on the line to Bonn.

'The job is done,' he told the Chancellor.

'How many dead?'

'None on our side. One or two of the terrorists.'

Schmidt broke down and wept. 'I'm not easily moved,' he said years later, 'but at that moment I couldn't help it. The weeks of tension caught up with me.'[2]

Most Germans were asleep when the hijack ended. Hours later, they hardly had time to delight over the morning news bulletins when there was a new shock. Three terrorists in Stammheim jail had committed suicide. Baader and Jan-Carl Raspe shot themselves. Gudrun Ensslin was found hanging from the cross-bar of her cell window. A fourth, Irmgard Moeller, stabbed herself but recovered from her wounds. Even in death the terrorists had mocked the system. Somehow they had gained access to weapons and a transistor radio. One of them had evidently heard a newscast about the Mogadishu raid and told the others, via a secret communications network using wires in the prison walls. With their hopes of freedom all but gone, the four decided to kill themselves.

'I can't find the words for these bloody and tragic events, this devilish round of violence and death,' President Scheel said in a broadcast to the nation that night. He appealed to the kidnappers yet again to free Schleyer – but in vain. The next evening, police in the French town of Mulhouse, just across the border from Germany, received an anonymous phone call. They followed it up and found Schleyer dead in the boot of a car. He had been shot in the back of the head.

'Something has changed for the worse in this Republic,' said a leading West German television commentator during those final, emotionally exhausting days. 'People will look back and divide the history of our country into the period before the Schleyer kidnapping and the period after it.'

Many liberal Germans feared he was right. While Schleyer was being held the cabinet approved big new sums to boost the state's fight against terrorism. At the same time, the Bundestag hastily passed a law barring lawyers from contact with jailed terrorist clients if society was under a particularly grave threat. The law took effect at once, though it was either too late, or not enough, to stop the Stammheim prisoners from acquiring weapons and a radio. More far-reaching legal steps were being discussed too. In the feverish atmosphere of the time, those who warned that the state might be going too far were often called terrorist sympathizers by conservatives.

Schmidt faced a new and drastic variation of an old problem. He had to try to steer a middle course which was rejected as too weak by the political Right and viewed with deep reserve on the Left of the SPD. His difficulties were underlined when the Bundestag debated proposed new government measures to counter terrorism four months after Schleyer's death. One step gave police widened powers of search. They would have the right to gain entry throughout a whole apartment block, not just to a single flat, if terrorists were thought to be inside. Other measures sought to make still more difficult criminal collaboration between terrorists and their lawyers. Several SPD rebels said the steps would strike at basic freedoms without getting to the roots of terrorism. The opposition felt the proposals had been so watered down in the committee that nothing really effective remained. In the end the measures were passed, but only with a majority of one.

Opposition speakers stressed that the tougher provisions they felt necessary were already the norm in other Western democracies, including France, Italy and Switzerland. That was true, but Schmidt knew that even the more moderate steps he advocated were being viewed critically abroad. As usual West Germany, because of its Nazi past, was a special case. Few foreigners were ready to condone terrorist violence. But quite a lot wondered whether, after all, there might be something in the Baader–Meinhof charges against the state. Could it be that the Germans were gradually moving towards fascism again, despite the Federal Republic's model democratic form?

The terrorists were mostly aware of these foreign concerns and of the troubled liberal conscience at home. They skilfully exploited the situation by making accusations of 'isolation torture' against their jailers, and by demanding recognition as 'political prisoners'. International bodies like the European Commission on Human Rights rejected these claims, but suspicions of maltreatment did not wholly die down.

German authorities partly had themselves to blame for the fears that the Federal Republic might be on an illiberal path. In 1972 Brandt and the prime ministers of the *laender* had agreed on a decree to bar extremists from public service. The object was to prevent people who wanted to destroy the democratic system from getting high posts in the government, education or the judiciary.

Despite the good intentions of those who passed it, the decree was applied with an often unimaginative perfectionism which created an atmosphere of intimidation and, sometimes, of farce. In Germany, train drivers and postmen are classed as public servants, like judges and teachers. One cartoon of the time showed a charwoman being dismissed because her membership of the (legal) communist party threatened 'the basic democratic order'.

The decree was an error. Its abuses could only be undone bit by bit and it gained the federal and state governments a bad press for years at home and abroad. But that is a long way from suggesting that the terrorist claims about the state had substance, whatever their superficial credibility.

The Schleyer affair was indeed a watershed in post-war Germany, but not in the way that television commentator meant at the time. Schleyer's kidnapping and murder turned out to be the peak of a wave of terrorism. It was not the last such atrocity, but gradually the authorities gained the upper hand; one by one the killers were caught. Politicians and businessmen began to lead more normal lives again. The atmosphere calmed. More than that, a sense of confidence emerged which had not been present before. For one thing the anti-terrorist laws finally emerged as moderate and sensible in the main, despite the honest misgivings of their critics. For another, the tension over Schleyer and the Lufthansa hijack brought the country and its elected representatives together as rarely before.

It had long been fashionable to talk about the Federal Republic as 'an artificial state', 'a country without a soul' or 'a haunted land'. Suddenly there seemed to be something more to be proud of than a relatively successful economy. A German force had acted abroad to protect the weak, not to conquer. Its success had won applause across the world. When the returning GSG–9 commandos stepped from their plane in Bonn and the national anthem was played, many of those present were hard put to blink back tears. It was a red-letter day in the history of Federal Germany.

Opinion polls showed Schmidt's popularity was greater than that of any Chancellor since Adenauer. He was called the 'hero of Mogadishu', which was perhaps less than fair to the many others who had been vital to the operation's success. But Schmidt had borne the final responsibility, just as he had during the weeks of unavailing search for Schleyer. He had not been able to save Schleyer's life, but most Germans clearly felt he had done everything possible short of giving in and inviting yet more terrorist attacks.

Schmidt paid tribute to the murdered industrialist in a speech before a solemn Bundestag on 20 October. He spoke softly, and looked more tired and older than he had a month earlier. At the end of his address Schmidt said: 'A man who knows that, one way or another, he is bound to be burdened with guilt and omission, whatever he does and however hard he tries – that man won't claim to have done everything, and that everything was right. Nor will he try to shuffle off responsibility for guilt and omission onto others, because he knows that they face the same inevitable dilemma.' Schmidt added that 'the government will take the opportunity later to explain in public its decisions, its reasons and its doubts. We accept our responsibility. God help us.'

Little more than a week after that scene in the Bundestag, Schmidt gave a speech to the International Institute for Strategic Studies (IISS) in London.[3] The address about 'New Dimensions of Security' did not have the popular appeal in England of 'Superschmidt's' appearance at the Labour Party conference three years before. In Germany, most minds were still too filled with the Schleyer and Mogadishu affairs to take in new strategic matters. But that IISS speech, especially the part about nuclear missiles, was one of the most important Schmidt ever gave. It foreshadowed a decision by the Western alliance which had big repercussions for East–West relations and for domestic German politics well into the 1980s.

Schmidt was speaking against a background of growing friction between Bonn and the new US administration of President Carter. Many people put the difficulties down to a personality clash between the evangelical Carter and the pragmatic Schmidt. There was something in that; the relationship had begun on the wrong foot when Schmidt prematurely congratulated the incumbent President Ford on victory in the 2 November 1976 US election. Later returns showed that Carter had won after all. Oddly, a similar mistake had happened seven years earlier, but that time the American side had been to blame. President Nixon had phoned Bonn on election night in 1969 to praise Chancellor Kiesinger for a victory which had actually gone to Willy

Brandt. Nixon passed the error off later with a laugh, saying he had been given a wrong number.

But there was much more to the US–German strains than the inability of Schmidt and Carter to get along well. A lot of the problems pre-dated Carter, though they became more acute during his unhappy presidency. Moreover, many of them were European–American difficulties, not solely Bonn–Washington ones. But they showed up most clearly between West Germany and the US because of the marked change in the relative political weight of those two countries.

When the Germans and Americans had differences in the 1950s and 1960s, it was almost always Washington which won the argument. The US was the protective superpower, the Federal Republic the overwhelmingly dependent ally. Things changed in the 1970s. The Germans became more vital to the NATO alliance, militarily and financially. Simultaneously they won more room for foreign policy manoeuvre, though their scope to strike out alone was far less than most non-Germans seemed to think.

That much had been inevitable since the 'economic miracle'. Naturally it was accompanied by a generation change. Germans and Americans who had the vivid shared experience of the Marshall Plan and Berlin airlift gradually retired from public office. Their successors lacked that emotional bond. The Germans did not become anti-American, let alone pro-Russian, as opinion polls made clear time after time; but they did start to articulate more clearly what they perceived to be their interests (though still much less trenchantly than, for example, the French).

Apart from the generation change, there was an increasingly rapid turnover in US leadership. In the first sixteen post-war years, the Germans had to come to terms with only two US Presidents, Truman and Eisenhower. In the next sixteen they faced five: Kennedy who was shot, Johnson who gave up over Vietnam, Nixon who was forced out over Watergate, Ford who was a (good) stop-gap, then Carter. Moreover, the double trauma of Vietnam and Watergate weakened the presidency, and brought a period of intense American introspection. Germany thus gained more weight in Western councils just as the US became less able, or less willing, to exercise a steady and calculable leadership role.

In the early 1970s the German government still applauded much in Nixon's (and Henry Kissinger's) foreign policy. It found Ford to be a reliable partner too. The main German criticism in those days was directed at the US Congress. At least from the late 1960s, NATO was in principle agreed on a policy of 'carrot and stick' towards the Russians. This meant offering economic co-operation from a basis of military strength and prompt response to communist pressure. But it seemed to the Germans that Congress was undermining that policy by circum-scribing presidential power. That tempted Moscow and its allies to go in for adventures (in Angola and elsewhere) which they might not have tried if the risks of a firm US response had been higher.

Then came Carter and things got a lot worse. Bonn partly blamed the President's advisers, the so-called 'Georgia Mafia', most of whom had no foreign affairs experience. The policy influence of East Coast Americans with close knowledge of European problems declined, that of the 'new boys' from the South increased. The process continued into the Reagan presidency too. One exception to the rule was the national security affairs adviser, Zbigniew Brzezinski. He had a great knowl-edge of European and Soviet matters, but Bonn distrusted what he made of it. He often seemed to be pulling in one hard-line direction on foreign policy while the State Department professionals sought to pull in another. Schmidt disliked Brzezinski and felt his influence on policy to be pernicious. The feeling seems to have been mutual.

Most of all, though, Schmidt quickly concluded that Carter was an amateur, a leader who, as he later put it with a wan smile, 'was just not big enough for the game'. The tale of the policy differences between the two would fill a book in itself. There was a dispute, which surfaced the moment Carter came to office, about a DM12 billion civil nuclear deal the Germans had signed in 1975 with Brazil. Carter felt the Brazilians, who had not signed the nuclear non-proliferation treaty, might use the facilities the Germans were supplying to make bombs. Bonn insisted that tough safeguards had been built into the contract and, despite extraordinarily strong pressure from Washington, Schmidt refused to give way and the deal went ahead.

Then there was Carter's human rights policy, above all his public efforts on behalf of Soviet dissidents. Schmidt said later 'the aim was idealistic, the prospect of achieving it small, the methods used dilettantish'.[4] He shared Henry Kissinger's view that 'a policy of state-to-state confrontation on human rights with the Soviet Union can bring nothing but a demonstration of Western impotence, a worse condition for the dissidents and no significant progress on human rights'.

Kissinger had managed by quiet diplomacy to win permission for the emigration of thousands of Soviet citizens. Successive governments in Bonn had quietly and methodically secured the release of hundreds of thousands of ethnic Germans from communist states. Schmidt feared that by overt action, which would cause the Soviet Union loss of face, Carter would achieve the opposite of what he wanted. Carter's good intentions, his genuine concern, were never in doubt. His judgement and ability were.

Then there was the affair of the so-called 'neutron bomb', not in fact a bomb at all but a weapon able to emit very high doses of radiation over a relatively short range. It could halt a tank attack in a built-up area by killing the crews without emitting a blast which would bring down buildings and crush civilians. It might thus be an especially useful defence weapon in West Germany, with its high urban concentration and long common border with the Warsaw Pact.

But many people, especially in Schmidt's SPD, did not see it that way. They were thoroughly alarmed when Carter said the US was going to produce the weapon. One leading Social Democrat called the 'bomb' a 'perversion of thought' because it killed people without destroying property. Schmidt recognized the weapon's value but felt Carter had launched his plan in a ham-fisted way, evidently unaware of the impact it would have on European, and especially German, public opinion. Schmidt had finally swung many in the party and the country round to the idea when Carter decided not to go ahead with construction after all. Again, the President's original aim seemed sensible, his methods counter-productive.

One issue in particular might have almost been designed to show off all these problems simultaneously – Carter's inexperience, Schmidt's impatience, the bad blood between both leaders, the lack of consistent top-level communication between Washington and Bonn and, not least, the system of 'dynamic tension' between 'Zbig' Brzezinski and the State Department. This issue was the superiority of the Soviet Union in nuclear missiles of continental range, and the need for a Western response. The problem pre-dated Jimmy Carter's presidency, but it came into the open during his term, above all because of Schmidt's IISS speech in 1977.[5]

The origin of the problem even goes back to the start of the 1960s. At that time the Soviet Union had close to 300 nuclear missiles variously described as of 'medium' or 'intermediate' range. The real point is that they could hit much of Western Europe direct from Soviet territory, but did not have the range to reach the US. They are thus, perhaps, best called 'Euro-strategic' missiles. The Americans had about fifty similar weapons in Europe, but they withdrew them bit by bit starting in 1963. The US had clear superiority over the Russians in missiles of intercontinental range. Moscow therefore could not risk a nuclear attack on NATO Europe, without expecting a response from the numerically superior weaponry on US soil.

By the start of the 1970s the balance changed. Moscow drew level with the US in intercontinental range weapons while increasing the number of its Euro-strategic missiles. The Strategic Arms Limitation accord of 1972 (SALT I) in effect codified the nuclear balance between the superpowers in the intercontinental range, but it did nothing about the imbalance in Soviet favour in the Euro-strategic field. Of the larger European countries, the dilemma was one for the Germans above all. The British and French had their own nuclear forces, and were determined to keep them as a last-resort deterrent against Moscow. West Germany had no nuclear weapons of its own and wanted none, but with the new intercontinental 'balance of terror' it could no longer be as certain as before of the US nuclear shield. Put bluntly, would the US be ready to risk losing Chicago, by replying with an inter-continental missile to a Soviet attack on Hamburg with a Euro-strategic weapon? Not that the Germans believed the Russians really planned to obliterate Hamburg or anywhere else, but by building up weaponry in a field where there was no real Western equivalent, Moscow could well subject Europeans to political blackmail and drive a wedge between the US and its allies.

It was the old question of 'balance'. Schmidt was one of those who saw the problem gradually emerging during the 1960s. In 1965 he wrote a new preface to his book *Verteidigung oder Vergeltung*, stressing that eventual superpower parity would mean an added danger for Europe unless the Euro-strategic imbalance were corrected. What virtually no one (probably including the Russians) foresaw at that time was the ss–20. This Soviet missile was observed on test flights round about 1975, and greatly intensified the potential threat to the Europeans. Its predecessors the ss–4 and the ss–5 had ranges of 2,000 kilometres and 4,000 kilometres respectively, had one nuclear warhead apiece, and were stationed in silos where they were relatively vulnerable to attack. The ss–20 had a range of up to 5,000 kilometres, was mobile and therefore almost invulnerable, and had three nuclear warheads which could be programmed to hit three separate targets. The nuclear yield of each warhead was less than that of the ss–4 or ss–5, but was still enough to 'take out' a large town. All the missiles were fast enough to reach European targets within fifteen minutes or so.

During President Ford's visit to West Germany in July 1975, Schmidt stressed his deep concern about the Euro-strategic imbalance. In a private talk with Ford (even Kissinger was not present on that occasion) Schmidt urged that the United States take up the problem with the Soviet Union. Ford and the Soviet leader Brezhnev had met at Vladivostok in November 1974, and had agreed on the broad outlines of a second Strategic Arms Limitation accord (SALT 2) which was then to be negotiated over the coming few years. Schmidt wanted the Euro-strategic weapons, above all the ss–20 and a new long-range super-sonic Soviet aircraft called the Backfire bomber, to be drawn into SALT 2.

Schmidt gained the firm impression that Ford understood the problem and was ready to take account of it, but then domestic US politics intervened. Ford faced a national convention of his Republican party and a hard-line rival in Ronald Reagan who seemed wholly opposed to SALT. Ford's tactic thus seemed from Bonn to be to back-peddle on SALT, and hence on the Euro-strategic issue too, until he had won the election. But Ford lost. Schmidt then sought to win Carter's understanding of the problem, but for a long time felt he got nowhere. He recalls Carter saying, in so many words, 'This is none of your business. America is the great strategic nuclear power and will maintain an overall balance. So why should you worry about the ss–20?'

By this time it was 1977 and the Soviet Euro-strategic arsenal was growing steadily. In October, Schmidt decided to 'go public' on the issue, stirring a debate and, he hoped, convincing the US of the sincerity of European, as well as German, fears. To those who knew the background, and that must have included many in his audience at the Strategic Studies Institute that night, Schmidt's warning was clear. Schmidt also has good cause to believe that the Soviet Foreign Minister Andrei Gromyko quickly realized the crucial point of that London address. Schmidt said, 'SALT neutralizes [the superpower] strategic nuclear capability. In Europe this magnifies the significance of the disparity between East and West in nuclear tactical and conventional weapons.' He went on to stress that NATO must be ready to maintain the *full range* of its deterrence strategy. This might have to involve a build-up on the Western side to match the East, but it was preferable that overall balance at a lower level should be reached by negotiation.

But what was clear to Gromyko and the experts of the IISS was not immediately plain to many politicians and the press. Schmidt did not specifically mention the ss–20 (of which ten had been deployed by that time, with thirty warheads) and naturally he did not say he was speaking out because he felt he could not get his message across to Carter. In retrospect it might have served his purpose better if he had emphasized still more firmly what he had on his mind. However, his speech was still enough to make some senior US officials furious. They felt that the American nuclear shield, including submarine-based Poseidon missiles, was quite strong enough to deter Soviet aggression, and believed Schmidt could only create unnecessary alarm by saying otherwise in public.

Naturally, the Chancellor was not only trying to convince Carter to bring the problem into the SALT 2 talks. He repeatedly sought to convince the Soviet Union that its continued Euro-strategic build-up threatened co-operation with Europe and, indeed, peace itself. He evidently felt he got this message across to Brezhnev when the Soviet leader visited Bonn (and Schmidt's Hamburg home) in May 1978. A joint declaration issued after the talks said, 'Both sides consider it important that no one should strive for military superiority. They assume that approximate equality and parity are enough to guarantee defence.'

When Brezhnev put his name to that statement the Soviet Union had deployed sixty ss–20s with 180 warheads. Even after it, Moscow continued to deploy at the rate of about one missile a week. Did Brezhnev dupe Schmidt or was he up against strong domestic rivals determined to strengthen the Soviet advantage at all costs? Schmidt believes there were fierce arguments in the Soviet Politburo on the missiles issue, and that later Brezhnev pressed successfully for negotiations with the West when other members of the Moscow leadership were against it.

Naturally, it is impossible to be sure. There is some evidence that the ss–20 was a development of an intercontinental missile, banned under SALT but perfect, as it were in modified form for Europe. Once the build-up began it gained its own momentum, with the enticing possibilities for political blackmail of the West outweighing the potential danger of an eventual NATO response. Perhaps some Politburo members felt NATO would never respond. They were wrong.

The next round of the missiles drama emerged, to Schmidt's surprise, during talks between the leaders of the 'Big Four' Western nations on the Caribbean island of Guadeloupe in January 1979. The Guadeloupe meeting can fairly be called historic for two reasons. For one thing, until then such talks had been held only among the 'Big Three' Western wartime victors – the US, Britain and France. At Guadeloupe the Federal Republic at last joined in. It was the formal acknowledgement of what had been clear at the latest since Schmidt became Chancellor: West Germany was wholly indispensable to the alliance and deserved an equal place at the top table.

Further, it was on Guadeloupe that basic accord emerged at the highest level for what later became known as NATO's 'twin-track' decision on Euro-strategic missiles. The odd thing is that when Schmidt arrived he had received no firm word in advance that Carter would raise the Euro-strategic issue, he was expecting talks on a range of other alliance problems, but not that one. It seems that the two other participants, Prime Minister Callaghan and President Giscard d'Estaing, were in much the same boat.

Carter told the other three he recognized European concern about the Soviet Euro-strategic weapons build-up. The US was therefore prepared to provide similar weapons to deploy in Western Europe as a counterbalance.

Schmidt says that, as the representative of the only non-nuclear weapons country present, he waited for his two European colleagues to react first. He recalls Callaghan saying there was probably no alternative to Western deployment, but urging that there should first be negotiations with Moscow. Giscard d'Estaing added that the Russians would only negotiate if they had cause to be sure that if they did not do so then new Western missiles would indeed be stationed.

Schmidt agreed, but made an important proviso. He would support an alliance decision in which responsibility was fairly shared among the partners, but not one in which Bonn was given a unique role. This meant that the Federal Republic would be ready to have new missiles on its territory if negotiations with Moscow came to nothing, but it must not be the only non-nuclear weapons state in Europe to do so. In other words, Italy, or Holland or Belgium, ideally all of them, must be ready to accept some of them as well.

Schmidt's position was understandable. West Germany already had a bigger concentration of nuclear weapons (American ones of relatively short range) on its soil than any other nation. Schmidt was not looking for more weaponry in Europe but, in the first place, for less in Russia. He certainly did not want new missiles packed into his country alone, making it still more clearly the prime Soviet target in any future war.

By this time, a SALT 2 agreement between Washington and Moscow was almost ready for signature, but it did not take account of the Euro-strategic weapons problem. It would therefore have to be the job of a new series of superpower talks to deal with the issue along the lines sketched out by the 'Big Four' in Guadeloupe. Five months later, from 15–18 June 1979, Carter had talks with Brezhnev in Vienna and they signed the SALT 2 agreement. Schmidt assumed that Carter had taken the opportunity to stress the importance of the Guadeloupe accord and warn Brezhnev that the alliance meant business. But he soon found out, in a curiously roundabout way, that he was wrong.

Another of the annual Western economic summit meetings (which began with the Rambouillet conference in 1975) was being held from 26–29 June in Tokyo. Schmidt decided that on his way there he would stop over in Moscow for talks, partly about the oil crisis but also about missiles.

He remembers arriving at the airport to be greeted by Prime Minister Alexei Kosygin and Foreign Minister Gromyko who promptly offered him a welcoming banquet. 'Let's talk politics first,' Schmidt said and launched into the Euro-strategic weapons issue. There were blank faces all round (though of course Gromyko knew very well what was on Schmidt's mind). The Russians insisted that the matter had not been raised by Carter in Vienna, and they were not in a position to talk about it.

Schmidt was shocked. As soon as he arrived in Tokyo he recalls contacting the US Secretary of State, Cyrus Vance, a member of the Carter team whom he admired for his dedication and professionalism. Vance confirmed that the Guadeloupe agreement had not been discussed. Later evidence emerged suggesting that the Euro-strategic issue had come up between the Soviet and US side during a brief talk in a lift in Vienna – but that did not make things seem much better. Schmidt felt a golden opportunity had been lost.

For the rest of the year, NATO continued preparations for a formal decision on the Euro-strategic weapons problem. At the same time the debate on the issue intensified in West Germany, and above all in Schmidt's SPD. Many members of the party feared that a new and dangerous twist to the arms race was in the offing. Schmidt was able to swing a majority to his view during a dramatic SPD conference in West Berlin from 3–7 December, but it was a battle which had to be fought time and again in the next few years.

Schmidt helped his case in Berlin by announcing that he would shortly meet the East German leader, Honecker. News that an inter-German summit was in the offing persuaded some delegates that Schmidt was doing his best to keep *détente* alive, and that he deserved the benefit of the doubt on the missiles issue, at least for the time being. In fact, the German summit meeting was postponed because of the Soviet invasion of Afghanistan that same month.

The week after the SPD gathering, on 12 December, NATO foreign and defence ministers meeting in Brussels approved the 'twin-track decision'. They agreed that a maximum 572 Euro-strategic missiles should be deployed in Western Europe, but called on Moscow to begin negotiations. The more the Russians were ready to cut back their arsenal of similar weapons, the fewer missiles NATO in its turn would feel obliged to deploy. By this time Moscow had deployed 140 ss–20s with 420 warheads, and still had about 450 older missiles of the ss–4 and ss–5 type.

The ideal was what later became known as the 'zero solution'. Under that, Moscow would scrap all its Euro-strategic weapons and therefore the West would not have to deploy a single one itself. No serious policy-maker thought that very likely, but it was a nice thought and one to which the SPD attached itself like a limpet.

NATO also agreed on a formula which took account of Schmidt's insistence that West Germany should not be the only non-nuclear weapons country earmarked to take new missiles. But the Germans did find themselves in a special position all the same. Of the 572 new weapons planned, 464 were cruise missiles which would take up to two hours to reach the Soviet Union. The Germans would deploy a few of these, but they also agreed to take up to 108 Pershing–2 missiles, which were able to reach Soviet territory in about fifteen minutes and hence were the biggest worry to the Russians. No other country would take Pershings.

In retrospect this looks like a cardinal political error. When Schmidt opposed a 'singular' role for the Federal Republic during the Guadeloupe talks, there was no detailed discussion of missile types. Later on Bonn agreed to take 108 Pershing–2 missiles because it already had that number of Pershing–1s on its territory. It thus seemed a natural, cost-effective matter to withdraw the old weapons and put the new ones in their place. It was also felt that such evident 'arms modernization', rather than installing something wholly new, would be less likely to inflame domestic oppostion to deployment.

But the big political, as well as military, difference is that while the Pershing–1s had a range of only about 750 kilometres and could not reach the Soviet Union, the Pershing–2s have one of about 1,800 kilometres, enabling them almost to hit Moscow. The NATO decision spread the burden of deployment a bit, but it was the West Germans alone who accepted the fastest, most deadly weapons and hence took on the heaviest part of the political load.

The new Pershing and cruise missiles could only start to be made available by the US for installation from the end of 1983. That meant there was a maximum of four years available for negotiation. But at first Moscow rejected talks on the Euro-strategic problem and Carter, shocked and angered by the Soviet invasion of Afghanistan, felt there was little point in pressing for negotiations. He embargoed grain and other supplies to Russia, advised US athletes not to take part in the Moscow Olympic Games scheduled for the summer of 1980, and urged his allies to do the same.

It is not surprising that Carter called that period the worst of his life. In November 1979, supporters of the Iranian leader Ayatollah Khomeini had taken more than fifty Americans hostage in the US embassy in Teheran. They were only freed more than a year later. Carter again imposed economic sanctions and sought support from the Europeans.

The US administration felt that it did not receive the quick and firm allied backing it wanted. There is something in that. The European Community dithered on Iran sanctions (as on so many things), though individual European states did much diplomatically to try to win the hostages' release. On Afghanistan, European divisions were most clear over Carter's call for a boycott of the Olympics. Britain's Conservative Prime Minister, Mrs Margaret Thatcher (who had succeeded Callaghan in May 1979), quickly expressed strong support for Carter's stand. That naturally warmed many hearts in the US. Schmidt was more cautious. He spoke out in principle for a boycott, but gave the Russians longer to show signs of withdrawing from Afghanistan. The US evidently felt that the Germans were dragging their feet and, in contrast to Britain, finally would not support the boycott.

In the event British athletes ignored Mrs Thatcher and went to Moscow, while West German ones agreed not to go. Schmidt noted with some irony that the British could evidently win more American goodwill with strong words than Bonn could win with action. But for him the Olympics issue was not the heart of the problem. He had sympathy for Carter's plight over Iran, and he deplored the Soviet invasion of Afghanistan, but he felt that there had been serious US policy failures too. For years Washington had not acted firmly and consistently in the face of Soviet adventures, notably in Africa. This had surely been one factor which encouraged Moscow to think it could get away with intervention in Afghanistan. But Carter then altered his stance from that of a dove to a hawk, simultaneously putting in question the whole superpower dialogue, not least on nuclear arms control.

Schmidt's criticism was shared in large part by Giscard d'Estaing and, it seems, by Britain's Foreign Secretary Lord Carrington (though evidently not to the same extent by Mrs Thatcher). To Carter, and to many other Americans, it must have seemed that the Europeans (particularly the acerbic Schmidt) were putting the wrong country in the dock. After all, it was the Soviet Union, not the US, which had invaded Afghanistan, sown unrest in the developing world and increased its arms build-up. Whose side did the Europeans think they were on?

This was a misunderstanding of the European criticism, but it was one to which the Europeans themselves greatly contributed. The US lack of a consistent strategy was matched by the petty-minded bickering of its allies. Likewise, in the next bizarre round of differences over the Euro-strategic weapons problem neither Carter nor Schmidt was wholly free of blame.

In May 1980, the *Frankfurter Allgemeine Zeitung*, a widely respected conservative newspaper, carried an editorial accusing Schmidt of suddenly weakening his stand on Euro-strategic missiles.[6] The paper had often suggested before that Schmidt, and above all his party, were being too accommodating to the Soviet Union. But the terms of the latest criticism made Schmidt so furious that he fired off a sharply worded telegram to the paper and simultaneously made the text public. He denied changing his position on the missiles and stressed that 'since a lot of notice is taken of your newspaper abroad your false statement of facts could lead to serious misjudgement of Federal Government policy and damage our country'. The paper retorted that Schmidt's charge was unjustified and that it would continue to criticize as and when it felt it should.

Behind the dispute was a public remark by Schmidt in April that 'both sides [East and West], for a certain number of years, give up installation of new or additional intermediate range missiles and use this time for negotiations'. Many in the West were baffled by Schmidt's statement, and some were suspicious – especially in Washington. Schmidt talked about 'both sides', although the West so far had no such missiles of its own. He also talked about 'a certain number of years', whereas NATO's missiles were expected to be ready in about three years. It looked to many people as if Schmidt was trying to slip out of the NATO commitment which he had done so much to bring about.

The fears were understandable, but groundless. Schmidt's comments were well-intentioned, but unclear. The Chancellor was trying to make a signal specifically to the Soviet Union along the lines of 'For God's sake at least stop *deploying* your missiles (even if you continue to produce them) so that talks with the West can get off the ground. Otherwise another round of the arms race is absolutely certain.' Put that way, of course, the onus is on Moscow. Schmidt deliberately wrapped up the proposal in circumlocutions which might help Moscow accept without losing face. He could hardly admit this later in public, and his tactic (like his telegram to the *Frankfurter Allgemeine*) was counter-productive. Schmidt spoke at an SPD gathering in Hamburg for which no advance text was available. It was hard enough for the press in Bonn to find out just what he had said, let alone for Moscow to realize a signal was being sent. When it did realize, it refused.

About three weeks after the brush with the *Frankfurter Allgemeine*, Schmidt received what he called an 'astonishing and superfluous letter' from Carter. The President recalled the NATO missiles decision and mentioned press reports querying Bonn's position. He evidently wanted to warn Schmidt not to undermine the NATO stand in German–Soviet talks to be held in Moscow on 30 June and 1 July. Carter had first been presented by his advisers with a tougher draft letter than the one he finally sent, but even the toned-down version infuriated Schmidt. He was due to meet Carter shortly at the Western economic conference, being held on 23 and 24 June in Venice. Besides, he had recently sent Washington further details about his position on the missiles, to clear up any doubts Carter might have had. Had the President never received this information, or not read it, as his reference to 'press reports' suggested?

Close aides to Schmidt believed Brzezinski was behind the affair. They felt confirmed in that view by a report appearing in the *Frankfurter Allgemeine* during the Venice economic summit conference and headlined, 'Everything is now fine with Schmidt for the man from the White House.'[7] Brzezinski had evidently sought to clear the troubled US–German atmosphere in a background briefing given to the paper in Venice. Whether he acted on his own initiative or at Carter's bidding is not clear.

Meanwhile, in a Venice hotel room Carter was having a talk with Schmidt. The President later called it one of the most unpleasant encounters he ever had with a foreign leader. The Chancellor, Carter stated, had worked himself into a frenzy over the letter, believing his honour had been impugned. 'Eventually he [Schmidt] said why don't you go outside and tell the press that you have confidence in me. So we went outside and I made the comment.'[8]

A week later Schmidt went to Moscow. The foreign and domestic political stakes were high. The US and some of Bonn's European allies had strong reservations about top-level German–Soviet talks when Moscow was still showing no signs of budging on Afghanistan. The West German political opposition, and part of the press, was saying much the same. Moreover, Schmidt faced a general election in the autumn; if the Moscow trip came a cropper, it could easily undermine his position at the polls. Giscard had already had a hurriedly arranged meeting with Brezhnev in Warsaw which brought no clear results, and the French President's popularity then dropped at home; this was probably one reason for his failure to gain re-election in 1981.

Despite the risks, Schmidt felt he had to go ahead with the Moscow trip. He judged that the superpowers had hardly been talking to one another since the Afghanistan invasion; yet it was at just such periods of crisis, Schmidt believed, that a dialogue between the US and Soviet Union was most needed, however sharp the exchanges. Without talks, the danger of further miscalculation would increase. Moreover, Moscow had still not agreed to negotiate on the Euro-strategic missiles problem. The Russians needed jogging.

On the night of 30 June, the visiting German delegation and almost the whole Soviet Politburo attended a banquet at the Kremlin. Schmidt proceeded to give what he later called (with more than a hint of pride) 'the toughest speech any Western leader has given in the Kremlin, although I delivered it in a courteous tone.'[9] He urged the Russians to withdraw all their forces from Afghanistan and to start talks, without pre-conditions, on the missiles problem. He remembers that, 'Next to me on the left sat [the Soviet chief ideologist] Suslov, following the Russian text with a finger. He was clearly shocked. Opposite me sat Leonid Ilyitch Brezhnev, also following the text with a finger. But at the end he stood up and clapped, so Suslov had to get up and clap too.'

After the meal the Politburo members went into a huddle in a corner of the hall and the Germans realized that the evening was over. The next day Schmidt remembers that the scheduled German–Soviet talks began late, 'but then it became clear that Brezhnev had got his way and that the Russians were, after all, ready to negotiate on the missiles. The effect of that speech was apparently very strong.'

Could it all have been a put-up job? Had the Russians perhaps already decided before Schmidt turned up that they would have to negotiate anyway? 'I don't know,' Schmidt says simply. 'I can't tell you.' The only certainty is that after 1 July 1980, both superpowers were ready in principle to negotiate, but it was another sixteen months before they began to do so. By that time, November 1981, Moscow had deployed 250 ss–20s with 750 warheads.

Most people in the West gave Schmidt credit for speaking firmly to the Russians and helping bring the superpowers to the conference table. But the US and part of the West German press were unhappy about a long-term economic agreement signed between Bonn and Moscow during Schmidt's visit. The accord did not undermine the specific sanctions Carter had imposed, but it was embarrassingly timed, to say the least. The Germans seemed to recognize that, and insisted that the agreement be signed only by ambassadors, not at high level as Moscow wanted. It would surely have been better if the signature had been postponed altogether. In the long history of US–German friction, it was not only Washington which displayed insensitivity to its partner's concerns.

Some Western journalists who accompanied Schmidt on the visit will remember being taken aside by a high Soviet official for a 'friendly chat'. The official was very well-informed about US affairs, claimed even to read the US congressional record before he went to sleep at night. His message was, broadly speaking, 'We are baffled and worried by the twists and turns in Carter's policy. We know that you Europeans are too. We thus have a clear, mutual concern.' The official went on to say that Moscow would prefer a president with a comprehensible policy line, even if it was a hard one. He was soon to get his wish. On 4 November Carter lost the US election to Ronald Reagan.

Like a killer whale, the nuclear missiles problem repeatedly reared up and vanished again during the Carter era (and beyond). The US–German disputes over nuclear exports, the neutron weapon and human rights policy flared fiercely, but fairly briefly. It may seem a big jump from all that to Schmidt's efforts to create a zone of monetary stability in Europe, but in fact there is a close connection.

From mid-1977, that is half a year after Carter took office, the US dollar began to drop like a stone, above all against 'hard' currencies like the Deutschmark. The decline had set in much earlier, but the speed became breathtaking. In 1949, $1 would buy you DM4.20. Two decades later, thanks to the almost fixed exchange rate system, a dollar was still worth DM4. When the transition was made to floating rates in 1973 the dollar bought less than DM3 and by mid-1977 it was worth DM2.35. By the end of the year it had plunged to DM2.11 and in 1978 it sank well below the psychologically (as well as financially) important DM2 level.

The immediate reason for the dollar's sharp fall in 1977–8 was the emergence of a US balance-of-payments problem for which Carter could not fairly be blamed. In 1976, during the last year of the Ford administration, the US visible trade balance went into deficit, although the current account remained in surplus thanks to US 'invisible' earnings abroad. The situation was worsening as Carter took over. During 1977, the trade deficit became so big ($31 billion) that invisible earnings could no longer compensate for it, and the current account dropped into the red too. Hence the dollar's weakness, especially against the currencies of countries with relatively big surpluses like Germany and Japan.

Some people argued that this was just the sort of situation which floating exchange rates were intended to cure. In theory the dollar would float down until US goods became cheap enough to trounce the competition on foreign markets. The American trade balance would then go back into the black and the dollar would strengthen. On the other hand to the Germans and a lot of others, the dollar seemed not so much to be floating as drowning.

There was another side to the problem too. Many Americans stressed that the US deficit meant a corresponding trade surplus for other countries, thus helping them to pull themselves out of recesssion with strong export business. But it was now time, in the US view, for those who had benefited – especially West Germany and Japan – to do more to boost their own economic growth and suck in extra imports. That in turn would help other states, including the US, to increase their exports and so further encourage a general economic upswing.

That, in simple terms, was the 'locomotive theory' which the US sought to press on the Germans and Japanese before and during the Western economic summit conference in London in May 1977. Even at that time, Schmidt thought little of what he later called 'this ridiculous little locomotive theory'; but he did pledge orally that West Germany would do its best to reach a real economic growth rate of 5 per cent in 1977. The Japanese made a similar promise. Both fell short of the target.

Schmidt's pledge was part of an effort to placate the new US President, and indeed the London conference ended with greater apparent harmony than many people had expected. But basic differences had only been papered over. The German side had managed to have a phrase inserted in the communiqué saying, 'Inflation is not a cure for unemployment, on the contrary it is one of its basic causes.' That precisely expressed the view Bonn had held for years, and later most other countries came to regard it as almost self-evident, but at the time it still seemed a rather daring idea. It only got in the communiqué at all after a long tussle. Herr Schmidt's personal representative who prepared the summit meetings, Karl Otto Pöhl (later President of the Bundesbank), fought long but unsuccessfully for inclusion of the phrase. He then left the room where the communiqué was being drafted to stretch his legs. When he came back the wording he wanted had been inserted and another point was under discussion. Senior officials of the other summit countries thought Pöhl had walked out in a huff. Worried that the meeting might stall, they decided to agree to Bonn's wish. So a small piece of economic history was made.[10]

Schmidt had promised to seek stronger economic growth, but it was hard to see how that could be done without increasing German inflation. And inflation, according to the London communiqué, was 'a basic cause of unemployment'. Moreover, neither West Germany nor its partners were wholly convinced by the argument that the US deficit was of great economic help to the rest of the world. One main reason for America's plunge into the red was its huge increase in oil imports. As the dollar fell, so the US oil import bill increased, pushing the country further into deficit and forcing the US currency down again. That encouraged the oil producers, who were paid in dwindling dollars, to raise prices to maintain their earnings. This problem of oil and the dollar played a major role at the next economic summit conference in Bonn in July 1978. But already in 1977 Schmidt felt that a large part of the answer to the dollar problem lay in a US energy programme which cut the American oil bill.

Schmidt had little hope that Carter could bring in such a programme quickly. His brushes with the US President on other policy matters had warned him to expect the worst. In the second half of 1977 his fears were realized. The dollar plunged, speculative funds flooded into the Deutschmark, and US authorities seemed divided on what to do. Some, like the Chairman of the Federal Reserve Board Arthur Burns (whom Schmidt greatly admired), were opposed to further sharp depreciation. Others like the Treasury Secretary, Michael Blumenthal, apparently thought the opposite. In Bonn the sick joke made the rounds that Blumenthal was following an 'open-mouth policy'. Every time he spoke, the dollar dropped another few points.

Whatever virtues Schmidt had seen in floating exchange rates in 1973, the dollar's collapse in 1977 helped persuade him that an effort had to be made to regain more stability. In theory the floating system was meant to bring relatively painless balance-of-payments adjustment. In practice, Schmidt felt by late 1977 that the dollar's plight reflected not so much economic factors as a crisis of confidence in US leadership.

Giscard d'Estaing fully agreed. He and Schmidt had already expressed concern to one another about Carter's emerging policies at a meeting in February 1977. As time passed their worries increased. Moreover, Giscard needed no convincing about the virtues of stable exchange rates. He had always been hostile to floating and clearly welcomed Schmidt's conversion under the pressure of the 'Carter effect'. If the US was not willing, or able, to stabilize the dollar, the

Europeans would have to try to shield themselves against the worst of the dollar-induced currency shocks. 'The Nine [European Community countries] build a fortress', is how a West German newspaper later described the initial moves to set up a European Monetary System (EMS). The headline was a bit premature. Not all nine Community countries became full members of the EMS, and the fortress turned out to have gaps in its walls. But certainly the instinct for self-preservation against the vagaries of American policy played a key role in the European decision.

The dollar crisis was not the only reason for creation of the EMS. Right back in 1970 the European Community had produced a plan which aimed for a full Economic and Monetary Union and, ideally, a single European currency by 1980. A start was made in 1972 with an arrangement intended to stop European currencies from fluctuating much against one another. But the strains of trying to maintain the system among countries with diverging inflation rates and balance-of-payments performances proved too great. Britain and Italy left the arrangement – called the currency 'snake' – within the first year. France drifted in and out again, keen on the principle of the 'snake' but unable in practice to turn in an economic performance which would keep the franc strong. The hard-core members of the 'snake' were West Germany, the Benelux countries and (most of the time) Denmark, plus the associate members Norway and Sweden.

When Schmidt and Giscard decided that there should be a European Monetary System, they were thus not starting from scratch. Moreover, some other far-sighted European leaders believed that closer monetary and economic co-operation had become essential if the Community itself were to hold together. One person who believed this, and who made his view clear in a speech in Florence in October 1977, was the President of the European Commission, Roy Jenkins. He was widely derided at the time as a 'dreamer'. Yet, only six months later, Schmidt and Giscard broached a similar monetary scheme to their astonished European colleagues.

For all the close co-operation between France and West Germany which made the EMS possible, there was a competitive element too. Giscard made plain more than once that he wanted to see his country draw level economically with its neighbour across the Rhine. A quarter of a century earlier, the European Coal and Steel Community had been formed above all to bind German and French production together so that another war between the two countries would become impossible. Giscard saw French economic health in a Europe moving towards integration as a further insurance policy against the danger of a strong and restless Germany. If France were to compete it had to force down its inflation rate to something close to the German level and boost its rate of real economic growth. Giscard felt the EMS would help achieve both. He thought it would be easier to impose tough anti-inflationary policies at home with the argument that otherwise the franc might have to suffer the ignominy of devaluation in the EMS.

Schmidt agreed. He felt that if France fell further behind Germany economically it could well turn protectionist, starting a chain reaction in Europe and beyond with serious political as well as economic consequences. It might destroy that special Franco–German *entente* on which Schmidt, disappointed by Britain's performance in the Community, greatly relied.

There were thus a lot of weighty economic and foreign policy arguments for Schmidt and Giscard to go ahead with the EMS, but domestically both leaders were in a strong position too. By late 1977 Schmidt was on a peak of popularity at home following the Mogadishu affair, Giscard had four more years to run before he had to face election. Those factors too spoke in favour of a daring initiative. When it came, it was kept so secret that even prime ministers and central bankers initially had no idea what was happening.

Schmidt and Giscard felt the scheme was far too important politically to be put in the hands of monetary experts alone. They feared that if the plan went first to lower-level European Community bodies it would simply run into the sand. Schmidt was also well aware of the opposition he would meet at home, not least from a Bundesbank worried about possible threats to Germany's price stability. It was thus essential to get a big political head of steam behind the plan first, so that potential opponents would not be able to block progress.

After preliminary talks, the German and French leaders pinned down their strategy at a meeting at Rambouillet on 2 April 1978. It was agreed that the monetary scheme would be brought up at a session of the European Council (summit conference) due to be held in Denmark five days later. But the topic would only be raised when the European heads of state and government were alone together, without foreign ministers or officials who might afterwards spill the beans.

That was more or less the way things happened. On the night of 7

April, after dinner at Marienborg Castle, Copenhagen, Schmidt and Giscard outlined the plan to seven bewildered Prime Ministers and a delighted Roy Jenkins (who as Commission President was allowed into the talks). There was also a note-taker, which was just as well since several of those present were baffled by what they heard but naturally were not keen to admit it at the time.

Schmidt led the assault, complaining that the US had 'flooded the world with greenbacks' (i.e. dollars). He underlined what he felt to be the link between currency instability and weak economic performance and warned of the danger of growing European unemployment. He even mentioned in passing that Britain might have two million jobless in the foreseeable future. It seemed a horrific figure at the time, but was later far surpassed not only in Britain but in France and West Germany too. In detail, Schmidt proposed the creation of a new European Monetary Fund, the partial pooling of the official reserves of the member states, less use of the dollar for currency intervention, and gradual development of a new European reserve asset. Giscard backed up Schmidt, saying the time had come for a 'new course in European monetary affairs'.

Britain's Prime Minister, Jim Callaghan, at once raised objections. He feared the scheme could be interpreted as aimed against the US, however much its authors themselves might see it as self-defence against the vagaries of American policy. Callaghan (like Schmidt and Giscard an ex-Finance Minister) was well aware of the dollar problem, but he felt that efforts to solve it should in the first place be made through the International Monetary Fund (IMF). The IMF already had its own fledgling reserve asset, called Special Drawing Rights (SDRs). In time, SDRs might be able to take over part of the role in world monetary affairs so far played by the dollar. A competitive European currency such as Schmidt had mentioned might complicate the situation and undermine the future role of the SDR. Callaghan was also remarkably blunt about the British economy, describing its general weakness as a 'hardening of the arteries'. He felt the kind of exchange rate system being discussed might hold down the Deutschmark, thereby making German exports more price competitive. The Germans might plunge ahead and the British would be left floundering behind.

With the benefit of hindsight, it is clear that the new European reserve asset hardly emerged as a challenge to the SDR, or indeed to anything else. Moreover, the Deutschmark was unusually weak from

1979 to 1981 for reasons which had nothing to do with the EMS. It would be unfair to blame Callaghan for not foreseeing this, but it seems certain that behind his objections, Callaghan was anxiously wondering what the 'anti-Common Marketeers' in his Labour Party would say when they heard about the Franco–German scheme.

Callaghan's remarks did not come as much of a surprise to Schmidt and none at all to Giscard. The French President had felt from the start that the 'special relationship' between the US and Britain would mean more to Callaghan than any European scheme. The British evidently believed that US leaders with varying degrees of intellectual and political capacity came and went, but that Anglo–American friendship was immortal.

Despite those differences, an initial effort was made (above all at Schmidt's insistence) to have West Germany, France and Britain work together on the EMS. The following morning, Schmidt, Giscard and Callaghan had breakfast together and agreed that their special representatives should discuss the scheme further.

Thus a group emerged whose existence was initially known to almost no one. Its members were Horst Schulmann, Schmidt's senior economic adviser at the Chancellery, Bernard Clappier, governor of the Banque de France (the French central bank), and Ken Couzens, a British Treasury official. Later, the group became popularly known as the 'three wise men'. Then Couzens dropped out as British reservations about the scheme grew.

It was an extraordinary situation. The Danes, who at that time held the (rotating) chairmanship of the European Community council, wrote to Schmidt asking what they should do about the monetary discussions begun in Marienborg castle. They received no reply, because the 'three wise men' were already working away secretly. The West German Finance Minister Hans Matthofer, the Economics Minister Count Lambsdorff, and the Bundesbank President Otmar Emminger, were told what was in the wind but knew little in detail. Various European Community bodies went on talking about prospects for monetary integration, without realizing that a European Monetary System was being prepared under their noses.

Word about the 'three wise men' gradually leaked out, but the monetary scheme only emerged fully into the open at the European Council meeting in Bremen on 6 and 7 July 1978. Once again it was a performance largely written and directed by the French and Germans.

In the preceding week Schulmann and Clappier toured Europe explaining to other governments details of what the Chancellor and President had in mind. Earlier on 24 June, Schmidt and Giscard had met with advisers in Schmidt's home in Hamburg–Langenhorn to settle their approach for the Bremen meeting. What Rambouillet palace had been to the Copenhagen council, Langenhorn was to Bremen.

By that time, the British were no longer playing an active role in the work, though Couzens was given the draft of a Schulmann–Clappier paper on the proposed monetary system a few days after the Hamburg talks. This paper was distributed to the other heads of government in Bremen and was published, with minor changes, as an Annex to the official declaration at the end of the conference.

The paper contained many of the technical points about a monetary fund, intervention and so on which Schmidt had already mentioned informally in Copenhagen. It also referred for the first time to a European Currency Unit which would be 'at the centre of' the new monetary system. Many people felt that this unit would eventually emerge as 'Europe's dollar'. For Giscard the name, unexciting though it was in English, had a very big advantage. The first letters made up the word ECU, which was the name of an old French coin. So he could hope that one day (however far off) the ECU would regain vanished glory as a medium of exchange throughout Europe. *Vive la France!*

The Annex published in Bremen did not mean that all heads of government agreed with every detail, or even that all were determined to set up the new system. The official declaration said 'decisions *can* be taken [not must be] and commitments made' at the next European Council meeting in Brussels in December. Callaghan remained very wary. So did the Irish and Italians for different reasons. But the French and Germans remained ahead of the game, there was only one detailed paper on the table, and that was their own.

From the Bremen meeting on, the monetary issue dominated all others in the European Community. Councils and committees produced long reports on the topic, newspapers were full of articles about currency paraphernalia like 'crawling pegs', 'warning indicators' and 'parity grids'. Some people insisted that the proposed new system, insofar as it could be understood, would never work properly. Others felt the Community was at last back on the road to economic and monetary union.

In Britain, many feared the EMS was a Teutonic plot concocted with the aid of the tricky French to undermine the British economy still further. So-called 'Pro-Common Marketeers' feared that if Britain did not join the EMS it would lose a big chance, as it had done when it failed to become a founder member of the European Community in 1958. The government, torn between a desire not to miss the bus and the fear of buying a pig in a poke, hedged its bets in a report on the EMS issued only ten days before the December summit meeting. 'Government not ready to decide whether it is in Britain's best interest to join' is how one newspaper headline summed up the report's contents.[11]

Schmidt and Giscard tried to ensure that what they felt to be the historic importance of their initiative should not be lost in a welter of technical detail. Two months after the Bremen meeting they held consultations in Aachen (Aix-la-Chapelle), the city of the Emperor Charlemagne and rich in tradition for Germans and French alike. On the first evening the two leaders attended a concert in the 1,000-year-old cathedral – a scene recalling the symbolic gesture of national reconciliation between de Gaulle and Adenauer in Reims sixteen years earlier.

Afterwards, both Schmidt and Giscard, visibly moved, spoke of their common heritage and said efforts for greater monetary integration were an essential step on the road to European unity. The President stressed that the EMS would help to increase the stability of 'our old and dear continent'. The Chancellor urged sceptics not to rely 'on the premature view of experts who tend to judge things quickly, but to see it [the EMS] in the major political context of the next fifteen or twenty years – or still longer. . . . I want to state very clearly that I don't see these as technical monetary questions alone, but as political, economic and psychological matters of the very first importance.'[12]

Schmidt was particularly cutting about journalists who had written before the Aachen meeting that differences had arisen over the EMS between Germany and France. 'I'm terribly sorry to disappoint you,' he sourly told a press conference, but Bonn and Paris were wholly at one – as future discussion of the issue with other European partners in Brussels would prove.

In fact, the two sides had run into a problem before Aachen – highly technical like so much to do with the EMS, but potentially serious. Put simply, France was pressing for an EMS rule which, if accepted, would have involved the Bundesbank in more currency intervention than was strictly essential to hold the system together. As usual the French had cogent arguments, but Schmidt had little room for manœuvre. The Bundesbank had reservations about the EMS on several other scores which it seemed ready to swallow, but it was not ready to accept the kind of intervention commitment the French wanted. The central bankers felt if they gave way there would be a new danger of increased German money supply and inflation. As an independent body, the Bundesbank could dig in its heels and the Schmidt–Giscard plan could not be put into practice. Governments could decide on the EMS, but central banks were needed to make it work.

Schulmann and Clappier stayed up most of the night in Aachen trying to find a compromise. They finally produced a series of options for their bosses, and it was Giscard who saved the day by agreeing to a formula which took account of the Bundesbank's fears.

The incident proved what the British in particular had long been aching to know – that the Germans and French were not as agreed on all details, even quite big ones, as their public statements indicated. That is not surprising. There is no reason to doubt that Schmidt and Giscard were wholly in accord on the political need for the EMS, and that their emotional comments about Europe in Aachen were genuinely felt. But even for two ex-Finance Ministers, the technical problems raised by the system were obscure – the more so since Schmidt and Giscard had to discuss them in their only common language, English. Sometimes particularly intricate points needed repeating – but there comes a time at which it seems impolite to go on making the same point, even if there is still no certainty the argument has been fully understood.

In the circumstances it is surprising that there were not more gaffes. One reason there were not is that Schulmann and Clappier worked well together from the start. The forty-five-year-old German Social Democrat and the French central banker close to retirement age did not look tailor-made for easy co-operation. There were initial comments in private from critical (and perhaps envious) German officials that Schulmann might be led up the garden path by a wily adversary. The Chancellor, it was said, was putting too many eggs in one basket. But, in the event, Schulmann and Clappier trusted and evidently respected one another, and that paid dividends.

The Aachen meeting turned out to be the high-point of the EMS story. Franco–German ties had never seemed closer, Schmidt and

Giscard appeared to have confirmed that technical problems would not deflect them from their main political aim. Yet by year's end the 'grand design' had almost disappeared behind a sordid squabble about a problem almost no one foresaw.

In the weeks leading up to the Brussels conference which was due to decide formally on the birth of the EMS, most things seemed to be going Schmidt's way. Domestically he had been able to calm (if not remove) many of the fears among bankers and academics about the new system with a campaign of public and private persuasion. On one notable occasion, Schmidt arranged a 'discussion' with EMS sceptics over a meal. While the others present had their mouths full, the Chancellor ignored the food and gave a dramatic lecture on the perils of currency instability for the world economy, jobs and social peace. At first none of the diners could answer back and later, when the meal was over, most of them felt too chastened by Schmidt's gloomy vision to raise their original objections.

Abroad, Schmidt could rely on the currency 'snake' members (the Benelux countries and Denmark) to join the EMS from the start. He became almost certain that Italy would join too after holding talks in Siena in November with Prime Minister Giulio Andreotti. The Italian leader was guarded in his comments so long as his own sceptical central bankers were nearby. But in private he told Schmidt that Italy, as one of the founder members of the European Community, could not afford politically to stay outside the new system. On the other hand, Andreotti made it clear that Italy needed more economic aid from its partners, and the chronically weak lira would have to be bound by less strict rules in the EMS than those applying to hard currencies like the Deutschmark. Schmidt was not happy about the conditions but he felt a compromise could be found. The same applied to demands for more Community cash from Ireland as its price for EMS membership. That seemed to leave only Britain firmly on the sidelines – and the Chancellor, for all his irritation, still hoped Callaghan might turn up trumps on the day.

Schmidt was mostly right in his assessment. The Brussels summit conference of 4 and 5 December confidently announced that 'A European Monetary System will be set up on 1 January 1979.' Italy and Ireland did not pledge right away to join, but both did so a few days later. Britain agreed to become, in effect, a non-playing participant, it would not accept the EMS exchange rate rules, but formally speaking it was a member and thus had its foot in the door should the EMS really become a going concern.

Yet, after all the months of preparation, the battles with the doubters and the fine speeches about European unity, it turned out to be France which stopped the EMS emerging on time. Amazing though it may seem, farm policy problems were behind the delay.

This is not the place to go into the mind-boggling intricacies of the Common Agriculture Policy. It is enough to say here that the Europeans have sought for years to guarantee common agricultural prices to farmers throughout the Community, although there is no common European currency and the exchange rates of the national currencies are constantly altering. To try to even out the impact on prices (and hence on farmers' incomes) of the currency ups and downs, a system of Monetary Compensatory Amounts (MCAS) has been introduced in cross-border agricultural trade. The whole affair recalls the mad scientists in *Gulliver's Travels* who set a sundial on a weathervane, then tried to ensure the right time would always be shown no matter which way the wind blew. The key point in the EMS connection is that the French had long felt German farmers were gaining unfair export benefits through the application of MCAS. The start of a new system aimed at currency stability seemed to Paris to be a good moment to start phasing out MCAS altogether.

Giscard had drawn attention to the farm policy point at the Brussels summit, and the closing communiqué had a few ambiguous words on the topic.[13] A few days later, other French spokesmen became more specific, saying that if any new MCAS were created they would have to be dismantled again within a year. The French made it clear that, if accord could not be reached on the timetable, they would not agree to the technical arrangements allowing the EMS to start on 1 January. The dispute simmered on over Christmas but most people believed the German and French leaders would intervene personally at the last moment. It seemed unthinkable that they would allow their brainchild, the EMS, to stay in limbo. But the unthinkable happened.

The French President evidently found himself under greater domestic pressure on the farm issue than he had bargained for. In any case the two leaders were badly placed in the last days of 1978 for a *tête-a-tête*. Giscard had gone on a visit to Africa and Schmidt was in the Caribbean. Urgent messages were in fact sent from Bonn, via Paris to Africa – but if the President received them he did not respond; 1

January came and went without the EMS.

All eyes then turned hopefully to Guadeloupe where Schmidt and Giscard were due to meet with Carter and Callaghan on 5 and 6 January. But the 'Big Four' meeting brought other things to bother about than the EMS. Carter produced his Euro-strategic missiles offer, thus nudging the problem of compensatory amounts in farm trade down the list of Franco–German priorities.

The dispute drifted on for another two months, then the French gave way and the EMS formally began operation on 13 March. By that time it was hard to recall without irony Giscard's comments six months before in Aachen about the 'spirit of Charlemagne'. In retrospect, Schmidt had come closer to the mark when he stated with a wan smile that 'nothing in the world is conceivable without risk, not even love, let alone monetary policy'.[14]

Schmidt's international prestige was never higher than in 1978 and early 1979. Although the EMS had begun with a whimper and not a bang, Schmidt could hardly be blamed for the delay. The European monetary show was on the road and, according to the Brussels communiqué, was due to take a big institutional step forward in 1981. In fact, that deadline was not respected either, but few at the start of 1979 foresaw the new political and economic obstacles just around the corner.

Even a public with little interest in arcane European monetary matters was aware that Schmidt had scored a hit as host of the Western economic summit conference in Bonn in July 1978. To the surprise of many of the participants, Schmidt turned out to be a relaxed, almost modest, chairman of the seven-nation gathering. Jimmy Carter, who combined the summit with an official visit to West Germany and Berlin, emerged all smiles from a friendly chat with the Chancellor. 'I always learn so much from Helmut about economics,' he admitted.

The conference resulted in a 'package deal' to tackle unemployment and inflation in which the Western leaders made unusually specific commitments. Japan pledged to cut its trade surplus, the US to lower energy imports, and West Germany to boost its economic growth rate by taking steps costing the state around DM12 billion. Not every country kept its promise, however. Germany did, but, by increasing spending and foregoing tax revenue, it gave itself still bigger budget problems, which later were to strain the SDP–FDP coalition to breaking-point. Some people already saw that danger looming, but if Schmidt had not pledged his share, the summit deal would have collapsed and German inflexibility would have been blamed.

On the broader foreign policy front too, statesman Schmidt in 1978 looked like the European leader other countries could least afford to ignore. Two months before Carter's visit, Brezhnev had been in town talking about long-term industrial co-operation as well as military matters. A stream of other foreign notables passed through Bonn – sometimes from opposing sides in this or that regional conflict, but almost all hoping from Schmidt for a special hearing and support.

'I am speaking on behalf of a country that cannot and will not act as a big power,' said Schmidt in a speech to the United Nations general assembly that year.[15] But many of his listeners felt the statement underplayed if not West Germany's power then at least its influence. Indeed, Schmidt went on to give a grand survey of world dangers and how to handle them, which hardly seemed to fit in with his humble opening remark. No doubt with Carter especially in mind, Schmidt stressed the need for 'predictability and calculability of political and military conduct'. And, wagging a finger at both superpowers, he called for the political will to respect four guidelines, 'to avoid provocation; to make one's own options unmistakably clear; to defuse dangerous situations through readiness to compromise; and to enable those concerned to save face'. No one could honestly be surprised when, months later, Schmidt was invited to take a seat with the other 'Big Three' Western nations at the Guadeloupe summit conference table.

Despite the acclaim abroad, and his widespread popularity at home, Schmidt had grave problems holding his coalition together. A restive group of parliamentarians on the left wing of his SPD posed a constant danger to the slim majority the coalition parties had won in the 1976 election. Even as 'the hero of Mogadishu', Schmidt had barely gained Bundestag approval for the government's new anti-terrorism measures. The liberals of the FDP looked on nervously at SPD in-fighting, stressed that if the coalition collapsed it would not be *their* fault – and started to eye the opposition CDU–CSU more favourably as a possible future partner.

On one big issue, nuclear power, the leaders of both government parties faced strong opposition from the rank and file. Schmidt was more than ever convinced after the oil crisis of 1973–4 that West Germany, dependent on imports for all its energy supplies bar coal, had to build more atomic power-stations. But a strong minority in the country was violently against, staging sit-ins and battling with police at the construction sites of nuclear plants. Some of the opponents later joined 'The Greens', the party of ecologists, pacifists and other radicals which won seats in local parliaments from the late 1970s and entered the Bundestag after the 1983 general election. But many others, claiming safety problems of atomic plant operation and waste-disposal had not been solved, stayed in the SPD and FDP and sought to swing the government to their view. In conferences of both parties in November 1977, the leadership had to make awkward compromises on the issue. At the SPD party conference in December 1979, the topic was almost as fiercely debated as nuclear missiles policy. Again a compromise emerged with which Schmidt felt he could live, involving priority for coal but grudging tolerance of nuclear power to plug an energy gap which could not be closed any other way.

This stand hardly seemed an adequate response to the new problems emerging on the energy and economic front. Even as the Social Democrats debated, the revolution in Iran was in full swing, posing a big threat to oil supplies to the West. Earlier in the year the oil producers had agreed on new price increases which ushered in the second oil crisis and helped plunge the West into its deepest post-war recession. West Germany had come through the first crisis better than almost any country, but it was much harder hit this time.

In 1974, the Germans had shrugged off the impact of the oil price rise on their imports by sharply boosting their exports. In 1979, they could not manage the same trick again. Exports went up by about 10 per cent (against nearly 30 per cent in 1974), but imports rose twice as fast. As a result the visible trade surplus slumped to DM22.4 billion compared with DM41.2 billion in 1978. After deducting deficits on 'invisibles', the country's current account went into the red for the first time since 1965. The shortfall was only DM11 billion (less than 1 per cent of Germany's Gross National Product) but the next year it plummeted to around DM30 billion, the biggest current account deficit in the Western world.

Dearer oil was one big reason for the swing into deficit but not the only one. Ironically, it seemed other countries had taken Schmidt's lectures about the evils of inflation too much to heart for Germany's own good. During the first oil crisis they had expanded their economies, sucked in a lot of German export goods, but fuelled inflation too.

During the second crisis they were much more cautious. This time Germany's economy and its imports expanded a bit faster than those of its partners, partly because of that boost to growth which Schmidt had pledged at the 1978 economic conference in Bonn.

That was not the only irony. In 1978, Schmidt had pressed for European monetary integration not least because the US deficit and the dwindling dollar seemed to signal a crisis of American leadership. But in 1979, the Deutschmark became less of a high-flier than it used to be, and in 1980 was unusually weak because the Germans themselves had begun to run into deficits. Meanwhile, the US, perhaps prodded into action by the impending creation of the EMS, had finally taken effective steps to support the dollar in November 1978. As a result, by the time Ronald Reagan defeated Carter in the November 1980 presidential election, the US economy looked in some key respects to be in better shape than before, while West Germany's seemed to be in difficulties.

Many people (not least Germans) exaggerated the change, saying the Federal Republic might be moving into chronic deficit. In fact, it returned to surplus in 1982. But there was an undeniable shift in the relative economic status of the US and Germany, which tended to strengthen Reagan's political position and weaken Schmidt's.

It was thus against an uneasy background that Schmidt approached the general election of October 1980. Moreover, he was at last facing the political opponent most worthy of him, the irrepressible Franz Josef Strauss who had emerged at the head of the CDU–CSU forces. The direct confrontation between the two temperamental ex-Defence and Finance Ministers seemed bound to make the sparks fly as they had hardly done since the days of Adenauer and Schumacher. The election campaign was therefore billed in advance as a 'battle of the giants'.

The mere thought of Strauss as Chancellor sent shudders through the government coalition parties and helped them forget for a while their problems in working together. Both SPD and FDP felt that if the impulsive Bavarian got the top job he would smash social-liberal reform policy at home and put the *Ostpolitik* at risk. These fears were probably exaggerated, but many in the CDU, the senior opposition party, also had reservations about Strauss, with good reason.

Shortly after the 1976 general election, Strauss's CSU announced it was pulling out of the joint parliamentary group it had formed with the CDU in Bonn for decades. Strauss clearly felt that if he instead of the

CDU leader Helmut Kohl had been heading the combined Union parties in the election campaign, then Schmidt would have been tipped out of office. In a private speech which leaked out, Strauss referred to Kohl (who, in fact, had won a respectable 48.6 per cent of the vote) as lacking the character and brains to become Chancellor. He also talked about 'pocket-sized' politicians in the CDU who were unable to find the right strategy to bring about election victory.

Strauss's big problem was that his CSU existed only in Bavaria (where the CDU presented no candidate). His party could always be relied on to bring him a big victory in his home state, but that only amounted at best to about 10 per cent of the national vote and some fifty seats in the Bonn Parliament. Strauss thus toyed with the idea of creating a new party beyond Bavaria to extend his hold and scoop up extra right-wing support. The break with the parliamentary CDU seemed to be a first step in that direction.

But Kohl called Strauss's bluff, making it clear that if a new national party emerged, then the CDU would for the first time put up rival candidates to the CSU in Bavaria. Strauss backed down, the new party never emerged (at least not in a form Strauss desired), and the CDU–CSU stuck together in Bonn. But the skirmishing between the two 'sister parties' left deep scars.

Hence the astonishment when, in July 1979, both CDU and CSU agreed on Strauss as their 'Chancellor candidate' for the 1980 election. Some in the CDU reluctantly gave Strauss their support because, like him, they thought Kohl a dunce. Others (no doubt Kohl among them) felt Strauss should be given his head, that he would probably lose the election but that the CDU would then be rid of him. Strauss himself, by then in his mid-sixties, was fully aware that the stakes were high. If he could not oust Schmidt this time he would almost certainly never get another chance. For a while he was undecided whether to seek the Union candidacy, and finally did so only after pressure to go ahead from ambitious CSU colleagues.

Strauss often seemed uncertain of his tactics during the campaign too. Once in a while the old fire emerged as he stumped from one public meeting to another, urging the nation to choose 'freedom instead of Socialism'. Tie loosened, face glistening with sweat under the arc-lights, Strauss on top form could still mesmerize the crowds with his scornful salvoes against the government. But on other occasions he seemed consciously to check himself as though feeling a more statesmanlike showing better suited a potential Chancellor. The result was that Strauss, to the surprise of many old foes and fans, sometimes became dull.

Schmidt naturally had his good moments too, especially when he was attacking Strauss. He only had to mention his opponent's name to bring titters from his audience, then an expectant hush. 'That man can't even control himself,' Schmidt would whisper sadly into the microphone. Then he would step back, stab a finger in the air and shout to an approving roar, 'He *must not* have control over our country.'

But, especially in the last weeks of the campaign, Schmidt was off form. He developed a bad cold which affected his speeches and temper. Sometimes he looked as though he had something worse than a cold. Few people knew that Schmidt had had a bad illness the previous winter and that his doctors had urgently, but unsuccessfully, warned him to take things easier. In 1981, Schmidt's health grew worse and again almost no one was aware of it, until he was rushed to hospital for an operation which made front-page news well beyond Germany.

So it was that the 'battle of the giants' turned out to be something of a damp squib. Instead, two other political leaders extracted unexpected benefit from the campaign. One was Kohl, who supported Strauss loyally in public, whatever his private feelings, and gained credit for doing so even from opponents and rivals. The other was the FDP leader, Genscher, who could profile himself as a moderate liberal, helping to guard the nation against the excesses of Strauss on the one hand and the far Left of the SPD on the other. One FDP slogan urged voters to support the liberals (and hence the coalition) 'so that Schmidt can stay Chancellor'.

Genscher was to have that slogan rammed down his throat by furious Social Democrats when he pulled out of the alliance two years later. But, in 1980, his approach paid off handsomely. On election night, 5 October, it turned out that the SPD had won 42.9 per cent of the vote, only 0.3 per cent more than it managed in 1976. Genscher's FDP jumped to 10.6 per cent (7.9 per cent before), thus ensuring continuation of the government coalition.

Strauss was the loser. Under his leadership the CDU–CSU had picked up only 44.5 per cent, clearly less than the Union had managed under the 'ineffectual' Kohl four years earlier. In a television interview, a crestfallen Strauss agreed that he might have made some mistakes; but he added there was only one German politician who, according to himself, never made mistakes 'and that is Helmut Schmidt'.

INTERLUDE
Schmidt and the Arts

It was not all politics! Despite election campaigns and coalition strains as well as international economic and strategic problems, Schmidt still found time for another, less hectic, world. His surprising appearance as speaker at a conference on Kant has already been mentioned. But he emerged in a still more unusual role during a trip to England in December 1981, during his last term as Chancellor. One journalist who got wind of the visit in advance sought to find out the point of it from a Chancellery official and was told 'to record Mozart'. That wildly unlikely explanation turned out to be true.

Schmidt went to Abbey Road studios in North London with two young pianist friends, Christoph Eschenbach and Justus Frantz, and recorded Mozart's *Concerto in F-Major for Three Pianos* (KV242) with the London Philharmonic Orchestra. All three devoted their earnings to Amnesty International.

Schmidt is no Paderewski (to name one statesman who was at the same time a master pianist) and has no illusions that he ever will be. Hence, when Eschenbach and Frantz first suggested recording the Mozart concerto, Schmidt was inclined to turn down the idea. But the more he thought it over the more he felt attracted by the challenge.

He had been fond of music ever since his Hamburg childhood, with the madrigal singing at home and the piano lessons at the Lichtwark-Schule. Even as minister and government leader he occasionally found a few minutes in the evenings to sit and strum at the piano. He liked Bach above all, for the clarity and logic of the writing, the emotion which did not overwhelm form. The elevated lightness of Mozart was less close to his own temperament and a recording naturally a very different proposition from picking out pieces privately at the keyboard. True, the 'third piano' part of the Mozart concerto can be mastered even by those whose fingers are none too nimble, but a good sense of timing and rhythm, concentration and teamwork are essential all the same.

Schmidt finally dropped his reservations, practised hard and the recording sessions went well; so well, in fact, that the Eschenbach – Frantz–Schmidt trio later recorded the work again, this time in Zurich for television. At the Zurich rehearsals, the shirt-sleeved Schmidt conveyed so deep an air of concentration and professionalism that a reporter was moved to ask whether he planned to develop a second career as a pianist. 'I fear, sir,' replied Schmidt with heavy irony, 'that it is just a bit too late for that.' Not everyone noticed the irony, however, and the remark helped add to the legend that there was absolutely nothing Helmut Schmidt felt he could not do – given time!

Quite apart from his own pianistic efforts, Schmidt held 'house concerts' in the old Chancellery building, the Palais Schaumburg, while he was government leader. They were scheduled for Sunday evenings (the moment when Schmidt was least likely to be called away by affairs of state) and were given little publicity. Any guest, however eminent, who tried to use the occasion too obviously to talk about politics tended not to be invited again.

It was thanks to four string players from the Israel Philharmonic Orchestra that those Sunday musical oases emerged in the desert of political Bonn. A few months after he became Chancellor, Schmidt was offered a house concert by the four Israelis. Behind the offer was the hope that those who attended might also give financial and other support to the orchestra. Schmidt at once liked the idea, perhaps because of his own part-Jewish background as well as his belief that the orchestra deserved backing.

That first concert, held in January 1975, was followed by about a dozen others over the years. The range was wide – from Bach to Bartók, from Telemann to Villa-Lobos – and the standard of performance high. There were expected triumphs from world famous artists like the violinist Yehudi Menuhin; and there were happy surprises, for example from the outstandingly gifted but relatively little-known Czech pianist Ivan Moravec, who delighted his audience with a concert of Beethoven, Schumann, Debussy and Janáček. Afterwards, Schmidt sat up talking with Moravec until after midnight, apparently oblivious to his heavy political schedule only a few hours away.

Alongside his fondness for music, Schmidt has a special love of the visual arts. That too dates back to his early years – the schoolboy talent for drawing, the thwarted ambition to become a town-planner and the admiration for painters the Nazis called degenerate. While on pre-war military service in Bremen he often spent the little spare money he had on what amounted to weekend artistic pilgrimages. He would take a train into the country, then walk for miles across the flat, swampy North German countryside to the villages of Worpswede and Fischerhüde where many painters and sculptors had made their homes. For a couple of days at a time the military and the Nazis seemed far away.

For Schmidt in those days Art was both a hope and a refuge. Later, as parliamentarian and minister, he wanted to show his appreciation of what Art had given him, and above all to salute those painters who had suffered under the Nazis. But it was only after he became Chancellor that he got a really good opportunity – both because of his influence and because of the new building into which he and his staff moved.

For his first two years as government leader Schmidt had precious little room in his Chancellery, the Palais Schaumburg, for art exhibitions. The move in 1976 to the new Chancellery changed all that. The seemingly endless corridors and spacious offices cried out for paintings and sculpture and Schmidt seized the chance. On the wall opposite the desk in his own office, Schmidt set a particularly fine seascape by Emil Nolde, the German Expressionist whom he most admired. Pictures by other Expressionists, including August Macke and Franz Marc, were placed in the cabinet room after an unexpected, intense meeting between Art and Politics. Schmidt had called in experts to recommend which paintings might be hung where. Suddenly a policy talk between senior ministers became necessary at the same moment. Experts and ministers found themselves together in the same room, and for more than two hours they swapped impressions of colours, positioning and lighting.

Schmidt put on about ten major exhibitions in the new Chancellery during his term as government leader. They began with paintings from the Berlin of the 1920s and continued with, among others, fine collections by Max Ernst, Nolde, Macke, Kollwitz and Dolbin. The most personal was a display of works by those who lived and worked in Schmidt's beloved Worpswede. The Chancellor opened each exhibition himself with a speech to up to 1,000 guests. When he arrived he already had a heavy day's work behind him, and looked tired and often grim. But from the moment he began with the greeting '*Liebe Kunstfreunde*' – 'Dear Friends of Art' – his weariness vanished. After the speech he went from picture to picture, arguing points of detail. The longer he stayed the more animated he became.

Schmidt constantly rejected the view that he was trying to give the Germans 'cultural leadership'. He stressed that, in the light of the Nazi experience, any political leader had to beware of the temptation to thrust his personal artistic preferences down the throats of his countrymen. But with both the semi-private concerts and the art exhibitions he wanted at least to offer a signal for the receptive. 'I would like people to have a true picture of Germany,' he said once, 'and not just one determined on the one hand by Holocaust on televison and on the other by an efficient economy and armed forces.'[1]

In fact, by far the biggest art work at the Chancellery is not by a German but an Englishman, Henry Moore. It is the huge bronze sculpture 'Large Two Forms' which stands on the Chancellery lawn; a symbol, as Schmidt put it, of 'nature and intelligence, of power and elegance – of the contrast between those elements and, at the same time, of the possibility for harmony between them'.

Schmidt and Moore first met in Bonn in 1977 to discuss prospects for a sculpture and got on well right away. Within a few weeks the Chancellor had paid a (largely unnoticed) return visit to the seventy-nine-year-old artist's Hertfordshire home to follow up the idea. Two years later, 'Large Two Forms' was formally inaugurated in the Chancellery grounds in Moore's presence. For Schmidt it was a special satisfaction to have acquired, in personal friendship, a major work from an artist who nearly four decades earlier had produced such moving 'Shelter Drawings' – of London under the Luftwaffe blitz.

Would that Schmidt had always got on as splendidly with British politicians as he did with Henry Moore: Soon after 'Large Two Forms' was in place, the Conservative Prime Minister, Margaret Thatcher, visited Bonn to seek Schmidt's aid in winning a better European Community budget deal for Britain. Schmidt felt the talks got nowhere – a 'wholly wasted day' in fact. That evening, at a supper for the visitors, he sought to retrieve the situation by abandoning his official text about politics and stressing instead the cultural links between Germany and Britain. Naturally Moore and his 'Large Two Forms' came in for special mention.

Mrs Thatcher did not take the outstretched olive branch. She agreed that the 'Large Two Forms' was most impressive – far bigger, in fact, than a work of Moore's she had seen at home. Indeed, the Moore sculpture which she knew bore about the same relation to the one on the Chancellery lawn as Britain's Gross National Product did to German GNP. 'And while we're on the subject of money, Chancellor. . .'

8

CHANCELLOR
Over the Top, 1980–82

On the face of it the 1980 election left Schmidt firmly in the saddle. Strauss had been trounced, the dejected Union parties had gone down at the polls for the fourth time in a row. The government coalition now had a majority of forty-five Bundestag seats instead of only ten. Almost all the gains had been made by Genscher's FDP not by the SPD, but that did not look like a problem for Schmidt. His popularity in the country far exceeded that of his party, and few doubted that without him the SPD would have fared much worse. Now he had greater room for parliamentary manœuvre and could more safely ignore pressure from the SPD's left wing, or so it seemed.

Immediately after the election, Bonn was buzzing with speculation about how Schmidt, Prometheus Unbound as it were, might use this increased scope over the next four years. Many political commentators and foreign diplomats reasoned this way: 'Schmidt has already prodded the superpowers into agreeing to talk about missiles. In Europe he can still reckon with support from his friend Giscard. For all the economic problems afflicting Germany as well as other countries, Schmidt has greater prestige and experience than any other Western leader. By late 1984, when the next election is due, he will be nearly sixty-six and will have been Chancellor for more than a decade, longer than any of his predecessors apart from Adenauer. So this could well be his last full term as head of government. Surely he will seek to launch initiatives which will ensure his place in the history books!'

Only a month after his election victory, Schmidt made a trip to the United States which seemed to fit this ambitious vision. His first stop was New York where he conferred with bankers and businessmen and received the top award of the Society for the Family of Man, a widely respected philanthropic organization. Previous recipients included John Kennedy and Jean Monnet. In the award ceremony at a luxury hotel, Schmidt was praised for his 'untiring fight for peace and *détente*' and his 'leadership of the European Community of nations'. The latter citation seemed to the Europeans present to go a bit far, but the Americans evidently had no doubts and applauded with gusto.

The next day, Schmidt went on to Washington for the more delicate part of the trip. Officially he had come for talks, long since arranged, with Jimmy Carter. But Carter had been defeated in the US election two weeks earlier and was thus a lame-duck President seeing out the last months of his one and only term. The man Schmidt really wanted to see was the victor, Ronald Reagan; but Reagan's staff had let it be known that the incoming President would not meet foreign leaders until after his inauguration in January.

In the event, Reagan chose to break his own rule and had an hour's chat with Schmidt in a building only a few minutes' walk from the White House. The meeting went well from the start. The 'arch hawk' Reagan, whose tough campaign talk about the Russians had made Bonn fear the worst for East–West arms talks, welcomed Schmidt like an old friend. He sat his visitor down near a table on which lay a book called *How to Entertain in Washington*, helped Schmidt prise the lid off his tobacco box and gently reminded him that smoking was bad for the health. Brezhnev had told Schmidt just the same in Bonn two years earlier, adding his doctors had forced him to quit the habit, but the Soviet leader also admitted slyly that he told his car driver to puff away at a cigarette so that he, Brezhnev, could sit behind inhaling as much smoke as possible.

More to the political point, Reagan vowed to consult intensively with the Europeans on all matters of common interest and laid as much stress on arms control as on defence readiness. Schmidt recalls him promising to 'negotiate and negotiate' to reach a fair settlement with Moscow. Naturally Reagan's *bonhomie* could not allay all German concerns either on defence or economic matters, but Schmidt came away from the meeting feeling that Reagan was sincere and capable (if so far unpractised in foreign affairs) and likely to be a much more predictable leader than Carter.

The talks with Reagan seemed the more satisfactory since they followed hard on Schmidt's dismal farewell to Carter. Both leaders appeared before the press at the White House to mutter a few friendly words, but their faces told a different tale. Schmidt stared poker-faced over the heads of his audience as though looking for the exit. Carter, white as a sheet, maintained a glassy smile as his aides shuffled unhappily in the background. Apart from losing the election, Carter had other woes. He was still trying to win the release of the US hostages held for more than a year in Teheran. In fact, the hostages were freed two months later, after Reagan's inauguration.

On the plane home, Schmidt worked with his aides on the declaration he was due to deliver to Parliament covering the government programme for the next four years. In it he urged, among other things, new efforts to find an East–West military balance, to develop the European Community, to modernize German industry and to reduce the country's dependence on oil imports. He praised Reagan's readiness to talk to Moscow and pledged that West Germany, despite budget problems, would do all it could to increase defence spending in line with NATO commitments. The declaration, called 'Courage to face the Future', sounded promising – too promising, sceptics said, in view of the big problems the country faced. But even the blackest pessimists could hardly foresee how many blows were to rain down on Schmidt and his government in 1981.

It turned out to be nearly a year before the Reagan administration got down to negotiations with the Russians on Euro-strategic missiles. This was not very surprising since the new President had to build up his government team, balance 'hawks' like the Defence Secretary Caspar Weinberger with (relatively speaking) 'doves' like the Secretary of State Alexander Haig, and reach an agreed strategy for dealing with Moscow. But by the time negotiations began there were only two years to go before the planned start in late 1983 of US missile deployment in Europe under NATO's 'twin-track' decision.

Just as worrying to Schmidt was the new shape of US economic and monetary policy. This relied on tight control of money supply to cut inflation, and tax breaks to help boost business and industrial activity. Schmidt feared that prescription, combined with higher defence spending, would in fact land the US with an ever-bigger budget deficit and increased government borrowing. That implied interest rates would stay high not only in the US but in Europe too, depressing investment and prolonging recession.

Schmidt was the first European leader to urge the US to change course (though the French were not far behind), but his words made little impact. The Americans felt the Germans were always moaning about something. A few years earlier Schmidt had been upset about

US inflation and the weak dollar, now he seemed to be making a fuss because a new US government was attacking inflation and because the dollar, boosted by high interest rates, was becoming unusually strong. Further, with its current account in deep deficit, Bonn's economic arguments carried less authority than before. Schmidt's hope, no doubt, was for a US which did not indulge in economic and monetary policy extremes – which roughly balanced its budget, kept its external payments more or less in equilibrium, held down inflation and interest rates and thus created the conditions for a stable dollar. At least he wanted the US to come much closer to this ideal than it apparently could manage under either Carter or Reagan.

In 1978, Schmidt and Giscard d'Estaing had combined to forge a defence against dollar turbulence in the shape of the EMS. Perhaps they might have taken new monetary steps to try to cope with the problems which emerged under the Reagan administration. But, in May 1981, Giscard lost the French presidential election to the Socialist François Mitterrand, who at once turned Giscard's economic strategy upside-down. The new French government went on a spending spree lasting more than a year, bringing a growing trade deficit, higher inflation and a weaker franc. The question for Schmidt became not whether new monetary initiatives could be developed with Paris, but whether the franc could stay in the EMS at all. It did – just.

With Giscard gone, Schmidt had no other similarly close ally in Europe. Britain under Margaret Thatcher seemed hardly nearer to joining the EMS than it had done under Jim Callaghan. Schmidt was infuriated by Mrs Thatcher's strident demands for a better European Community budget deal for Britain – 'my money' as she insisted on saying. He also mistrusted her judgement on how to handle the Russians. Later relations between the so-called 'Iron Chancellor' and 'Iron Lady' seemed to improve, but Schmidt's highest esteem always went to Mrs Thatcher's Foreign Secretary, Lord Carrington. Schmidt called him the most outstanding Western foreign minister of the late 1970s and early 1980s,[1] and deeply regretted his resignation in April 1982 over the Falklands conflict.

Giscard's fall virtually coincided with another foreign policy blow. In April 1981, Schmidt visited Saudi Arabia, valued by the Germans not just as a big supplier of oil and finance but as a force for moderation in the whole Gulf region. Schmidt was already under pressure from the Saudis to sell them Germany's highly sophisticated (and expensive)

Leopard–2 battle-tank. He made no promises, citing Germany's arms export policy which was especially restrictive because of the Nazi past. But the Saudi request raised a wider question. Western countries were discussing what steps they could take to help safeguard the Gulf region and its oil, following the Afghanistan and Iran crises and the Iran–Iraq war. If Germany, for moral and historical reasons, was to be barred from sending weapons or troops to the area, then what was its role to be?

At this point the Israeli Prime Minister, Menachem Begin, launched a ferocious public attack on Schmidt. He warned that German weapons might again be used to massacre Jews, accused Schmidt of arrogance and greed and linked him with the Nazi regime. Schmidt wondered for a while whether to make his own part-Jewish ancestry public for the first time, then thought better of it. He went before the Bundestag and announced he would not go into Begin's charges 'because I am, will be and always have been aware of the special moral and historical quality of German–Israeli ties'. The government spokesman had already described the attacks as 'misleading and insulting', Schmidt said. There was no more to add.[2]

Serious though these foreign policy problems were, Schmidt had to struggle with still greater difficulties at home. The coalition election victory did not work to his advantage in the way many people initially thought it would. The bigger parliamentary majority made Schmidt safer from the effects of a revolt by the left wing of the SPD, but it also encouraged left-wingers to show even less discipline than before because they knew their contrariness was now much less likely to bring down the government.

Moreover, the FDP, triumphant over winning the dizzying support (for liberals) of more than 10 per cent of the electorate, became too big for its boots. The post-election coalition negotiations were marked by bitter squabbles as the FDP tried to insist on bigger economic and social policy changes than its partner would accept. A large part of the SPD, not in this case the left wing alone, felt that the tail of the coalition was trying to wag the dog.

Schmidt papered over the cracks but the dispute erupted with new force a few months later. Party political tactics, genuine policy differences and personal mistrust began to form a dangerous and ultimately explosive mixture. There were three main actors in this last act of the coalition drama, apart from Schmidt himself. Two were in the

FDP, party leader Genscher and the Economics Minister, Count Otto Lambsdorff. The other was Willy Brandt.

In the Bonn political arena, Genscher had long since proved himself the star acrobat. Balanced on a wobbly high-wire he could carry on several different activities simultaneously with a speed which deceived the eye and generally held his audience enthralled. For a corpulent lawyer of late middle age (he turned fifty in 1977) and with a history of poor health, this was no mean achievement.

For the first five coalition years, Genscher cleverly skirted the minefields in the high-risk post of Interior Minister. In 1974 he switched to Foreign Affairs and still had the job well into the 1980s. No other Western foreign minister of the time was in office so long, but then Genscher was in a specially strong position. Because he was head of the junior coalition party in Bonn, no one could try to remove him from his ministerial post without threatening the government itself.

Genscher had a quick mind, an almost unerring sense of timing and a sure instinct for self-publicity. Shrugging off any hint of jet-lag, he flitted from one country and problem to another with a speed which brought gasps of ironic awe even from hardened colleagues. 'A day without a flight is a lost day for Hans Dietrich,' opposition leader Kohl once joked. He and Genscher were friends and close neighbours in the hills above Bonn, a fact which caused unease (rightly as it turned out) among supporters of the social–liberal coalition.

Despite his years in public life, Genscher's personality and political convictions remained hard to define. He was said to have developed a loathing of totalitarianism during his childhood in what is now East Germany. He also had undeniable tenacity, making it to the top in politics after spending more than three years in hospital with tuberculosis.

Schmidt believed that Genscher had courage. As Interior Minister Genscher had offered himself in exchange for hostages taken by Arab terrorists during the Munich Olympic Games in 1972. Schmidt praised Genscher's action at the time, and he still spoke privately of it with admiration even after his fall as Chancellor a decade later.[3]

However, over the years, Schmidt gradually concluded that for all his abilities Genscher was 'a tactician without a concept'. Until the 1980 election he felt he knew more or less where he was with the FDP leader. Schmidt realized that the smaller party needed to show a clear identity within the coalition or vanish on polling-day, so he constantly worked for fair compromise with liberal demands. That was not difficult for Schmidt personally, since FDP views were often closer to his own than were those of the SPD's left wing.

But after the election Genscher's conduct seemed to imply more than just a desire for a clearer profile. First there were the unusually tough negotiations on the new government programme. Then there were the coalition talks the following summer to put together the budget for 1982. Genscher appeared to be out for confrontation. It was not so much that he demanded a cut in government borrowing, which Schmidt and at least part of the SPD felt was necessary too; it was the way in which he insisted the problem should be tackled. Genscher urged spending cuts in unemployment pay and sickness benefit, the very heart of SPD social policy. He also said publicly that an SPD plan for a temporary extra tax was 'dead and cannot be deader' although in private the coalition partners were still discussing it.

In the middle of the budget dispute, in August 1981, Genscher issued a statement saying West Germany faced an economic and social challenge similar to that of the reconstruction after the Second World War. 'Our country is at a crossroads,' Genscher said. 'A change of direction has become necessary.'[4] Did Genscher feel the SPD–FDP could bring about the change or had he decided to jump ship? Schmidt repeatedly tried and failed to find out what Genscher's real intentions were. 'You can't nail a jelly on the wall,' is how one senior member of the SPD graphically described the Chancellor's dilemma.

There is strong private evidence to suggest that, at any rate in 1981, Genscher was still aiming to keep the government coalition together. But after the 1980 election he faced a new problem. Part of the extra support the FDP had won came for middle-of-the-road conservatives who would have voted for the CDU if Strauss had not been running for Chancellor. With Strauss defeated, Genscher feared the FDP's extra support might flow back to the CDU under the moderate Kohl. If the FDP were to retain its gains, it had to find a policy stance 'conservative' enough for its new voters but 'liberal' enough for its traditional supporters. Even for acrobat Genscher this was a tall order – too tall, as it proved.

In contrast to Genscher, Count Lambsdorff was nothing if not direct. Long before he became Economics Minister in 1977 his trenchancy upset allies as well as scattered foes. After the war, during which he lost a leg fighting on the Eastern front, Otto Friedrich Wilhelm von der

Wenge Count Lambsdorff (to give him his very full name) went into banking, then insurance. He entered Parliament in 1972, became economics spokesman for the FDP and slipped easily into the ministerial job when Hans Friderichs resigned to become head of the Dresdner bank. Lambsdorff started late in politics (he was born in 1927), but he moved fast once he was in. By the late 1970s, he was widely tipped as a possible successor to Genscher as party leader.

Never one to suffer fools gladly, Lambsdorff would often rap out answers to questions before they were fully asked and tended to fiddle menacingly with a paper-knife when getting bored. In cabinet he sat almost opposite Schmidt, and from time to time there would be brief, explosive arguments between the two. The storms passed and neither bore a grudge. Despite differences Schmidt and Lambsdorff had, and have, respect for one another.

Most of the points Genscher made about less state intervention, a cut in government borrowing and the need to boost private investment had been pressed by Lambsdorff for years. But by the summer of 1981, Lambsdorff had become more convinced than his party leader that the necessary policy changes could not be achieved in alliance with the SPD. He knew that he, Schmidt and the SPD Finance Minister, Hans Matthöfer, were personally not far apart on what needed doing. But he also saw that Schmidt was under growing pressure from his party and the trade unions for more public spending to try to create jobs. The Chancellor's scope for compromise with the FDP was thus becoming steadily less as recession deepened and unemployment increased. Already the average jobless total was back to above one million, and next year it was likely to be higher still.

If Schmidt and Willy Brandt had been working hand in glove, the restlessness of the SPD might have been quelled and the FDP bound more firmly to the alliance. But Chancellor and party leader still had quite different views about how the SPD should develop. A decade earlier, Schmidt had deplored what he felt were Brandt's excessive efforts to scoop up young voters identified with the student revolt. He believed the contours of the party would become dangerously unclear and traditional support would decrease. Now Schmidt felt Brandt was letting the SPD drift too close to the stance of the new young protesters against nuclear power and missiles (especially American ones). Party discipline was being eroded and support for the government undermined.

Brandt's reply was that the SPD had always been tolerant of minority views within its ranks and that it had to be open to the worries of a new generation. Two events alone in 1981 made those worries clear. In February, some 80,000 demonstrators marched on Brokdorf in Schleswig-Holstein to protest the planned building of a nuclear plant there. There were violent clashes with police. Then, in October, 300,000 people gathered in Bonn to demand an end to the nuclear arms race. Brandt as party leader asked himself what would happen to the SPD if it stood by and let ever more support accrue to the overtly ecological and pacifist 'Greens' movement. Schmidt as Chancellor asked if the Russians would ever make negotiating concessions in Geneva, if they believed Bonn would buckle under domestic opposition to deployment of US missiles.

Once or twice in early 1981 Schmidt exploded. On one occasion in Bonn he harangued other SPD leaders so fiercely at a private meeting that his words easily penetrated to the gleeful press huddled in the corridor outside. On another occasion, in Bavaria, Schmidt attacked those in the party who allowed themselves 'to be conned into believing that the Americans are our enemies'. White with fury, he warned that he would resign if the SPD withdrew its support for the NATO 'twin-track' decision.[5] Genscher later gave a similar warning to his FDP, though his plight was less serious than Schmidt's

Despite these eruptions which recalled the 'Schmidt *Schnauze*' of old, there were persistent charges that the Chancellor was 'off form', 'not the man he used to be' or, perhaps most cutting, 'not very efficient any more'. One commentator even spoke of a 'bunker situation', implying that Schmidt had gone to ground as his government tottered about him.

These comments were not very wide of the mark. Schmidt had allowed too many changes among his closest staff in too short a period. All original members of the *Kleeblatt* had gone. 'Ben Wisch' had already left the Chancellery at the end of 1979 to concentrate more on party work. Klaus Bölling had stressed to Schmidt that he needed a change from his six-year job as government spokesman after the 1980 election. He got his wish, though his new post as West German 'permanent representative' in East Berlin was hardly more jolly than facing the Bonn press corps. The ever-efficient Manfred Schüler left at the same time to take a top bank post. Schmidt's senior foreign affairs and economics advisers went too in the course of the big, and disturbing, reshuffle. It took time for Schmidt to get used to the new team – and it to him.

More important, Schmidt's health became much worse. He began to suffer from blackouts. The first struck him down in his holiday bungalow in Schleswig-Holstein. One moment he was standing upright, the next he was flat on his back staring at the ceiling and wondering what had hit him. More attacks followed in the next few months. They remained a secret until after Schmidt was rushed to hospital in Koblenz on 13 October to have a pacemaker fitted to his heart.

Letters of sympathy poured into the Chancellery. Commentators wondered if Schmidt would be able to carry on as government leader. But in a few days he was back at his desk asking what all the fuss was about. 'When my pulse drops to below sixty beats a minute, then the machine does its job,' he explained scientifically to a visitor. 'I've already noticed once that it has sprung into action.'

Few people knew, then or later, that the blackouts had impaired Schmidt's memory. He could still recall perfectly well events long past, but some more recent ones vanished as though they had never been. He literally had to re-learn what had happened, a huge disability which nonetheless remained concealed from many friends as well as from his political foes. One close aide speculated that if Schmidt had had his pacemaker fitted immediately after the October 1980 election instead of a year later, he would have kept a tighter grip on the SPD–FDP coalition and stayed Chancellor longer. That is only one of the many 'ifs' in those last hectic two years.

Two months after his pacemaker operation, Schmidt made his long-delayed visit to East Germany. Initially the trip had been set for February 1980, but was then put off because of the Soviet invasion of Afghanistan. A new date was agreed, but in August Schmidt decided to shelve the visit again, this time because of unrest in Poland.

The Polish workers' movement, Solidarity, was gaining strength under its charismatic leader Lech Walewsa, urging more democracy and backing its demands with strikes and demonstrations. Soviet armed intervention seemed a real possibility. Even if Moscow held off, Schmidt felt the East Germans would have little room to negotiate with him about closer ties so long as the situation across their eastern border in Poland stayed explosive. Schmidt had also said in advance that he wanted to make a 'meet the people' trip to the East German port of Rostock. But the East Berlin authorities vetoed the idea. They evidently feared there might be demonstrations of sympathy in Rostock, while Schmidt and his party were there, for the strikers in Polish ports along the coast.

The Polish situation was still tense a year later, but by that time Schmidt had concluded he must not postpone his visit indefinitely. He was anxious to press the East Germans to use what influence they had with Moscow to help win a negotiated settlement of the Euro-strategic missiles problem in Geneva. He also wanted to make a new bid to improve economic and other contacts between the two German states. He expected no easy breakthrough, but he did want his first really good chance to size up Erich Honecker, who had been leader of East Germany for a decade.

In his seven years as Chancellor, Schmidt had met most East European leaders and got to know several well. He admired Hungary's Janos Kadar and liked Poland's Edward Gierek (who, however, lost the top job in that turbulent summer of 1980). But Schmidt had only twice met Honecker, once at the Helsinki security conference in 1975, then on the margin of the funeral ceremonies for President Tito of Yugoslavia, in Belgrade in 1980. There had been no chance for a thorough talk.[6]

Honecker seemed keen to meet Schmidt too. He hoped for more financial benefits from Bonn to help ease his country's chronic lack of foreign exchange. In domestic political terms, he also stood to impress his countrymen by showing he could hold his own in direct talks with an admired and popular Chancellor. But there was another, more personal, reason too.

Honecker was born in 1912 in Neunkirchen, an industrial town in the Saarland close to the border with France. Much of his early life was spent in what is now West Germany. He had even worked for a while with Herbert Wehner in the early 1930s when both were communists. Arrested by the Nazis in Berlin, he spent nearly a decade in jail, stayed in the East after the division of Germany and worked his way steadily to the top.

Once a dialogue was established with Schmidt, the next step would be a visit by Honecker to Bonn and, he hoped, to the Neunkirchen of his youth. Even for this tough communist boss, who among other things supervised the building of the Berlin wall in 1961, the prospect of a 'sentimental journey' had a strong attraction.

The trip to see Honecker had a 'sentimental' element for Schmidt too. The East Germans arranged for the talks to be held at a hunting-lodge and a government guest-house near Lake Werbellin, fifty kilometres north-east of Berlin in the wild and beautiful Schorfheide region. Schmidt knew it well; the road to Werbellin passed by Bernau, the little town where he had been stationed during his war service in Berlin. Nearly four decades earlier he and Loki, recently married, had gone hiking through the forests and across the moors of what is still one of the most unspoiled areas of Europe.

So it was that, on 11 December 1981, Schmidt flew into East Berlin's snow-swept Schönefeld airport for the first official inter-German summit for eleven years. It was a visit which none of the participants will easily forget. It ended in something close to tragedy, and began with near-farce.

Schmidt's grey Luftwaffe jet taxied to the end of a red carpet lined with members of the East German leadership, steps were wheeled out to the plane – and turned out to be too short. The Chancellor and his aides would have been unable to descend without an unseemly, perhaps dangerous, jump. All the members of the welcoming party looked thunderstruck – except for Honecker. He strolled across to the press perched on a makeshift stand nearby, waved a hand airily and assured them that 'Everything will be all right. Just have a bit of patience.' He smiled, so his underlings smiled too and the problem was quickly sorted out.

Repeatedly over the next two days Honecker was relaxed and open in public, in sharp contrast to his evidently suspicious leadership colleagues. In a speech after the first welcoming banquet at Hubertusstock hunting-lodge, Honecker abandoned his official text to sing Schmidt's praises in a way which left the East German officials present open-mouthed. East German television carried much of the trip live, and almost always when the camera alighted on Honecker he was beaming as though Schmidt's visit was the best imaginable Christmas present.

How much was 'show business' for domestic consumption, how much was influenced from Moscow, how much was genuine? Even in the private talks it was hard to say. As expected, Honecker repeated the central communist demand that Bonn recognize a separate East German citizenship. No Chancellor could agree to that since it meant giving up the concept of a single German nation, albeit one divided 'temporarily' into two states, and was hence against the West German constitution.

Schmidt reminded Honecker that a year earlier East Germany had drastically raised the minimum sum of money which West Germans had to exchange whenever they visited the East. As a result pensioners and others with limited means could rarely make the trip any more to see friends and relatives. Schmidt said bluntly he felt disappointed and deceived. Honecker gave no firm promise, but indicated there could be a change for the better if West Germany prolonged its trade credit arrangement with the East which was about to expire. The credit accord was, in fact, renewed and a few, small improvements on the visits issue followed in 1982.

The discussion of broader East–West problems proved tantalizingly inconclusive, but not wholly unproductive. Schmidt said he believed that neither East nor West wanted a war, but that the world might slip into one through miscalculation as it had in 1914. Both East and West Germany had to use their influence to try to ensure that the worst did not happen.

Honecker listened carefully. He praised Schmidt for his role in getting the Geneva missile talks going and agreed that 'never again must a war begin on German soil'. Did that imply he would press for more negotiating flexibility in Moscow, where he was said to have close personal relations with Brezhnev?

It was impossible to be sure, but the idea was not absurd. Honecker was wholly loyal to the Warsaw Pact as Schmidt was to NATO, but he knew as well as the Chancellor that Germany would be the first hit, and probably obliterated, in any future European war. He would naturally have loved to see the West cave in altogether on the missiles issue, but he could hardly rely on that happening. Honecker faced the real danger that without a Geneva accord, new US missiles in large numbers would be deployed next door in West Germany. He was certainly realistic enough to calculate that a Geneva agreement would only emerge if both the Russians and the Americans were prepared to budge.

By Saturday night, 12 December, the result of the talks already seemed pretty clear, although the visit still had another day to run. Movement on the main topics had been small, but a dialogue had begun which both leaders were keen to continue. Honecker was looking forward to a trip to the West, perhaps before the following Easter. But within hours a dramatic event cast a shadow not only over inter-German ties but East–West relations in general for months to come. Early on Sunday morning, sixteen months after the creation of the trade union Solidarity, a state of emergency was declared in Poland and martial law imposed. A military 'Council of National Salvation' took power claiming that Solidarity had brought the country to the brink of economic chaos and civil war.

When the announcement came, Schmidt was asleep at his quarters by Lake Werbellin, half an hour's drive from the Oder river which marks East Germany's border with Poland. A day later and he would have been back in the West. Did Honecker know in advance what was planned in Poland? Did he even lay a trap to try to implicate Schmidt in the affair, as some members of the political opposition in Bonn quickly claimed?

It is very hard to believe Honecker knew nothing – but it is also difficult to see what he stood to gain from a trap. Schmidt's position might well be weakened at home and Honecker surely had no cause to strengthen the hand of the conservatives in Bonn. The most likely explanation came privately a few days afterwards from an East German official who said the action in Poland had been expected – but only later, after the Schmidt visit. 'Evidently the Polish comrades couldn't wait,' he remarked sourly.

Schmidt's plight was already bad enough on that Sunday morning, but he made it worse at a press conference held in a draughty hall after a final round of talks with Honecker. He became more and more tetchy as Western journalists demanded to know what concrete results had emerged from the meeting. Asked about the latest events in Poland, Schmidt snapped that Honecker was just as 'shocked' as he was. He let slip that East Germany, as well as West Germany, had been aiding the Poles financially, a point not previously known. He also said that, although Bonn had backed credit for Poland no matter who was in the government there, it had come to the limits of the possible.

Schmidt could hardly have made more inept remarks, especially while on East German soil. They sounded like a complaint that Poland had slipped further into chaos despite the best aid efforts of Bonn and East Berlin. From that it was easy to conclude that Schmidt had as little sympathy for Solidarity as his communist host – that both German states had a common interest in seeing freedom in Poland crushed. It was a conclusion widely drawn in the weeks ahead, not least in Washington, as the US pressed for sanctions against Moscow and Warsaw but Bonn held back.

In fact, Schmidt had long made clear, privately and publicly, that he would like nothing more than to see a Poland in which Solidarity's aims could be peacefully fulfilled. But since the movement began, he had followed its development with mingled hope and anguish. He feared that Solidarity would try to go too far too fast and that the experiment might end in military intervention and a bloodbath. That would put paid to hopes of modest but real reforms in Poland on the lines of those in Kadar's Hungary. It would almost certainly mean a tougher line in all Moscow's satellites for years to come.

Schmidt was not only thinking of invasion by the Russians. He was haunted by the thought that other Warsaw Pact forces might take part too, including those of East Germany. Once again German troops would be on the march to crush the Poles! Well before the Werbellin meeting Schmidt had found ways of making plain to East Germany how much it stood to lose, not least financially, if Poland were invaded. The point was surely not lost on Honecker. Whether it was decisive is another matter.

That bleak Sunday the 13th ended with scenes which seemed to be from a bad dream. Schmidt's 'meet the people' trip had been rearranged from the port of Rostock to the small town of Güstrow thirty kilometres to the south. By the time Schmidt arrived, it was growing dark and still more bitterly cold; but the West German party had other reasons to shiver. The local people had been told to stay indoors and away from their windows. Hundreds of armed police and state security officials lined the pavements. In the market-place, filled with Christmas stalls and decorated with coloured lights, 'passers-by' shouted 'Erich, Erich' in perfect unison. They were fervent party supporters, driven in by bus from far around to take the place of the absent population.

Schmidt knew he was the victim of a grim charade. With Honecker at his side, he plunged through the shouting 'extras' to the church as though seeking sanctuary. Inside it was quiet. High above him Schmidt could see the carving of the 'Soaring Angel' by Ernst Barlach, one of his favourite sculptors whom the Nazis had called degenerate. Barlach had studied in Hamburg and later lived in Güstrow, well before the division of Germany.

The local Bishop welcomed his extraordinary visitors. In this church, he said, they prayed for the Marxist Erich Honecker as well as for the Christian Helmut Schmidt. Today they particularly remembered the leaders and people of Poland too. Schmidt sat down in a pew alone. There was surely much to remember – his wartime life near Bernau, his son buried in East Berlin, the efforts to reduce tension between East and West, the successes and failures.

The same evening Schmidt took a special train home across the border to Hamburg, little more than 100 kilometres distant. Honecker saw him off at the station and handed him a cough sweet through the window just before the train left. A photographer snapped the scene. The picture was long prized by critics of Schmidt's visit as an illustration of 'appeasement politics' on Poland's 'black Sunday'.

By the end of December, the US had imposed economic sanctions on the Soviet Union on grounds it had instigated the crackdown in Poland. Bonn retorted that sanctions would not help the Polish people. Instead it appealed to Warsaw to end martial law, release all detainees and resume the dialogue with Solidarity. The government indicated more official economic aid could be expected if this were done. Privately, West Germans were already sending food and clothing to the Poles and soon the deliveries swelled to hundreds of thousands of parcels monthly.

Schmidt came into the public firing-line on both sides of the Atlantic. One French magazine carried a cartoon showing him polishing Brezhnev's boots. The *New York Times* in a sharp editorial said that '*détente* lives on as a powerful chimera in West German eyes. Gradually, those eyes will have to be re-focused on the real world.'

Truth to tell, the US sanctions (including a ban on export of some high technology goods) were quite modest in scope. But if Washington's bark was initially worse than its bite, the European allies (not just Bonn) hardly bared their teeth. After a lot of bad-tempered debate, the European Community agreed to cut back imports of some Soviet goods including caviar and binoculars as a 'political signal'.

As months passed and there was no sign of a real change for the better in Poland, Washington increased the pressure on its allies. One key US demand was that there should be an end to state-subsidized credit for trade with the East. Bonn was happy to agree to that since it gave no subsidies anyway but other European countries, especially

France, dug in their heels. A typically woolly compromise on the trade issue was found between the US and its main partners at the Western economic summit conference held in Versailles in June.

The Europeans breathed a sigh of relief, but too soon. A fortnight later, Reagan suddenly announced new steps to try to block a huge Soviet–West European natural gas pipeline deal. European firms, including German ones, were to supply pipes and pumping facilities, and the Russians would provide the gas – around forty billion cubic metres a year. Some of the key pumping components were made either by US companies or by Europeans under US licence. Reagan forbade supply of these crucial parts.

It was one of the rare moments when the European Community quickly reached a united stand. It condemned Reagan's action as 'contrary to the principles of international law' and made it clear that the pipeline project would go through, even though it might be delayed. The Europeans also complained that there had been no consultation by Washington, which was formally true although the US had long made it plain that it opposed the scheme. It felt that Europe, especially West Germany, would become too dependent on Soviet gas and that Moscow would get foreign currency which it could use to help finance its military effort.

The dispute worsened when, soon after the action against the pipeline deal, the US agreed to deliver more grain to the Russians. Washington explained that Moscow would have to pay cash for the grain and so would have less money available for weaponry. Scornful Europeans replied that Russia could now stop building combine harvesters and put the funds it saved into tank production instead. The crude arguments which swept to and fro across the Atlantic showed that the West was no closer to a joint view on how to handle the Soviet Union than it had been after the Afghanistan invasion.

Schmidt resolved to try to put Germany's, and Europe's, views across to a wider American audience. He well knew that the power-centre of US politics had moved away from the East Coast, and he thought little of the press coverage in Washington and New York. So in July he spent ten days on a swing across the South and up the West Coast of the US pulling no punches as he defended the gas deal and dialogue with the communists.

'My house is only fifty kilometres from the point where the Soviet sphere of influence begins,' he told an audience of high-level politicians and businessmen in California.[7] 'Our country lies within the range of Soviet intermediate-range missiles. It is no bigger than the state of Oregon, but six thousand nuclear warheads are deployed there which are not under our control. Anyone who talks about the psychological situation in the Federal Republic should try to understand these facts. They are the reasons why we insist on peaceful solutions and negotiations. Idealism tends to increase in direct proportion to one's distance from the problem.'

As for talk of German dependence on Russian energy, Schmidt said this was a 'malicious exaggeration'. Even after the pipeline deal had gone through, West Germany would be taking less than one third of its gas imports, representing about 6 per cent of its total primary energy needs, from the Soviet Union.

Schmidt could hardly convince all the sceptics. But on the sidelines of the trip he also had productive talks with George Shultz, the Californian who had just become Secretary of State. The two were old friends from a decade earlier when both had been Finance Ministers. Schmidt admired the American's common sense and quiet persuasiveness. He knew Shultz faced a tough struggle with the US administration 'hawks' who had contributed to the downfall of the previous Secretary of State, Alexander Haig. But if anyone could gradually bring a more balanced approach in Washington to foreign affairs, Schmidt thought, then surely it was George Shultz.

The Chancellor ended the visit in better spirits than when he began it. On a train ride through the Rocky Mountains he even told an interviewer he thought the pipeline dispute might be sorted out by the end of the year (which it was).

Back in his Hamburg home, Schmidt at once called in Genscher for a long talk. He passed on his good impression of the discussion with Shultz, then turned to domestic affairs. An election was coming up in the state of Hesse in September. The Hesse FDP had finally taken the plunge from which Genscher at national level had so far drawn back, agreeing to drop its local coalition with the SPD and seek an alliance with the CDU. Despite this step, Schmidt said he felt the SPD and FDP should conduct their campaigns in Hesse in a way which would not make the government partnership in Bonn unnecessarily harder. Genscher fixed the Chancellor with his cool blue eyes and replied that he felt the same.

* * *

That talk in Hamburg on 31 July was given little publicity at the time; but one government official, unusually well-placed to observe both leaders, believes that the meeting was crucial for the future of the Bonn coalition. He feels that if at that moment Schmidt and Genscher had made a personal pact to carry on to the next general election in 1984, then the coalition would have stuck together despite all other objective difficulties. His belief is that Genscher was open to conviction and that Schmidt in any case wanted the alliance to soldier on. The two parted politely but coolly, and the chance was missed.

That is only one view, not necessarily right but at least unbiased. Future historians who try to pin down exactly why the coalition collapsed when it did, who was responsible and whether it could have been saved, will find themselves wandering into a mine-studded maze. Certainly Schmidt tried again in Hamburg to pin down Genscher, and failed for the umpteenth time. That failure may partly be blamed on communication problems between two men of opposite temperaments. But when one partner often has to seek loyalty pledges from another, the marriage is probably on the rocks anyway.

Leaving aside personal differences at the top, there was plenty of other evidence that the coalition was crumbling. The rot which set in badly after the 1980 election triumph was still spreading in 1982. In February, Schmidt called for a parliamentary confidence vote after differences within the coalition on economic policy. He won the support of every SPD and FDP deputy, an apparent triumph but for the fact that Schmidt felt he needed to seek the vote at all.

In April, the SPD held its national congress in Munich, the Bavarian capital of its arch-foe Franz Josef Strauss. Schmidt raised a cheer from the 'comrades' when he donned a Bavarian hat and conducted a brass band in a local beer hall, but otherwise he had little to be happy about. The congress reluctantly passed its by-now ritual resolutions of heavily guarded support for the NATO missiles decision and atomic power. Moreover, the delegates, evidently sick of compromise, let off steam on economic policy, demanding tax increases and state-backed 'job creation' measures. Count Lambsdorff, never at a loss for a graphic phrase, at once called the proposed steps 'torture instruments from the socialist chamber of horrors'. The SPD stood no chance of realizing them with the FDP, he declared.

Two months later, the ruling SPD suffered big losses in elections in Hamburg and the FDP failed to win the 5 per cent minimum that would allow it seats in the local parliament. Instead 'the Greens', campaigning on their usual anti-nuclear and ecology issues, jumped the 5 per cent hurdle in Hamburg for the first time and started talking to the SPD about co-operation. Willy Brandt looked on this development with benign tolerance. Schmidt deplored it. Genscher felt still more under threat from this new third party which many in the SPD evidently preferred to the liberals.

Schmidt rushed from one point to another trying to plug the holes. He re-established much of the tried old *Kleeblatt* team at the Chancellery, drawing back Wischnewski from his SPD work and Bölling from East Berlin. He reshuffled the cabinet, putting in his top aide Lahnstein as Finance Minister to replace Hans Matthöfer whose health was poor. He also urged the coalition partners to a big new effort to get the divisive talks on the budget for 1983 over by the summer break. Goaded on by Lahnstein too, and much to its own surprise, the coalition kept to the deadline despite new battles about social security cuts and government borrowing. With the budget obstacle apparently out of the way at the start of July, most members of the government went on holiday breathing more easily.

The relief did not last long. Until about mid-year, the economy had been performing pretty well. The current account of the balance of payments was returning to surplus after three years of deficit, the Deutschmark was looking its strong old self again and the inflation rate was falling. Economic growth seemed likely to be over 1 per cent in real terms (after inflation) in 1982, and more than double that in 1983.

It was on that basis that the coalition reached its budget deal in July; but no sooner had it done so than things began to look more gloomy, especially export prospects. It became plain that economic growth would be less than hoped, unemployment would be up and government revenue down. That meant the coalition faced yet another tussle in the autumn, this time over how the newly emerging hole in the budget was to be plugged. The SPD was firmly against more cuts in government spending. The trade unions were complaining fiercely over the cuts already decided. Those with long memories recalled that in a similar budget situation in 1966, the FDP ministers had resigned, leading to Ludwig Erhard's fall as Chancellor.

The SPD put the blame for the faulty forecasts on Lambsdorff. The opposition claimed that the government as a whole had closed its eyes to the economic dangers to avoid facing a serious budget clash. Both charges were unfair. Government calculations had been broadly in line with those made by independent economic institutes and leading banks. Virtually all the crystal-ball gazers turned out to be wrong, but the coalition faced the heaviest bill for the error.

The SPD–FDP alliance might just have found the strength to clear even that new obstacle if it had been buoyed by at least one major policy success. Spirits would have risen and the atmosphere would have become less tense. Ironically, just such a success came close that summer, but no one in Germany, not even Schmidt, was aware of it until after the coalition's collapse – the Russians and Americans hovered briefly on the brink of accord in their missile talks, then drew back.

The key day was 16 July, shortly before Schmidt began his US trip. After months of unproductive bargaining, the top American and Soviet negotiators, Paul Nitze and Yuli Kvitsinski, decided to take a walk together in the woods near Geneva. There they sketched out informally what looked like a mutually acceptable compromise and agreed to pass it on to their governments. The main elements were a drastic cut in the number of Soviet ss–20s, fewer Western cruise missiles than planned and no deployment at all of the Pershing–2s.

Nitze would hardly have submitted a proposal to Washington which he knew in advance stood no chance. Kvitsinski, an old hand in the international negotiating game, would not have sketched the compromise without backing from Moscow. But in the event the superpowers rejected the deal. Administration 'hawks' in Washington would not swallow the absence of the Pershing–2 and the fact that Moscow would still be allowed to deploy ss–20s in Soviet Asia.

What happened in the Kremlin is, as ever, largely a matter for conjecture. The West has some evidence suggesting that a Politburo group around Brezhnev, which initially supported the Kvitsinski initiative, lost control that summer to hard-liners. Brezhnev's health was poor again and he died in November. He and Reagan never met. A year later deployment of new US missiles in Western Europe began in accord with the timetable of the 'twin-track' decision, and Moscow suspended its participation in the Geneva talks.

Schmidt would quickly have welcomed a deal based on the Nitze–Kvitsinski formula, if he had had the chance.[8] A balance at a relatively low level would have been established, without the Pershing–2s which West Germany alone had agreed to have on its territory. It would have seemed a fitting climax to Schmidt's years of effort on the missiles issue, further boosting his prestige and taking at least part of the pressure off his coalition. But it was not to be. The SPD–FDP alliance, in agony for so many months, split with breathtaking suddenness. In late August, even pessimists in the government parties maintained that while the end seemed near it would not come before the Hesse election on 26 September. Yet, when the Hesse voters went to the polls, Schmidt was already heading a minority SPD government and the FDP was in opposition.

Genscher for one was surely shocked by the speed of the collapse. He well knew that a change of coalition partner would be hazardous under any circumstances. Many in the FDP still favoured the Social Democrats and Schmidt remained the most popular politician in the country. A premature bid to switch to an alliance with the Union parties might well tear the FDP apart and destroy its hopes of re-election. Moreover, Genscher must have pondered that while he could expect a warm welcome from his old friend Kohl and most Christian Democrats, Strauss and his CSU loathed the FDP and its leader. A three-party coalition CDU–CSU–FDP might well be even more uncomfortable for the liberals than the SPD–FDP alliance. Genscher could not even be certain of the Foreign Minister's job any more. Surely Strauss would be after that.

Genscher seems to have confided to no one about his political intentions that summer. He may well have been playing for safety, aiming to keep all his options open at least until after Hesse. If the CDU–FDP experiment succeeded there, it would be easier for the FDP to change partners in Bonn sooner or later. If the Hesse gamble did not come off, Genscher would have lost one throw but would not be bankrupt. If that was Genscher's attitude, and much from his political history speaks for it, why did things turn out so differently? The answer is that Schmidt and Lambsdorff, acting separately but in what must have seemed to Genscher like an unholy alliance, set a pace which left the FDP leader no more time for tactics.

Towards the end of August, Schmidt lost patience. Despite the talk with Genscher a month earlier, key liberals had been sniping at the Bonn coalition in the campaign run-up to Hesse. Schmidt could not be sure of their motives and he still wanted to preserve the social–liberal alliance. But he would no longer tolerate the creeping attrition of his government and leadership in the guise of provincial electioneering. If the FDP could be brought into line, well and good. If not, then the liberals would have to carry the blame for the coalition breakdown and take the rap from the voters, first in Hesse then in the country in a general election.

From then on things moved fast, certainly faster than Genscher's ability to control them. In his drive to smoke out the FDP, Schmidt approached Genscher again, and Lambsdorff, who had been demanding urgent new budget talks and more spending cuts. This time Schmidt sent Genscher a letter, carefully phrased with one eye on the history books.[9] Had Genscher produced a written answer he could hardly have avoided giving at least a sign (and hence evidence) for or against continuation of the coalition. But the FDP leader replied to the Chancellor by phone, and then had another inconclusive talk with him.

Schmidt got a far more direct response from Lambsdorff, to Genscher's obvious concern. Schmidt said that if Lambsdorff wanted economic measures which differed from those the SPD–FDP had adopted, he should put them down on paper and submit them within ten days (well before Hesse). It was a bid to force Lambsdorff to produce some good new ideas on which the coalition might agree, or to show his hand with drastic proposals clearly beyond fair compromise.

Lambsdorff took up the challenge saying he had been working on just such a document. The same day, 30 August, he gave a newspaper interview, throwing still more doubt on the future of the Bonn alliance. Schmidt hit back in cabinet on 1 September, calling Lambsdorff's remarks 'astonishing and irritating'. If any minister wanted to leave he should say so directly, not give hints in interviews.

Lambsdorff defended himself with his usual vigour. Genscher looked glum, the more so when Schmidt called on the government spokesman to make a public statement about the differences after the cabinet session. Genscher knew that if matters came to a head and Lambsdorff were dismissed, or forced to resign, the other FDP ministers would have to go too and the coalition would be finished.

An uneasy week passed, punctuated with heavy hints from the Economics Ministry that Lambsdorff's paper would be a bombshell. On the day Lambsdorff completed the document, 9 September,[10] Schmidt went before the Bundestag with a bombshell of his own. He praised Social Democrat–liberal achievements, deplored the current shilly-shallying by some of the FDP – then dared the CDU leader Kohl to bring a vote of no confidence against him the following week.

The challenge was aimed as much at Genscher as at Kohl. Surely now the FDP leader would be forced to make his attitude clear in public. But yet again Genscher produced a masterly display of sitting on the fence. He said he shared Schmidt's pride in the SPD–FDP record; but he recalled that the liberals had also achieved much with the CDU in the 1950s and 1960s, and he was proud of that too. Kohl failed to rise to the 'no confidence' bait and the Hesse election moved a step closer with the Bonn coalition still formally intact.

The advance reports about Lambsdorff's paper had not exaggerated. Within days the full text became public and was at once labelled 'a declaration of war' by the trade unions. Even some politicians of the Right were critical of the plan which advocated big social security cuts to finance lower taxes on business and more public investment. 'Less money for mothers, tenants, pensioners, jobless, pupils, the sick and students,' is how one right-leaning newspaper summed it up.

The break was not imminent. Schmidt rejected the Lambsdorff document saying it betrayed an astonishing lack of economic analysis.[11] On Wednesday, 15 September, he asked the minister whether he meant his paper to be 'a writ of divorce'. Lambsdorff replied that he supported government policy and was trying to be helpful. Schmidt told him to make the same pledge promptly in public. On Thursday, Lambsdorff made a statement which fell short of what Schmidt was after, but by that time the minister's words had become almost irrelevant. Schmidt had decided to end the agony, dismiss the four FDP ministers and call for new elections. He sketched his broad plan to the Federal President Karl Carstens, held a meeting with Kohl which brought little benefit to either side, then worked on the text of a parliamentary declaration until the early hours of Friday.

For all those who watched the social–liberal alliance during its thirteen years of government rule, the Bundestag on that Friday morning, 17 September, presented an eerie spectacle. Four gaps on the government benches marked where the FDP ministers had sat, being pilloried by the CDU–CSU in scores of debates. All four ministers had forestalled their dismissal by resigning a few hours earlier.

Now the political cards were being reshuffled. Helmut Kohl, the potential beneficiary as CDU leader, sat in the plenum with knitted brows. No doubt he was thinking of the hazards which still lay on the road to appointment as government leader. A few benches away, among the FDP parliamentarians, Genscher pored over papers with an ostentatious lack of concern. Wolfgang Mischnick, seated nearby, did not trouble to hide his deep dismay. As FDP parliamentary leader he had worked well with the SPD opposite number, the volcanic Wehner, since 1969. Time after time the pair of them had conjured accord among coalition deputies when compromise seemed all but excluded. Now he faced a new and bitter task – to swing as many FDP parliamentarians as possible onto Genscher's course. He hated the job, but he felt the party no longer had a viable alternative.

Schmidt's knack of finding the right tone for almost any occasion was never more evident than on that Friday. He might have let off steam with polemics, giving himself and the SPD incidental satisfaction but forcing the disorientated FDP closer together. Instead, he made a measured, statesmanlike speech, rarely raising his voice, making few gestures and gaining his main effect by an occasional, judicious pause. It was largely an appeal beyond Parliament to the voters, many of whom were watching Schmidt live on television; but it was also a subtle bid to encourage those FDP deputies who already opposed Genscher, and undermine further the confidence of those who feared the consequences of the coalition split.

Schmidt said he was sure Social Democrats and liberals still had much in common and with a new effort they could have overcome their problems. But ever since Genscher had first talked about the need for 'a change' in the summer of 1981, doubts had grown about whether the FDP would stick to the alliance. Liberal leaders had failed to end the uncertainty. 'A single clear sentence was always lacking,' Schmidt said, 'namely that the FDP stands firmly by the social–liberal coalition. . . . Co-operation is impossible on a basis of continuing, unspoken reservation.'

Turning to the liberals on his right, Schmidt recalled he had close personal ties with many of them and had long benefited as Chancellor from their goodwill. For his part he had tried his utmost to keep the alliance alive; but 'in the interests of our country, of our parliamentary democracy and not least of the Social Democratic coalition partner, I cannot and will not stand idly by and watch the government's reputation and room for manœuvre undermined bit by bit.'

Dropping his voice so that his listeners had to strain to hear, Schmidt added, 'Surely no one will blame me for not wanting to see myself taken to pieces.' He proposed new elections and announced that in the meantime Social Democrat ministers would take over the portfolios of their former FDP colleagues. With deadpan expression, but surely with deep inner satisfaction, he revealed that he would be taking over Genscher's job. Schmidt might have got the Foreign Affairs post if he had pressed in 1966 at the start of the grand coalition. Now he had the power to give it to himself – at least for a few days.

An exhausting fortnight followed, with one political side and then the other winning an advantage. Schmidt's plan that the country should go to the polls sounds simple but was not. The modern German constitution puts large obstacles in the way of holding premature general elections, to help avoid the constant changes and weak governments which marked the Weimar era. Schmidt had suggested one convoluted escape route. He said he would arrange a vote of confidence and make quite certain of losing it by having some in the SPD cast ballots against him. He could then ask President Carstens to dissolve Parliament. But that procedure would have allowed elections by the end of the year, which was too soon for Genscher. He feared that his party would be crushed if the voters had a chance for a say so soon after the coalition break. Kohl strongly sympathized. He was anxious to keep the moderate FDP as a partner in a future government, so that he was not left only in uncomfortable tandem with Strauss and his Bavarians.

Kohl and Genscher therefore agreed to try to topple Schmidt in Parliament through a so-called 'constructive vote of no confidence'. This was the procedure which Rainer Barzel had used unsuccessfully a decade earlier in his bid to oust Brandt. It meant that if a majority of the Bundestag voted for the motion against Schmidt, then Kohl would automatically become Chancellor right away. On the other hand, keen though he was to help the FDP, Kohl felt elections must not be delayed too long. He would face big problems as head of government and they might prove insuperable if he sought to cling to power without going to the country for a mandate.

He and Genscher finally agreed to aim for a vote of no confidence on 1 October and a general election on the following 6 March. It was a high-risk strategy; neither leader could be certain that enough FDP parliamentarians would support Kohl in the Bundestag. Even if that hurdle were cleared, Genscher faced a huge battle to hold his party together and leap the 5 per cent barrier in the election. But there was no less risky alternative.

Five days before the crucial Bundestag vote, the people of Hesse went to the polls and Genscher's worst fears were realized. After a final burst of fierce campaigning dominated by the coalition collapse in Bonn, the FDP saw its support halved and failed to win re-entry to the local parliament. The CDU slipped a little and the SPD did far better than anyone had imagined even a few weeks earlier.

The Social Democrats were cock a'hoop. Many of them crowed that 'treachery does not pay' and became more hopeful about the 1 October vote. 'Our job', a top member of the SPD had stated shortly before the coalition split, 'is to stick our foot out so that when Genscher jumps he will trip and break his neck.' After Hesse, the master FDP acrobat seemed still closer to a fatal political tumble.

Schmidt was a hero – not just in the country which was not unusual, but in his own party, which was. The crisis which split the coalition drew the Chancellor and the SPD closer than they had been for years. The 'comrades' in the parliamentary party had often groaned as Schmidt drove them on to yet another compromise with Genscher and Lambsdorff. Towards the end many began to feel that a return to opposition would be better than more concessions. Now the Chancellor had reached his tolerance limit too and the party welcomed him back, offering him 'the warmth of the nest'.

Schmidt basked for a while in the new glow of SPD support, but he was not deceived by it. Despite his eloquent public statements laying the blame for the coalition collapse on the FDP, he knew that Social Democrats as well as liberals were responsible. Genscher had shown duplicity for which Schmidt hoped he would pay with his political life. Lambsdorff had increased the friction, deliberately over-reacting to the SPD congress' economic policy resolutions to speed the coalition's end.

But, truth to tell, Schmidt too thought little of the resolutions. Moreover, the SPD was straining to break away from the NATO missiles decision, it was flirting with the Greens and Brandt gave quiet encouragement to both trends. Herbert Wehner, as usual, hit the nail on the head. He too had lost patience with the liberals, calling them openly 'the so-called Free Democratic Party' in the last weeks of the coalition. But a few months earlier he had privately forecast the downfall of the alliance because 'no one' – he slammed his fist on the table and growled again 'no one' – could keep 'those two' on a common line. The two he meant were not the coalition partners, but Helmut Schmidt and Willy Brandt.

Nor did Schmidt have false hopes about the result of the Bundestag vote, despite his efforts to court those liberals hostile to Genscher. Some in the FDP would not follow their leader on the day, but enough would do so to clinch victory for Kohl. Schmidt felt calm about his own fate, but bothered by the thought of Kohl as Chancellor. He did not believe his successor had anything like the talent or experience for the job, and he distrusted Kohl's pledge to hold early elections. As so often over the decades, Schmidt and Strauss had much the same view, but neither could change things.

On the night before the vote, Schmidt called in the diplomatic corps. With Hamburg understatement, he said he had invited everyone in for a talk 'at a moment when the domestic political situation in this country has started to change'. All the ambassadors knew he was saying goodbye – to them and to his eight and a half years as Chancellor. Very many were moved, some like the US Ambassador Arthur Burns had tears in their eyes. Schmidt called for trust in the steadfastness of the Germans, despite the shadows of their past. He praised the legacy of freedom of the American revolution and recalled he had been a 'critical partner' for four US presidents. He urged new efforts to halt the arms race, but repeated he would advocate deployment of American missiles in West Germany if the Geneva talks failed. He stressed his friendship for France and for the Poles, and his belief in a common European culture transcending political barriers.

Towards the end of what amounted to his political testament, Schmidt spoke more urgently. 'Today we all face a dual crisis – involving both the world economy and the hardening of fronts in East–West relations. I want to ask you never to allow the dialogue between governments and statesmen to be discontinued, especially in a crisis – however good your reasons may be for reproaching the other side. In this time of great danger for worldwide economic and financial co-operation, I warn against thinking that one can solve one's problems by a policy pursued at the cost of others. . . . Ladies and gentlemen, I wanted to outline to you again the precepts of our policy for peace. To ensure peace remains our primary task. Peace is not a natural state but one that must be ever re-established, as the German philosopher Kant put it. To strengthen confidence in the consistency of our policy for peace – that was the contribution I wished to make.'[12]

The next day, Friday, 1 October, at ten minutes past three in the afternoon, the President of the Bundestag, Richard Stücklen, gave the result of the 'constructive vote of no confidence'. It was only the second such vote in Federal German history and the first to be successful. Kohl had needed 249 votes. He gained 256, against 235 with four abstentions.

Schmidt had long been inwardly prepared. He already sat among other SPD parliamentarians, not even on the front bench. But when the announcement came he slumped a little, looked tired and – just for a second or two – defenceless. Then duty called. He dragged himself from his place, walked briskly over to the CDU benches and offered his hand to the newly elected Chancellor, Helmut Kohl. He even managed a smile.

EPILOGUE

Within a month of being voted from office Schmidt told his party he would not stand again as Chancellor candidate. He gave his uncertain health as the key reason; but he was also sure that the old divisions in the SPD, papered over during the coalition split, would soon erupt again.

Kohl made good his promise. The general election was held on 6 March 1983, and the CDU–CSU gained 48.8 per cent of the vote, the second best result in its history. The FDP struggled back from its trough to win 7 per cent. Kohl stayed as Chancellor, Genscher Foreign Minister and Lambsdorff Economics Minister.

The SPD under its new Chancellor candidate, Hans Jochen Vogel, who had been Justice Minister under Schmidt, won only 38.2 per cent and stayed in opposition. Wehner left the Bundestag. Brandt remained party Chairman, for better or worse the most durable of the 'Troika'.

Eight months later, the SPD voted against deployment of new US missiles at a special congress, thus rejecting the second part of the NATO 'twin-track' decision. Only fourteen party members from around 400 supported the NATO stand. They included the three Social Democrat Defence Ministers, Helmut Schmidt, Georg Leber and Hans Apel, as well as the former Finance Minister, Hans Matthöfer, and Schmidt's long-time trouble-shooter, Hans-Jürgen Wischnewski. The vote made no difference to Bonn government policy. Kohl and Genscher stuck to the NATO line, and by the year's end the first Pershing–2s arrived on German soil.

That dismal sequence might suggest that Schmidt spent his first year after losing office in deep gloom. But the truth is that for much of the time he thoroughly enjoyed himself, doing the things usually impossible when he was Chancellor. He slept longer (which improved his temper), read more and went to the theatre. He travelled a lot, wrote and lectured about major economic and security issues, and made a film of the Mozart *Concerto for Three Pianos* with Eschenbach and Frantz. He also began to plan two books. He gave few interviews and wryly noted the stream of speculation about what he was allegedly going to do next. Some reports said he was about to become NATO Secretary-General, others that he was planning a domestic political comeback, still others that he was sick of his party and about to quit.

All that was wide of the mark. Schmidt was easily returned for his Hamburg constituency in the March election, but he vowed not to stay in Parliament longer than another four-year term. He was naturally unhappy about the trends in the SPD, but that was nothing new. He had lived in a state of dynamic tension with his party since joining it nearly four decades earlier. He neither considered leaving it – nor playing a 'tragic hero' over whom the CDU could shed crocodile tears.

A few days after the SPD congress rejected his stand on NATO missiles, back-bencher Schmidt was spied in the Bundestag making a paper dart. With the glee of a naughty schoolboy, he tossed it towards the front of the house where it went into a nose dive. Closer examination showed the projectile had been fashioned from the text of a speech by Brandt.

On 22 December 1983, the day before his sixty-fifth birthday, Schmidt was made an honorary citizen of Hamburg – following in a line which includes Brahms and Bismarck. But the biggest tribute of all to Schmidt came that evening, in the diversity of the guests who attended his birthday celebrations in a simple hall on the outskirts of Hamburg.

Bosses and labour leaders, conservatives and socialists, actors and artists, writers and musicians turned up in hundreds. There were old friends like Willi Berkhan, old rivals like Karl Schiller, former political allies like Barzel and Mischnick, valued foreign contacts like Kissinger – all anxious to wring Schmidt's hand and wish him well.

As the clock struck midnight, Giscard d'Estaing – *cher* Valéry – stood up and paid a rare personal tribute to Schmidt in German. He joked for a while, recalling Schmidt's sudden bursts of anger with a pun on the 'Well-Tempered Clavichord' of Bach. 'I would call you the bad-tempered Chancellor,' Giscard said with a smile.

But he also called Schmidt 'the most esteemed German in the world', a man of great knowledge and goodness of heart. In the old days, Giscard declared, 'we worked together more as brothers than as statesmen'.

Schmidt was moved. Amid the applause he hastily bent his head and took a large pinch of snuff.

Giscard may well have been right in his view that Schmidt was 'the most esteemed German'. Certainly Schmidt stayed the most popular politician in Germany for long after he lost the Chancellorship. But what will historians say about him? It is a bit rash to speculate because they will be able to compare Schmidt with his successors as well as with his predecessors; but part of their assessment will surely be along the following lines.

Schmidt was the 'great professional' among post-war Germany's government leaders. As a former Defence and Finance Minister he brought unmatched political experience to the highest office. As a parliamentary debater he had few equals. None of his four predecessors as Chancellor had a greater capacity for hard work nor paid more punctilious attention to detail.

Of the first five Chancellors, two – Erhard and Kiesinger – were interim leaders and three made a decisive impact on their country's fortunes. Adenauer anchored the Federal Republic firmly in the West in the 1950s. Brandt pressed social reform at home and reconciliation with Eastern Europe in the early 1970s. Schmidt consolidated in hard times what his predecessors had built, steered his country with a sure hand through the economic storms which followed the first oil crisis, and won a crucial domestic battle against terrorism. His contribution may be called less 'original' than that of Adenauer and Brandt, but it was no less vital. It was not a foregone conclusion that the young German democracy would cope so well with the shocks of the mid and late 1970s. Schmidt's steady leadership, his clear-sighted defence of the middle ground in politics against dreamers and fanatics, helped bring his country stability and won it more respect abroad.

That said, the history books are almost bound to judge too that the final years of the Schmidt era did not fulfil the promise of the early ones. The high point came, arguably, in 1978. Afterwards, Schmidt's party became even more contrary and his coalition partner more restive. Above all, his health deteriorated and his grip loosened. Compare the Schmidt of 1974 with the Schmidt of 1982, his face lined, his hair almost white. He served eight and a half years as Chancellor, and seemed to age at least fifteen.

Adenauer too was well past his peak when he stepped down. Erhard was at his best before he became Chancellor. Brandt's high point, no doubt, was the election of 1972. But both Adenauer and Brandt saw many of their major international policy goals achieved while still in office. Schmidt left with at least two key aims unrealized. Despite his efforts over years, no accord had been reached between the super-powers on Euro-strategic missiles; and the European Monetary System had failed to develop beyond its first stage.

While that is a fact, it will be a sour judge who gives Schmidt all the blame for failing to complete tasks not dependent on him alone. No modern leader struggled more tenaciously for a safer world based on military balance and economic stability. For the rest, Schmidt can look to his favourite stoic Marcus Aurelius: 'What shall be a complete drama is determined by him who was once the cause of its composition and now of its dissolution; but you are the cause of neither. Depart then satisfied.'

Source Notes

Much of the material for this book was gained at first hand during my work as a correspondent based in Bonn in the 1970s and early 1980s. For example, the accounts of Schmidt's accession to the Chancellorship and his fall, of the trips to Moscow, to the United States in 1980, to Italy, France and to the summit talks in East Germany are based on personal experience.

I am grateful to Herr Schmidt for talking to me about his personal life and family background as well as about politics. I am also deeply indebted to many German government officials, politicians and foreign diplomats in Bonn for their help, and friendship, over the years – long before this book was even thought of. It would be invidious, and unwise, to single out anyone by name. Many thanks to them all.

1 YOUTH AND WAR
1 The Hamburg edition of *Die Welt*, 28 July 1962
2 West German television interview, 8 February 1966
3 Schmidt gave this account of his Jewish background in conversation with the author
4 West German television interview, 8 February 1966
5 Speech 'Mahnung und Verpflichtung des 9 November 1938' given on 9 November 1978
6 West German television interview, 12 April 1982
7 Schmidt in conversation with the author

2 TO BONN AND BACK
1 Klaus Harpprecht, *Willy Brandt, Porträt and Selbstporträt* (Kindler Verlag, Munich, 1971)
2 *Sozialist*, 1 April 1954
3 Speech to a youth conference of IG Chemie, the chemical workers' trade union, 1960
4 Bundestag Protocol, 22 March 1958
5 Schmidt in conversation with the author
6 Hamburg Bürgerschaft Protocol, 21 February 1962

3 DEFENCE AND UNITY
1 *Hamburger Morgenpost*, 12 November 1970
2 West German television interview, 12 April 1982
3 West German television interview, 8 February 1966
4 Bundestag Protocol, 5 November 1959
5 Speech to CDU conference, Düsseldorf, 30 March 1965
6 'Mögliche Stufen eines wirtschaftlichen und sozialen Wiedervereinigungs-

Prozesses', reproduced in *Beiträge*, dated 10 February 1959
7 Speech to s p d congress, Dortmund, 3 June 1966
8 *Sunday Express*, 1965

4 PARLIAMENTARY LEADER
1 Bundestag Protocol, 15 December 1966
2 North German radio address, 15 April 1962
3 Noted in, among others, Willy Brandt, *Begegnungen und Einsichten* (Hoffman und Campe, Hamburg, 1976)
4 Quoted in Ulrich Blank, *Helmut Schmidt – Bundeskanzler* (Hoffman und Campe, Hamburg, 1974)
5 Noted in Brandt, *Begegnungen und Einsichten*
6 Schmidt in conversation with the author

5 IN CABINET
1 'Politik als Beruf', Introduction to *Beiträge*
2 Speech to annual assembly of Hermann-Ehlers-Akademie, Kiel, 30 October 1971
3 Schmidt in conversation with the author
4 Speech to Deutsche Atlantische Gesellschaft, Stuttgart, January 1972
5 Schmidt gave this account of how he came to take the 'Superministry' job, and why he stayed on after the general election, in conversation with the author
6 West German radio interview, 14 May 1982
7 Speech in California, July 1982
8 In brochure called 'Zwischenbilanz', reprinted in H. Schmidt, *Auf dem Fundament des Godesberger Programms* (Verlag Neue Gesellschaft, Bonn–Bad Godesberg, 1973)
9 *Der Spiegel*, 17 December 1973
10 Address to s p d national executive committee meeting, 8 March 1974. Text later published in *Auf dem Fundament des Godesberger Programms* (enlarged, second edition of 1974)
11 Schmidt in conversation with the author
12 Schmidt in conversation with the author

INTERLUDE: Only a '*Macher*'?
1 West German radio interview, 14 May 1982
2 Speech 'Bemerkungen zu Moral, Pflicht und Verantwortung des Politikers' at congress 'Kant in unserer Zeit', Bonn, 12 March 1981
3 See, among others, the Kant speech noted above

6 CHANCELLOR – The Early Years
1 In an after dinner speech in Paris, February 1980
2 'Background' briefing of 23 October 1975
3 Government declaration in Bundestag, 17 May 1974
4 Schmidt in conversation with the author
5 Speech to the Hamburg s p d, 21 September 1974
6 'Der Brief eines zornigen Linken', in *Konkret*, 31 October 1974
7 *Foreign Affairs*, April 1974
8 Speech in Cologne, to mark the fiftieth anniversary of the founding of the German group of the International Chamber of Commerce, 4 June 1975
9 Speech in Munich on receiving the Theodor–Heuss Prize, 21 January 1978

7 CHANCELLOR – To the Plateau, 1976–80
1 Schmidt in conversation with the author

2 Schmidt in conversation with the author
3 Alastair Buchan memorial lecture of 28 October 1977
4 Article by Schmidt in *Die Zeit*, 17 June 1983
5 This account of events leading to NATO's 'twin-track' decision of 1979 is based largely on a conversation between the author and Schmidt, supplemented by information from West German, US and British officials
6 *Frankfurter Allgemeine Zeitung* editorial by Fritz Ullrich Fack, 23 May 1980
7 Article by Heinz Stadlmann, *FAZ*, 25 June 1980
8 Carter interview in *Stern*, 1982
9 Schmidt in conversation with N. Colchester and the author, *Financial Times*, 16 December 1982
10 Karl Otto Pöhl in conversation with the author
11 *Financial Times*, 25 November 1978
12 Banquet speeches by Giscard d'Estaing and Schmidt in Aachen, 15 September 1978
13 The fateful confusing passage of the communiqué ran: 'The European Council stresses the importance of henceforth avoiding the creation of permanent MCAs and progressively reducing present MCAs in order to re-establish the unity of prices of the common agricultural policy, giving also due consideration to price policy.'
14 Banquet speech by Schmidt, Aachen, 15 September 1978
15 'Sicherheit und Berechenbarkeit', speech to UN general assembly, 25 May 1978

INTERLUDE: Schmidt and the Arts
1 Interview by Schmidt in *Die Bunte*, 5 November 1981

8 CHANCELLOR – Over the Top, 1980–82
1 Article by Schmidt in *Die Zeit*, 6 May 1983
2 Schmidt in Bundestag speech, 7 May 1981
3 Schmidt in conversation with the author
4 Genscher letter to FDP party members, 20 August 1981
5 Schmidt speech to Bavarian SPD, Wolfratshausen, May 1981
6 For Schmidt's attitude to Kadar, Gierek and the East Germans, see article by N. Colchester and the author in the *Financial Times*, 16 December 1982
7 Schmidt speech at 'Bohemian Grove', California, July 1983
8 See, among others, Schmidt speech to SPD special congress on security policy, Cologne, 19 November 1983
9 Text of letter reprinted in Klaus Bölling, *Die letzten 30 Tage des Kanzlers Helmut Schmidt* (Spiegel Verlag, Hamburg, 1982)
10 Otto Graf Lambsdorff, 'Konzept für eine Politik zur Uberwindung der Wachstumsschwäche und zur Bekämpfung der Arbeitslosigkeit', 9 September 1982; (also reprinted in Bölling, *op. cit.*)
11 Schmidt speech to SPD parliamentary group, 14 September 1982
12 Schmidt speech to the Bonn diplomatic corps, 30 September 1982. The text of this and other key speeches by Schmidt during his last weeks as Chancellor have been reprinted in the booklet *Jederman darf und muss mit unserer Stetigkeit rechnen*, published by the SPD parliamentary group, 1982.

SELECT BIBLIOGRAPHY

BOOKS BY SCHMIDT
Verteidigung oder Vergeltung (Seewald Verlag, Stuttgart, 1961; English edition: *Defence or Retaliation*, London, 1962; US edition: *Defense or Retaliation*, New York, 1962)

Beiträge (Seewald Verlag, Stuttgart, 1967): a compendium of speeches, articles and interviews from the 1940s to Schmidt's period as SPD parliamentary floor-leader

Strategie des Gleichgewichts (Seewald Verlag, Stuttgart, 1969; English edition: *The Balance of Power*, London, 1971)

Auf dem Fundament des Godesberger Programms (Verlag Neue Gesellschaft, Bonn–Bad Godesberg, 1973)

Der Kurs heisst Frieden (Econ Verlag, Düsseldorf–Wien, 1979) and *Pflicht zur Menschlichkeit* (Econ Verlag, Düsseldorf–Wien, 1981): both contain speeches and articles on politics, economics and philosophy.

Ways out of the Crisis: 16 Theses on the World Economy, ed. Schmidt (Robinson Verlag, Frankfurt, 1983)

Weltwirtschaft ist unser Schicksal (Robinson Verlag, Frankfurt, 1983; published in English in the *Economist*, 26 February 1983, under the title *The World Economy at Stake*)

ALSO
Kunst im Kanzleramt (Wilhelm Goldmann Verlag, Munich, 1982): a compendium largely devoted to articles and speeches by Schmidt on the visual arts and music

Perspectives on Politics, ed. Professor Wolfram Hanrieder (Westview Press, Boulder, Colorado, 1982); a selection of speeches and articles by Schmidt, in English

BOOKS ABOUT SCHMIDT
Helmut Wolfgang Kahn, *Helmut Schmidt, Fallstudie über einen Populären* (Holsten Verlag, Hamburg, 1973)

Ulrich Blank, *Helmut Schmidt, Bundeskanzler* (Hoffman und Campe, Hamburg, 1974)

Nina Grunenberg, *Vier Tage mit dem Bundeskanzler* (Hoffman und Campe, Hamburg, 1976)

Hart am Wind, Introduction by Marion Gräfin Dönhoff (Albrecht Knaus Verlag, Hamburg, 1978): press articles on Schmidt during the 1960s and 1970s

Sibylle Krause-Burger, *Helmut Schmidt Aus der Nähe gesehen* (Econ Verlag, Düsseldorf–Wien, 1980)

Klaus Bölling, *Die letzten 30 Tage des Kanzlers Helmut Schmidt* (Spiegel Verlag,

Hamburg, 1982)

The following have lengthy extracts on Schmidt's life and career:

Terence Prittie, *The Velvet Chancellors* (Frederick Muller, London, 1979)

Marion Gräfin Dönhoff, *Von Gestern nach Ubermorgen* (Albrecht Knaus Verlag, Hamburg, 1981; English edition: *Foe into Friend*, Weidenfeld and Nicolson, 1982)

BIOGRAPHICAL DATA

Born 23 December 1918 in Hamburg; married; one daughter

1937 Matriculation at Hamburg's Lichtwark-Schule, followed by military service in anti-aircraft unit

1939–45 Wartime service, ending as First Lieutenant and battery commander

1942 27 June, married to Hannelore Glaser

1945–9 Studied political science and economics at Hamburg University, economics degree

1946 Member of the Social Democrat Party (SPD)

1947–8 Chairman of the Federal Executive of the German Socialist Students Federation (SDS)

1949–53 Member of Hamburg office for Economics and Transport, finally heading transport section

1953–61 Member of the Bundestag (lower house of the Federal Parliament)

1961–5 Senator for Interior Affairs in Hamburg

1965 Re-elected to Bundestag

1967–9 Floor-leader of the SPD Bundestag group

1968 Deputy Chairman of the SPD

1969 22 October, Federal Defence Minister

1972 7 July, Federal Economics and Finance Minister

1972 15 December, Federal Finance Minister

1974 16 May, elected Federal Chancellor (by Bundestag)

1976 15 December, re-elected Chancellor

1980 5 November, re-elected Chancellor

1982 1 October, unseated as Chancellor through 'constructive vote of no confidence' in Bundestag

INDEX